CASES IN
RETAIL MANAGEMENT

DALE M. LEWISON
University of Akron

JON M. HAWES
University of Akron

Merrill Publishing Company
A Bell & Howell Information Company
Columbus   Toronto   London   Melbourne

Cover Photo: Tom Stack

Published by Merrill Publishing Company
A Bell & Howell Information Company
Columbus, Ohio 43216

This book was set in Italia.

Administrative Editor: Pamela B. Kusma
Developmental Editor: Jim Kilgore
Production Coordinator: Molly Kyle
Art Coordinator: James Hubbard
Cover Designer: Cathy Watterson

Library of Congress Catalog Card Number: 88–64049
International Standard Book Number: 0–675–21083–6
Printed in the United States of America
1 2 3 4 5 6 7 8 9—92 91 90 89

To
Kristopher and Tyler
D.M.L

Lisa and Jennifer
J.M.H

Preface

The world of retail management is complex, ever-changing, and largely unstructured. The 30 cases in this book allow the student to work on problems often faced by retail managers in the "real world." Through active involvement in these cases, students can develop the analytical and decision-making skills they will surely require to succeed in their professional careers. The learning experiences the cases provide will give students an edge when confronted with similar situations that are certain to occur on the job.

The 30 cases present a wide variety of problems and opportunities, all of which meet the criterion of realism. All are sufficiently complex to require good analysis; none are too lengthy to be of practical use. Most of the cases conclude with an "analytical problem" to help the student focus on important case issues.

We would like to thank the many authors for contributing their intriguing cases, along with their extremely helpful teaching notes. We would like also to thank the editors and staff of Merrill Publishing Company for their vital contributions in making this book a reality.

Finally, the authors would like to thank Pat Johnson for her many administrative and technical skills. Pat's efforts played a large part in making our writing task easier. We thank the University of Akron for giving us the opportunity to engage in this type of pedagogic endeavor. In addition, we appreciate the comments of these reviewers: William Black, Louisiana State University; Paul Mackay, East Central College; Doris Nelson, Memphis State University; Dr. Elizabeth Taylor, Art Institute of Atlanta; Anthony Urbaniak, Northern State College; and Sandy Wilson, O'More College of Design.

Contents

Contents

PART NINE	**STRATEGIC RETAIL MANAGEMENT**

PART ONE
The Case Method

STUDYING WITH THE CASE METHOD

Introduction

Of the many ways to teach retail management, the lecture method has been used most frequently in college-level retailing courses. But other approaches—such as experiential exercises, role playing, computer simulations, internships, and cooperative education programs—are also useful and effective in learning about retailing, especially when used in conjunction with one another.

The case method is another important means for learning about retail management. In fact, many authorities argue that although lectures are most effective for learning about retailing facts and principles, the case method also should be used "because wisdom can't be told."[1] Merely knowing about retailing is not adequate preparation for managing a retail enterprise. The student must have opportunities to practice solving retail problems and making decisions, which is the essence of the case method.

Perhaps a comparison to a sport such as golf will make this point more clearly. After reading many books about golf and attending many golf-technique lectures—even after thoroughly understanding and mastering all of these materials, still you must go to the golf course and practice swinging the clubs yourself to fully develop your skills and abilities. In a very real sense, the same is true as you further develop your skills and abilities as a retail executive. To become proficient at retail management, you must practice making decisions about retail problems and opportunities.

Case analysis is useful in developing your ability to get to the heart of a retail problem, to analyze it thoroughly, and to indicate the appropriate solution as well as its implementation. An outstanding business education exceeds the transmission of important facts. The recipient of an outstanding college business education does not simply learn to acquire knowledge but learns to act. The case method is an excellent mechanism for developing this ability to its fullest.

---

[1]Charles I. Gragg, "Because Wisdom Can't Be Told," *Harvard Alumni Bulletin*, 19 Oct. 1940.

What Is a Case?

The case method evolved during the 1920s at the Harvard Business School. Other professional schools such as medical and law schools had earlier used the case method of instruction. One of the early proponents of the case method, Charles Gragg, defined a case used in the business school as follows:

> A case is typically a record of a business issue which actually has been faced by business executives, together with surrounding facts, opinions, and prejudices upon which the executives had to depend. These real and particularized cases are presented to students for considered analysis, open discussion, and final decision as to the type of action which should be taken.[2]

Cases vary tremendously in terms of length, complexity, and topical problems. But every case is similar in that all describe a company and the situation it faces. To a great extent, the student learning by the case method operates within a simulated business environment. Often the case will require you to assume the role of one of the retail executives and to "handle" the case problem or opportunity.

Some cases are extremely long and provide pages of details, facts, figures, historical information, forecasts, and many other types of data. Others are quite brief and provide very sparse information.

In both instances, some students are tempted to complain that "not enough information is provided to make a decision." Welcome to the real world of decision making! Retail executives never have as much information as they would like. It is not practical to achieve the goal of "maximum information" for three reasons. (1) *Research is very expensive.* Beyond some point, the value of additional information diminishes to far less than the cost of obtaining it. (2) *Research requires a lot of time.* Often, retail executives cannot wait for the research to be completed. Decisions must be made now. Furthermore, the original situation could change completely by the time the additional research is completed, thus making the study worthless. (3) *Information overload can be as troublesome as the lack of perfect information.* To analyze endlessly is to miss the opportunity to take action and to gain a competitive advantage.

Consequently, you need to learn to make retail management decisions under a variety of "information levels." Each case provides some degree of information, and you should work within that constraint. One of your greatest challenges will be determining which information provided is useful and which is irrelevant. Sometimes case writers will tempt you with data that have little bearing on the case to test whether you detect the irrelevant material and are not distracted from the main issues.

Cases involve real-world companies and the real-world problems they face. Most cases are written by professors who teach by the case method. Often, the case represents a previous consulting assignment. Frequently, the company, or the problem it faced, may have been of some special academic interest to the case

---

[2]Charles I. Gragg, "Because Wisdom Can't Be Told," *Harvard Alumni Bulletin,* 19 Oct. 1940.

writer. The names of the company and the people discussed often are disguised to "protect the innocent." Some companies are reluctant to provide case writers with access to confidential records if the real name of the company is used. It is important to realize, however, that cases are never intended to show good or bad examples of retail management. Case writers have a professional obligation to develop cases that are academically sound and useful in the education of managers. Cases written to gain favorable publicity for a firm or to express disapproval are unacceptable.

Purposes of the Case Method

Studying cases should help you to achieve the following:

1. Learn how to put textbook knowledge into practice.
2. Stop simply receiving facts, concepts, and techniques and begin diagnosing problems, analyzing alternative solutions, and developing implementation plans.
3. Solve problems on your own (or in a group), as opposed to relying on a professor or a textbook for "the right" answer.
4. Learn about a wide range of firms and problems or opportunities, establishing a basis for comparison that might take a lifetime of personal experience to develop.
5. Develop the ability to identify and comprehend the main and subordinate ideas in written material.
6. Develop the ability to separate your personal opinions and assumptions from those in the case and to distinguish between fact and opinion in the case itself.
7. Develop the ability to organize, select, and relate ideas and develop them into a coherent and effective written or oral presentation.
8. Develop skill in exchanging critical and constructive ideas, especially during class discussions.
9. Develop reasoning and logic skills.
10. Deal with constructive criticism and learn from it.

Once you understand the purpose of using the case method, you'll be less likely to be preoccupied with "what is *the right* (the one and only!) answer to the case?" Instead, you should learn to focus on approaches to the problem and should be aware that a number of solutions are usually feasible.

The Student's Role in the Case Method

Each student has an important role to play in a case-oriented retailing course. Each student is responsible for productively contributing to the class discussion; students usually do most of the talking. But you should be careful not to dominate the discussion. All too frequently, a small number of students carry the discussion for the rest of the class. Each student has a unique opportunity to provide a benefit to the class by offering his or her own insights into the case. Don't be afraid that you'll look dumb by asking a certain question or making a comment. It is critical that you participate and share your thoughts with the class.

Learning by the case method is hard work—both for the students and the professor. *It is imperative that you prepare well for each case.* If you haven't studied the case before class, it is unlikely that you will learn much from listening to the other students discuss it. Far more than in a lecture-oriented course, you get out of a case-oriented course exactly what you put into it. If you study extensively before class, concentrate on the discussion during class, contribute productively to this discussion, and reanalyze the case and its discussion afterward, you will benefit greatly from the experience.

It has often been suggested that preparing for a *case discussion* should consist of three steps. First, you should quickly scan the case from beginning to end to become familiar with the general nature of the case. Second, you should go back and read the case very carefully. You should take notes and make an effort to learn the facts relevant to the case. Finally, after extensive thought on the case problem and possible solutions, you should again read the case for details. After this reading, you should anticipate several questions that might be asked and make some notes on how you would respond. By this time, you should feel comfortable that you understand the facts of the case, the major problem, and several feasible solutions.

Most professors also require *written analyses of cases* during the course. Although preparing for a case discussion is hard, time-consuming mental effort, writing a case analysis is even more demanding. Every professor has his or her own preferences for the written report, and you should be very certain that you understand these. The next section offers some general guidelines, but be sure you know what your professor wants—it may be quite different.

How to Prepare a Written Case Analysis

First, realize that every case is different. Therefore, although we'd like to, we can't provide you with a structured list of steps that will enable you to deal with each and every case neatly, orderly, and consistently. Also, remember that your professor has his or her own rules and requirements that are well defined and specific to case analysis. We can, however, offer you some *general* guidlines to get you started.

Remember that very few cases have only one absolutely "right" answer. There are almost always numerous feasible solutions. Your job is to analyze these and make a recommendation that is fully supported by your logical reasoning, corroborating evidence found in the case, and other persuasive material that further contributes to your recommendation.

Next, plan your schedule so that you have adequate time to prepare the case report. Writing the report is hard work, and you should expect to devote considerable time and effort to it. Expect some delays, and plan your schedule so that you do not have to rush and attempt to prepare your report the day before it is due.

We would never argue that you should "sell the sizzle rather than the steak." It is critical that you recognize, however, that the "sizzle" is also very important. It greatly influences the reader's perception of the overall quality of your report—even if the reader tries to read for content with less concern for style. Consequently, you need to do an excellent job in preparing the written report. It should be well organized and should effectively use headings, figures, tables, and other visuals that enhance the paper's readability. The well-organized paper will "flow" nicely.

Obviously, your report should be neatly typed on white bond paper (no onion skin or erasable paper!). There should be no typographical, grammatical, or spelling errors. You should very carefully proofread your paper—then proof it again! We also recommend that you staple the paper in the upper left corner, rather than place it in a binder, which may not fit in a file drawer; furthermore binders often break apart while the paper is being read.

There are many ways to organize the written case analysis. Some professors want students to answer the questions at the end of the case, in the order given. Others may prefer, however, the problem-to-solution type of organization. Again, some cases may lend themselves to a particular format. A traditional approach to written case analysis follows.

Situation Analysis

The first section of the case report often includes a discussion of the situation confronting the company. An analysis of the firm's environment—specifically, its competitors, its customers, trends in the industry, and other relevant environmental information—often are included here.

The purpose of the situation analysis is to set the stage for subsequent analysis of the problem and its solution. In addition, the situation analysis should help the writer and the reader understand the relevant facts that have a bearing on the firm.

You should be careful, though, to *avoid simply summarizing or rehashing the case* in the situation analysis. As the phrase "situation analysis" indicates, there should be some *analysis*—some clear identification of what these facts mean to the company and to the case issue. Use the situation to show very clearly that you understand the context in which the firm operates. Show what this means to the firm and its impact on the firm's activities.

Identification of the Problem or Opportunity

In most cases, there is one central problem or opportunity that must be addressed. Often, there are also additional minor problems or opportunities. The purpose of this section of the report is to identify very clearly these problems or opportunities.

Often, the case writer makes it easy to find the "true" problem. Sometimes, though, evidence in the form of symptoms may be plentiful, but the search for and identification of the problem is left to you. Be sure that you have very carefully considered the case before you finalize your problem statement. This is very critical because *all of your subsequent analysis should be directed toward ultimately solving this problem* or showing how to best seize the opportunity.

Also, be careful to identify a problem that truly can be solved. For example, if you are assigned the role of a junior executive and you define the problem as "incompetent top management," you are hardly in a position to gain implementation of a solution that involves firing the firm's current top management team.

Identification and Analysis of Alternatives

After accurately and specifically defining the problem, the next step is to identify several creative and reasonably effective solutions. These alternative solutions should reflect actions that the firm could implement to solve the problem(s) you have defined. Often, the identification of these alternatives requires some creative thought and a deep understanding of the situation facing the firm. Brainstorming may help. Reading about how other firms have dealt with similar problems also may be useful. Asking "experts" in the field is another good way to generate a list of reasonable alternatives.

A useful way to analyze these alternatives is to list the pros and cons of each solution. Remember that each alternative must address the specific problem you have defined. The alternative solutions also should be mutually exclusive; they should not overlap. Ideally, the list would be totally exhaustive, but such a list may be unmanageably long.

Recommendations

The next part of the report should indicate which of the alternatives you would recommend as the preferred solution to the problem. More importantly, you should very clearly and convincingly explain *why* this is the best solution. You should provide a very persuasive argument that is supported by evidence from the case, statistics and references from other sources, and obvious logic and reasoning skills.

As previously discussed, your goal is not to find the one and only "right" answer. It is critical, however, that you hold yourself accountable for convincing the reader of the wisdom of your decision. Remember that several of the alternatives have merit; your job is to choose the optimal solution and support your decision to the best of your ability.

Implementation

Your recommendation also must be implemented. This is often a stumbling block for students. They devise what they think is a great solution, only to find out that it would be far too costly to implement, or that it would take too long, or that it would be impossible to convince important stakeholders to accept the solution; or they find that other implementation constraints make the previously viewed "great" solution unacceptable.

This final section of the report therefore should specify the implementation plan in great detail. It should answer such questions as who, what, how, when, and where. In addition, a cost estimate of implementing your solution usually should be included.

A useful checklist is provided in Table 1 to help you to prepare your written report. Please remember that your professor may require additional or alternative features.

The Team Approach to Case Presentations

Sometimes, professors form teams or groups of students who make case presentations to the class. Usually, the group also prepares a written case analysis. This is

TABLE 1
A Written Case Analysis
Checklist

Problem
1. Was the case problem (opportunity) correctly identified?
2. Are there any additional case problems that were not identified?
3. Is the problem description sufficient?

Situation analysis
1. Were any relevant facts or data overlooked?
2. Is the analysis of case facts and data appropriate to the case problem and alternatives?
3. Are there any misinterpretations of case facts and data?

Alternatives
1. Is there a complete identification of alternative solutions to the stated problem(s)?
2. Are the advantages and disadvantages of each alternative clearly enumerated and discussed?
3. Did the identified alternatives demonstrate creative thinking?

Recommendation
1. Was a clear decision made regarding the most appropriate alternative?
2. Is the selected alternative a logical and reasonable choice, given the defined problem and the firm's situation?
3. Is the decision sufficiently supported and justified?

Implementation
1. Are the plans necessary for implementing the recommendation clearly specified?
2. Have questions about the who, what, how, when, and where of the implementation been answered?
3. Is the cost of the implementation clearly specified and justified in relation to the value of the recommendation?

a very good learning experience for the students. Although it can be very frustrating, it is realistic because committee, group, or team work is a fact of life in many corporate environments. Learning to work with others is a very important skill that is likely to develop as a result of this experience. Learning to work together, to delegate, and to cooperate is critical to success in a corporate environment. While some frustrations are bound to develop, life-long friendships also may result from group case work.

If your professor allows you to form your own groups, you may improve your group's cooperative efforts by considering the following. Essentially, the goal is to form a team whose members have common goals and complementary skills, talents, and resources.

1. Do group members have similar grade objectives?
2. Do group members have similar topical interests?
3. Do group members have complementary talents, resources, and organizational skills?

4. Do group members have schedules that will permit frequent meetings to plan case strategy and to conduct the other necessary case-work activities?
5. Can group members be trusted to fulfill obligations?
6. Can group members be expected to work together effectively, harmoniously, and cordially?

In presenting the case and its solution to the class, a number of formats are possible. Again, your professor may have a specific set of requirements. There are several issues, however, that are common to all professional business presentations. To help you prepare, plan, and evaluate your case presentation to the class, we have designed a checklist for you (see Table 2).

A Final Note

Case work is interesting, challenging, and rewarding. Even though you will have to work hard to earn these benefits, we are sure that it is worth the extra effort. Many of our country's top retail managers were educated by the case method. We are confident that this tradition will continue.

TABLE 2
Checklist for Reviewing Case Presentations

Content
1. Was everything that was presented technically correct?
2. Were any important points or relevant information overlooked?
3. Did visuals clearly relate to the presentation?
4. Was the material clearly presented?
5. Was the material presented at a suitable level of detail?

Organization
1. Was enough background given to prepare the audience?
2. Was the problem clearly defined early in the presentation?
3. Was the organization clear and easy to follow?
4. Were visuals used to help you follow the organization?
5. Did the speakers move clearly and naturally from point to point?
6. Did the organization seem logical?
7. Did the conclusion come as a surprise?

Delivery
1. Did the speakers appear to be relaxed, confident, and in control?
2. Did the speakers use effective nonverbal communication?
3. Did the speakers rely too extensively on notes?
4. Did the presenters speak clearly?
5. Did the presenters speak at an appropriate pace and use a suitable level of volume?
6. Was the delivery monotonous?
7. Were the speakers dressed appropriately?
8. Did the speakers make effective eye contact with the audience?
9. Were questions from the audience effectively handled in a constructive and supportive style?

Good luck with your case studies! We wish you all the best as you engage in this stage of your preparation for a career in retail management.

Additional Information on the Case Method

Andrews, Kenneth R. *The Case Method of Teaching Human Relations and Administration.* Cambridge, MA: Harvard University Press, 1955.

Barach, Jeffrey A. "Performance Criteria Used in the Evaluation of Case Courses." *Collegiate News and Views,* 28 (Winter 1974–1975): 19–20.

Gunn, Bruce. "The Competitive Case Presentation and Critique Training Method." *Journal of Marketing Education,* (Spring 1983): 22–32.

Lehman, Donald R., and Russell S. Winer. *Analysis for Marketing Planning.* Plano, TX: Business Publications, Inc., 1988.

McNair, Malcolm P. *The Case Method at the Harvard Business School: Papers By Present and Past Members of the Faculty and Staff.* New York: McGraw-Hill Book Co., 1954.

O'Dell, William F. "And Once Again . . . The Case Method Revisited." *Collegiate News and Views,* 29 (Winter 1975–1976: 17–21.

O'Dell, William F., Andrew C. Ruppel, Robert H. Trent, and William J. Kehoe. *Marketing Decision Making: Analytical Framework and Cases.* 3rd ed. Cincinnati: South-Western Publishing Co., 1984.

Raymond, Thomas C. *Problems in Business Administration: Analysis by the Case Method,* 2d ed. New York: McGraw-Hill Book Co., 1964.

Ronstadt, Robert. *The Art of Case Analysis: A Student Guide to the Diagnosis of Business Situations.* Needham, MA: Lord Publishing, 1978.

Schnelle, Kenneth E. *Case Analysis and Business Problem Solving.* New York: McGraw-Hill Book Co., 1967.

Towe, Andrew R. *To Study Administration by Cases.* Boston: Harvard University, Graduate School of Business Administration, 1969.

PART TWO
The Retail Consumer

CASE 1   METRO BANK:
Adapting Consumer Services to Consumer Behavior Patterns

The Metro Bank of Capital City was chartered in 1920 and was the second-largest commercial bank (in total deposits) in the state. The bank's facilities consisted of a central bank and twenty-seven outlets. The central bank served as the center of banking operations and was located in the downtown area. Metro's statewide facilities consisted of a centrally located outlet in each of the state's eighteen principal cities (populations ranging from 32,000 to 280,000).

In its early years, the bank's management philosophies were quite conservative under its now retired founder, J. P. Homestead. Although the board chairman, Arthur B. King, and the president, Malcom S. Hargrave, followed a somewhat more aggressive management philosophy, Homestead's conservative influence was still prevalent in many of the major policy decisions. Several of the bank's top managers felt that Homestead's conservative influence helped Metro avoid the recent problem of overextending on high-risk loans, which had led to the collapse of several banks.

Metro's current operating philosophy was described accurately by one competitor as " progress through discretion." In past years, Metro's management had adopted banking innovations when sufficient evidence demonstrated that the innovation was in the best interest of the bank and its customers. These policies have created a consumer image of reliability, an image most managers felt was one of the bank's strongest assets. Recently, however, some of the bank's younger managers had exerted considerable pressure to initiate more progressive policies. Janet F. Peterson, vice president of marketing and research, felt that the bank's management should be more receptive to banking innovations. Peterson believed that increasing competition, in terms of new competitors and new competitive marketing strategies, would require early adoption of new technologies and approaches if Metro were to maintain or increase its present growth. The trend in recent years has been toward greater competition among commercial banks as well as intensi-

This case was revised and updated by Dale M. Lewison and Kenneth E. Mast, University of Akron, as adapted from Dale M. Lewison and Roger Cannaday, "The Second National Bank of Capital City: The Adoption of Service Innovations," in *Retailing: Cases and Applications*, ed. D. M. Lewison and M. W. DeLozier (Columbus, OH: Merrill, 1982): 49–60.

fied competition with other financial institutions. This competition extends across all facets of the banking business.

Commercial banks offer a wide array of financial services to individuals, firms, institutions, government, and other organizations. These services include storage of funds in interest-bearing accounts (savings accounts) and in interest and noninterest-bearing accounts (checking accounts) for day-to-day transactions; loans for a variety of purposes; trust services; safe deposit boxes for valuable personal items; financial planning; and investment counseling. While commercial banks offer a wide range of services to both commercial and retail consumers, not all banks offer all services. The product–service offering of each bank facility is shown in Exhibit 1–1.

The general state of the economy affects the level of checking and savings deposits, the demand for personal and commercial loans, and the costs of resources. Banking operations are affected by cultural and social factors such as atti-

EXHIBIT 1–1
Product–service offering by facility

Service	Full-Service Bank	Limited-Service Bank	Automated Teller Machine	Point-of-Sale Terminal
Open accounts	X	X		
Make loans	X			
Cash withdrawals	X	X	X	
Deposits	X	X	X	
Transfers	X	X	X	
Loan payments	X	X	X	
Credit card payments	X	X	X	
Other bill payments	X	X	X	
Determine current balance	X	X	X	
Trust services	X			
Safe deposit boxes	X	X	X	
Financial counseling	X			
Cash third-party checks	X	X		
Purchase traveler's checks	X	X		
Purchase cashier's checks	X	X		
Purchase money orders	X	X		
Check authorization	X	X		X
Credit card authorization	X	X		X
Debit card authorization (to allow immediate transfer of funds from buyer's to seller's account)	X	X		X

tudes toward the use of credit, attitudes toward women as customers, pressure for greater social responsibility, and the continuing redistribution of the population into the suburbs.

As a quasi-utility, the banking industry has been subject to a high degree of government control and regulation. Regulatory agencies include the Federal Reserve Board, the Federal Deposit Insurance Corporation, the Comptroller of the Currency, and state banking authorities. As an example, national banks must obtain approval from the Comptroller of the Currency for the location of new branch banks.

Major technological changes affect the competitive environment of the banking industry. The Electronic Funds Transfer System (EFTS) is an example. The EFTS is an electromechanical method of transferring value, partially replacing the method of paper transfer of value (i.e., cash and checks).

One of these EFTS components has been classified as customer–bank communication terminals (CBCT) by the Comptroller. These terminals may be located on the site of an existing banking office or off-site such as in a shopping center. They can be staffed (operated by a bank employee) or unstaffed (operated by the customer), on-line (connected directly to the bank's central computer) or off-line (self-contained). One type of CBCT is the automated teller machine (ATM), which typically allows customers to make deposits, withdraw cash, pay on loans, and make account transfers. Another type of CBCT is the point-of-sale (POS) terminal, which can be used at checkout counters in supermarkets, department stores, and other business establishments. Retailers use POS for check or credit-card authorization and for debit-card authorization, which allows immediate transfer of funds from the purchaser's account to the store's account.

Metro's Current Situation

In recent months Metro's top management had devoted considerable discussion to the need for additional banking outlets. The management consensus was that potentially profitable sites existed in the rapidly expanding suburban areas of Capital City. Moreover, management felt that additional profit potential existed in several of the state's eighteen other principal cities and smaller cities (10,000 to 30,000 people). Although senior management generally agreed that expansion was necessary to increase market share, they disagreed considerably as to what form the expansion should take.

The need for a decision on the expansion issue had acquired greater importance in recent weeks. Two of Metro's competitors, First Central Bank (the state's largest) and first Farmers' Bank (the fourth largest), had expanded their service offerings through the use of ATMs in conjunction with their existing branch facilities. Just recently, Peterson learned that First Farmers' intended to limit further construction of traditional brick-and-mortar branches and embark on an ambitious expansion program of off-site ATMs in shopping centers, employment centers, and other major activity centers. Its expansion program was based on the belief that banking services are primarily convenience goods; therefore, banking facilities should have the greatest possible geographical distribution. Since ATMs were available to customers 24 hours per day, 7 days a week, the marketing strategy appeared to be one of creating greater spatial and time convenience.

Metro's senior management was concerned about a recent report showing that market share of deposits peaked in 1980 and had declined slowly since then. Management's assumption was that market share of deposits was correlated closely with share of the total number of branches. Metro's share of branches, however, continued to increase in 1984 and 1985 while share of deposits decreased. Many of the larger banks in the state experienced a similar trend. The exceptions to this trend were First Central and First Farmers', which experienced substantial growth.

One of Metro's stated goals was to maximize market shares subject to a rate of return of at least 15 percent. In 1985, the market share fell to 19.5 percent, under 20 percent for the first time since 1977, although the rate of return remained slightly above 15 percent.

In light of the situation, Hargrave asked Peterson to develop and evaluate alternative expansion plans that would increase Metro's market share and rate of return. In addition, Hargrave instructed Peterson to consider the following issues:

1. Construction of a brick-and-mortar branch would cost a minimum of about $250,000, or about five times as much as the cost of an ATM.
2. The chairman of the board had expressed repeatedly the opinion that ATMs cannot be cost justified in terms of the profits they generate, an opinion shared by some experts.
3. Several of Metro's large commercial accounts had expressed a wide range of views as to the desirability of the EFTS.
4. At the recent conference of the National Association of Bank Managers, several experts expressed strong feelings concerning the problems of fraud, security, and malfunctioning of ATMs.
5. Recent consumer surveys showed considerable mixed reactions to the use of ATMs.
6. Several of Metro's senior bank officials were concerned that any radical departure from current modes of operation might have considerable negative effects on the bank's image.
7. Pricing concepts in the banking industry were undergoing significant changes; whereas most banks sought to make each application of each service profitable, some banks would adopt pricing strategies based on the profitability of the total customers and/or a total class of customers.
8. Point-of-sale terminals were in use at checkout counters in retail stores and generally were installed with one terminal per checkout counter, or anywhere from one to twenty terminals per store.

In her initial meeting with the bank's Marketing Research Department, Peterson outlined the major issues of the problem as presented in the previous discussion. She expressed the following opinion:

"Innovative expansion is the key to regaining and increasing the bank's market share. For any expansion program to meet the bank's market-share goals, we must develop expansion alternatives incorporating product–service mixes that not only satisfy the needs of our existing customers but also provide the opportunities for attracting new customers. In my opinion, the only way to attract large numbers of new customers is to create the image of a modern, progressive bank. This type of image requires fresh and imaginative marketing programs. Today's banking customer chooses and continues to patronize a bank for many different reasons; however, all of these reasons are strongly related to today's modern life-styles. What I need from this department are innovative alternatives of expansion that not only are conducive to the consumer's modern way of life but will be acceptable to the dated gentlemen upstairs.

"I believe that our current research files" (see Exhibits 1–2 to 1–7) "are sufficient for the initial development of these alternatives. We can always collect additional data later that would be more suited to whatever alternative we come up with. If you have any ideas about additional information that might be required, or if there are any specific aspects to the problem you feel should be drawn to my attention, submit them to me in writing by the end of the week. Otherwise, within the next 6 weeks, I expect from the department recommendations as to the most feasible expansion alternatives. Now, are there any questions?"

Bob Sidewood: How many alternatives do you want?

Peterson: I'll leave that up to you.

Sidewood: Are there any specific issues you wish us to consider?

Peterson: I think I have at least mentioned most of the issues pertinent to the problem. Again, I would think that consumer needs and responses might serve as the focal point in developing the alternatives. But you shouldn't overlook all of the other issues I've noted. Also, I'm sure that there are additional issues that you might consider.

Sidewood: One last question. How extensive an area should we consider?

Peterson: The entire state.

Cheryl Armstrong: As a resident of this state for 55 years and a banker for 27, I feel that I know the people of this state and the customers who bank with us. Although we want to think progressively, let's not forget that this state's population is quite conservative. These people are bound in tradition. It has taken

EXHIBIT 1–2

Bank patronage reasons: Retail and commercial consumers

Patronage Reason	Importance (%)						
	First	Second	Third	Fourth	Fifth	Sixth	Totals
Location	42	5	19	25	3	6	100
Hours	34	4	22	20	10	10	100
Services	10	43	15	13	11	8	100
Personnel	7	20	9	17	22	25	100
Reputation	5	7	10	6	21	51	100
Facilities	2	21	25	19	33	0	100
Totals	100	100	100	100	100	100	

Source: Statewide Consumer Survey, Marketing Research Department, Metro Bank.

EXHIBIT 1–3
Consumer banking trip behavior: Retail and commercial consumers

	Type of Consumer (%)	
Shopping Characteristics	Retail Consumer	Commercial Consumer
Type of trip: I conduct my banking business in connection with:		
Trips between home and work	32	10
Special trips from home	30	8
Special trips from work	17	57
Shopping trips	18	—
Business trips	2	23
Other	1	2
Total	100	100
Trip frequency: I visit the bank:		
Less than once a month	1	—
Once a month	8	—
More than once a month (less than weekly)	21	—
Once a week	51	1
More than once a week (less than daily)	19	11
Once a day (weekday)	—	69
More than once a day	—	19
Total	100	100

Source: Statewide Consumer Survey, Marketing Research Department, Metro Bank.

this long for them to trust dealing with us. How long will it take to get them to trust dealing with a machine?

Peterson: You have a point. But people have changed. We have an influx of people from all parts of the country into this state. The newcomers don't have the same life-styles.

Doug Robeson: As research analyst, I have data that support both of your contentions. People in this state have been slow to adopt banking in general, and innovative banking practices in particular. The population's composition, however, has changed in the states' major cities. Out-of-state companies have opened major branches of their businesses here and have relocated many of their personnel as well. Although they represent a small percentage of the state's population, these outsiders have learned the advantages of using the new technologies in banking.

Peterson: Well, it is true that these people have been exposed to new banking techniques and do adapt to change more rapidly, but they are a minority. I think we should consider educating the rest of the population to the advantages of

EXHIBIT 1–4
Demographic characteristics of automated equipment users and nonusers

Demographic Characteristics	Nonuser (%)	Infrequent User (%)	Frequent User (%)	Total User (%)
Sex				
Male	53.9	64.0	64.9	59.1
Female	46.1	36.0	35.1	40.9
Age				
21–34	36.8	49.3	54.5	43.4
35–49	47.4	44.0	39.0	43.4
50 and over	15.8	6.7	6.5	13.1
Social class				
Upper-middle	27.6	14.7	33.8	23.7
Lower-middle	38.2	53.3	39.0	45.6
Upper-lower	34.2	32.0	27.3	30.7
Marital status				
Married	86.8	85.3	87.0	86.9
Single	7.9	10.7	9.1	8.4
Widowed, divorced	5.3	4.0	3.9	4.7
Education				
Postgraduate	13.2	13.3	14.3	12.8
College graduate	23.7	32.0	29.9	27.7
Some college	<u>28.9</u>	<u>32.0</u>	<u>28.6</u>	<u>30.3</u>
Subtotal	65.8	77.3	72.8	70.8
High school graduate	25.0	17.3	19.5	22.6
Some high school	6.6	5.3	6.5	5.5
Eighth grade or less	2.6	—	1.3	1.1
Income				
Under $5,000	2.6	4.0	2.6	2.9
$5,000–$7,999	3.9	6.7	2.6	5.1
$8,000–$10,999	21.1	22.7	10.4	17.2
$11,000–$13,999	19.7	24.0	15.6	20.1
$14,000–$17,999	13.2	10.7	18.2	16.1
$18,000 and over	34.2	22.7	44.2	32.8
Refused	5.3	9.3	6.5	5.8

Source: Statewide Consumer Survey, Marketing Research Department, Metro Bank.

EXHIBIT 1–5
Consumer bank selection criteria

Selection Criteria	Customer Type and Importance Rank (%)					
	Retail Consumers			Commercial Consumers		
	First	Second	Third	First	Second	Third
Recommendation of friends or relatives	3	4	8	—	—	2
Recommendation of a professional acquaintance	2	6	1	11	9	8
Good reputation	4	3	—	9	8	14
Located near where I shop	10	8	3	—	—	—
Located near where I work	11	10	14	16	10	10
Located near where I live	18	16	10	—	1	1
Offers full service	11	13	11	29	22	13
Helpful personnel	8	7	4	6	15	10
Open during the evening hours	5	7	4	11	6	8
Open on Saturdays	7	4	6	4	12	6
Attractive facilities	—	6	3	—	—	—
Convenient automatic services	5	6	12	4	5	11
Interest charges on loans	1	—	1	6	7	9
Interest paid on savings	3	3	3	—	—	1
Availability of credit	—	1	—	4	5	5
Overdraft privileges on checking accounts	3	4	6	—	—	—
Premiums or gifts for new accounts	7	2	9	—	—	—
Convenient parking	1	—	2	—	—	1
Convenient entrance/exit	1	—	3	—	—	1

Source: Statewide Consumer Survey, Marketing Research Department, Metro Bank.

new banking technology. Just look at the strides First Central and First Farmers' have made.

Greg Lucas: Ms. Peterson, it is true that those banks have increased their market shares, but I agree with Ms. Armstrong. The people of this state are staunch conservatives, and particularly the customers who bank with us. If we try to become 'progressive,' as you call it, we will lose the solid image we have built with our loyal customers and they'll go elsewhere. People are reliable and trustworthy; machines are nothing but metal and electrical circuits.

Peterson: But the people of this state are changing, and people from out of state with more progressive views are coming in. We cannot continue to manufacture the horse-drawn carriage! Does anyone have any final comments before we adjourn?

EXHIBIT 1–6

Likelihood of using automated teller equipment

Characteristic	Very Likely (%)	Somewhat Likely (%)	Somewhat Unlikely (%)	Very Unlikely (%)
Age				
18–34	34.1	21.7	11.2	29.2
35–49	33.2	18.6	11.3.	33.2
50–64	19.8	12.5	14.7	49.6
65 and over	10.9	7.8	14.7	51.9
Income				
Under $7,500	15.2	11.0	11.0	51.7
$7,500–$10,000	25.8	20.8	11.9	37.7
$10,000–$15,000	34.8	17.4	12.1	32.6
$15,000–$20,000	34.1	20.3	14.8	26.8
Over $20,000	28.9	12.3	15.8	41.2
Sex				
Male	26.8	16.7	15.0	37.0
Female	28.0	16.2	10.5	40.0

Source: Statewide Consumer Survey, Market Research Department, Metro Bank.

Robeson: If I may make one last comment, let me say once again that I can see both sides to this question. As I view it, we are concerned with several issues. Each must be analyzed. We must consider the changing life-styles of bank consumers in this state. On the whole, are consumers changing rapidly enough to accept modern banking techniques in the near future? Second, what image do we convey and to whom? Third, can we educate people to accept and use machines? Their prior learning habits may not be easy to change. I don't presently have answers to these questions.

Peterson: You've raised some good questions, Mr. Robeson. And as project director, I know you will have answered these in the report I expect from this department.

Analytical Problem

As director of the project, prepare an appropriate expansion plan that identifies and evaluates the most feasible alternatives for Metro Bank. As stated by Peterson, that plan must be predicated on meeting existing customers' needs as well as attracting new customers.

What are the possible effects of your recommended alternatives on the bank's (1) internal operations, (2) promotional programs, (3) product–service mix, and (4) pricing strategy?

EXHIBIT 1–7
Automated teller equipment: Advantages versus disadvantages

Characteristics	Advantages Outweigh (%)	About Equal (%)	Disadvantages Outweigh (%)	Advantages Outweigh Plus Equal (%)
Occupation				
White collar	31.6	38.6	29.8	70.2
Blue collar	25.4	12.8	61.7	38.3
Professional	12.9	45.2	42.0	58.0
Housewife	23.6	31.1	45.3	54.7
Retired	23.5	5.9	70.6	29.4
Other	41.2	35.3	23.5	76.5
Age				
18–23	40.0	40.0	20.0	80.0
24–34	27.5	25.8	46.7	56.3
35–44	16.7	33.3	50.0	50.0
45–55	20.3	29.7	50.0	50.0
56–64	16.7	16.7	66.7	33.3
65 and over	33.4	13.3	53.4	46.6
Income				
Under $5,000	12.5	25.0	62.5	37.5
$5,000–$10,000	32.6	30.2	37.3	62.7
$10,000–$15,000	38.2	21.8	40.0	60.0
$15,000–$20,000	25.0	36.5	38.5	61.5
Over $20,000	29.2	33.3	37.5	62.5
Refused	17.1	31.4	51.4	48.6

Source: Statewide Consumer Survey, Market Research Department, Metro Bank.

THE FRUITCUP RESTAURANT:
Adjusting Policies to Better Service Consumer Needs

Background

Sue Johnson recently was promoted from Assistant Manager to Manager at The Fruitcup Restaurant. Johnson's promotion was well deserved; she had worked very hard over the past 3 years. She would miss the former manager, Bob Smith, who was retiring after 22 years of service, but Johnson looked forward to the new challenge. She especially looked forward to the opportunity to have a greater impact on The Fruitcup's growth and development. She wanted to establish an action plan that would guide the restaurant over the next several years. As Assistant Manager, she had been vitally engaged in many of the day-to-day problems. Now, she hoped to have a chance to make her mark on The Fruitcup Restaurant's total business operation. She wanted to develop policies that would enable the restaurant to prosper over the long run.

The Fruitcup Restaurant was a single-unit operation, not part of a franchised chain. Sam Mallory owned the restaurant, as well as many other businesses, some of which were also restaurants. He lived in a community several hundred miles away. Consequently, Mallory depended heavily on the restaurant manager and would allow Johnson to have a free hand in the management of the facility. Mallory and Johnson had a good working relationship, and Mallory was willing to help Johnson get off to a good start in her new role. Johnson understood, though, that Mallory was a devoted believer in the profit motive and expected considerable long-term improvement in the restaurant's bottom line. Johnson supported this view because her compensation plan included a portion of the restaurant's profit.

The Fruitcup Restaurant was a 200-seat, full-menu, table-service operation located in an urban area of almost 100,000 people. The business was open from 6:00 A.M. to 1:00 A.M., 7 days a week. While The Fruitcup was not luxurious, it had been remodeled about 2 years ago and was definitely not in poor condition. In fact, Johnson thought that the restaurant's physical appearance was somewhat "upscale" in comparison to competitors.

The Fruitcup Restaurant was located on a major thoroughfare in a southern community. The population had grown over the past several years and now approached 100,000, including the nearly 15,000 university students. The community could be described as being somewhat progressive. Other community characteristics of interest included the following:

- ☐ Approximately 40,000 family units
- ☐ Average annual household incomes of $34,000
- ☐ Above-average levels of education
- ☐ Yellow-pages listing of 165 restaurants
- ☐ Nearest major metropolitan area about 60 miles away

This case was prepared by Harry F. Krueckeberg, Colorado State University, and Jon M. Hawes, University of Akron. Although the case is based on a real company, several facts have been changed and the names are fictitious.

Student Survey

Because The Fruitcup was located within 5 miles of the university, Johnson thought that she might be able to work with marketing students to collect some information to help her determine the restaurant's current image. She made some phone calls and was eventually directed to Professor Williams, who taught marketing research. He agreed to encourage some of his students to work with Johnson as part of the course requirements.

The students were pleased to work with Johnson on the project. She tried her best to be cooperative and supportive. The group decided to examine the university community's perceptions of The Fruitcup. The students conducted 100 personal interviews using a convenience sample of students, faculty, and staff. The results indicated that 7 percent of the university respondents ranked The Fruitcup as a "favorite" eating place. Overall, The Fruitcup placed third in a list of sixty-one restaurants in the community that were rated in the study.

Additional survey findings include the following conclusions:

- Of the top fifteen "favorite" restaurants, eight were specialty and seven were traditional. The Fruitcup was one of the traditional restaurants.
- The type of food was ranked most important in choosing a restaurant; price was second.
- The respondents did not recall advertising by The Fruitcup.
- The single most important form of transportation to a restaurant was by motor vehicle (58.7 percent had cars).

Community Research Project

Although the student survey was very interesting and informative, Johnson knew that the sample was not designed to be representative of The Fruitcup's overall market. Consequently, she decided to retain Professor Williams as a consultant and continue the project by collecting additional information. It would be expensive, but Johnson and Mallory recognized the need and value of better understanding their retail customers.

After several meetings, Williams helped Johnson and Mallory agree on the following three research objectives:

1. Identify possible long-term and general issues regarding the awareness, attitudes, and opinions of The Fruitcup's customers and noncustomers.
2. Identify apparent weaknesses and strengths in management and marketing related to The Fruitcup's personnel and policies.
3. Develop information to assist in retail planning.

The research was also intended to help management know how to make decisions that would enable it to reach three company goals:

1. Increase the number of customers.
2. Increase average check size.
3. Increase profit dollars.

After an extensive analysis of all available sales data and The Fruitcup's accounting records, Williams suggested that a more extensive consumer survey should be conducted. It should use a more representative sample of the community. Management agreed and authorized Williams to hire some marketing students to administer the mall-intercept survey he had designed after conducting a focus group interview among ten Fruitcup customers.

The sample included 250 households randomly selected from the local telephone directory. The first part of the survey involved asking an open-ended question, "Which sit-down restaurants have you patronized within the past year?" For each named restaurant, the respondent was then asked to recall "reasons for eating there." These responses were then coded and tabulated. Exhibit 2–1 shows the outcome of this part of the research.

The next section of the survey involved an application of the semantic differential. The interviews showed the respondents' two bipolar adjectives (or phrases) separated by seven blank spaces. Each respondent was asked to rate The Fruitcup Restaurant on each scale by placing an "X" in the blank that most accurately reflected his or her opinion of this restaurant. These scores were then tabulated, and the mean value was calculated for each item. These research results are shown in Exhibit 2–2.

The last section of the study involved asking the respondent to indicate his or her perception of the importance of various full-service restaurant attributes. The response categories were very important (4), important (3), somewhat important (2), and not important (1). The results of this analysis are shown in Exhibit 2–3.

Analytical Problem

All of the surveys have been administered, the data have been tabulated, and the results are shown in Exhibits 2–1 to 2–3. Assume Professor Williams's role of a consultant to The Fruitcup Restaurant, and prepare a written report that is designed to help Sue Johnson and Sam Mallory understand the retail consumer so that they can develop retail policies that will ultimately improve the restaurant's "bottom line."

EXHIBIT 2–1
Reasons for Eating at Specific Restaurants

	Reasons for Eating There									Total for Each Restaurant
Restaurant	Good Service	Food Quality	Good Atmosphere	Was Taken	Preferred Food	Convenient Location	Liked the Place	"Good Place"	Other	
Age's	8	20	12	28	4		8	4	16	100
Basement	14	28	28	14	3		6		6	99
Benny's	5	19	24	8		3	5	8	27	99
Boot House	10	29	14	8	12	6	2	8	10	99
Cannery	15	44	11	7	7		4	8	4	100
Catamarand	9	42	19	12	2		2	9	5	100
Cool's	12	19	4	8	35	3			19	100
IN	16	32	19	10		3	6	13		99
Fruitcup		18	18	27	9	18			9	99
Total Reasons (%)	9.9	28.1	16.7	13.6	8.0	3.7	3.7	5.6	10.7	100

EXHIBIT 2–2
Semantic Differential Results for The Fruitcup Restaurant

	Very		Neutral			Very		
	1	2	3	4	5	6	7	
Friendly			●					Unfriendly
Good parking facilities	●							Poor parking facilities
Beautiful				●				Ugly
Clean facilities						●		Dirty Facilities
Good portion sizes				●				Poor portion sizes
Good service					●			Poor service
Interesting			●					Uninteresting
Well-known				●				Unknown
Uncrowded		●						Crowded
Reasonably priced					●			Unreasonably priced
Attractive plates		●						Unattractive plates
Enjoyable			●					Unenjoyable
Wide appeal					●			No appeal
Inexpensive				●				Expensive
Tasteful				●				Distasteful
Valuable experience				●				Worthless
Tender meat					●			Tough meat

EXHIBIT 2–3
Importance of Restaurant Attributes

Attribute Description	Mean Value	Rank	Rated Very Important or Important (%)
Quality of the food served	3.90	1	100.0
Quality of the service	3.78	2	99.2
Cleanliness of the dining room	3.77	3	99.2
Amount of wait-time before being seated	3.52	4	95.4
Restaurant atmosphere	3.48	5	96.9
Friendliness of the restaurant employees	3.47	6	95.3
Comfort of seating facilities	3.29	7	91.4
Reputation of restaurant	3.23	8	87.4
Variety of menu items	3.21	9	93.7
Amount customer may wish to spend	3.19	10	86.6
Convenient parking	3.19	11	91.5
"Specialty" or main type of food served	3.13	12	86.7
Serves food not normally prepared at home	3.02	13	81.3
Restaurant's decor	2.96	14	81.9
Recommended by friends	2.92	15	74.3
Previous customer	2.91	16	74.8
Casual atmosphere	2.87	17	78.6.
General economic outlook	2.86	18	69.1
Areas for nonsmokers	2.75	19	60.9
Alcoholic beverages served	2.71	20	66.7
Restaurant takes reservations	2.67	21	63.5
Adequacy for social occasions	2.61	22	56.2
Distance from home	2.59	23	59.4
Location relative to other activities	2.59	24	53.9
Ethnic foods	2.44	25	49.6
Discount coupons offered	2.37	26	41.8
Services provided for children	2.32	27	45.7
Advertising by restaurant	2.24	28	36.5
"Gourmet" menu items	2.21	29	34.7
Formal atmosphere	2.19	30	36.3
"In" place among friends	2.07	31	27.6
"Live" entertainment	1.95	32	25.7
Take-home services	1.83	33	18.0

AKRON DENTAL SERVICES:
Reconciling Firm Operations With Consumer Expectations

In 1964, Drs. Paul Jones, Mary Johnson, and Tom Marini merged their respective dental practices to form Akron Dental Services. Dr. Jones was an orthodontist, Dr. Johnson specialized in fitting dentures, and Dr. Marini practiced family dentistry. By combining their practices in the new downtown location, they saved a considerable amount of the overhead expense associated with operating a dental office. In fact, this cost-containment motivated the merger in 1964. Another attractive consequence of the merger was their combined ability to provide nearly a full range of dental services to patients.

These dentists were very skilled, dedicated professionals, and the practice flourished through the 1960s and into the 1970s. During the late 1970s, however, all dentists began to see a reduced consumer demand for their services. Fluoridated water supplies, mouth rinses, and dentrifices had become widespread. Consequently, the incidence of dental caries (cavities) was greatly reduced, especially among children.

At the same time, the number of dentists practicing in the United States increased. This increase exceeded the rate of population growth (see Exhibit 3–1). Furthermore, population growth in the Akron area began to level off. In fact, while the standard metropolitan statistical area (SMSA) grew somewhat, the city of Akron saw its population fall from 290,000 in 1960 to 275,000 in 1970, 237,00 in 1980, and 227,000 in 1984.

Jones, Johnson, and Marini were not pleased with the prospect of incomes that did not continue to increase, but they recognized this as possibly inevitable because they did not know how to overcome the environmental constraints on the provision of their professional services. Conventional wisdom during the 1970s and early 1970s in the dental services industry had suggested that any dentist who provided excellent dental care would be rewarded with many (perhaps *too* many) patients, who would go to great lengths to find and secure such services. Consequently, the dentists at Akron Dental services simply pursued their business of trying to provide the best possible dental care services to their patients.

By the early 1980s, however, the environment had changed so dramatically that many dentists were forced to "do something" to remain solvent. The nationwide trend toward increased oral hygiene was shifting from dental maintenance to prevention, diagnosis, and aesthetics. Besides caring for tooth decay, dentists began to emphasize preventive, reconstructive, and cosmetic dental care and thereby encouraged an increased rate of dental visits. The annual per capita number of dental visits increased from 1.5 in 1970 to 1.8 in 1983.

Excess capacity problems nevertheless persisted, and dentists became interested in marketing to retain or expand their customer base. They soon began to realize that marketing greatly benefited dentists as well as patients. In this highly competitive field, some experts claimed that dentists had to have as much "mar-

---

This case was prepared by Jon M. Hawes and Greg Heben, University of Akron.

EXHIBIT 3–1

U.S. Dental Demographics

	1950	1960	1970	1980	1984
Number of active dentists	75,000	85,000	96,000	141,000	153,000
Rate per 100,000 population	50	47	47	54	57

keting savvy as medical expertise"[1] to operate a successful practice. This should not be viewed as an indication that the quality of dental care would suffer, however. After all, the marketing concept simply suggests that dentists should understand and respond to the needs and wants of well-defined target markets. The dental practice should be operated like any other successful retail service. The primary objective should be long-run service and profit maximization by understanding and responding to customer needs and wants. When successfully implemented, a marketing philosophy results in higher levels of patient satisfaction and a more profitable practice for the dentists.

The dentists at Akron Dental Services began to develop an interest in marketing after meeting Dr. Sally Simpson at a country club party. Simpson is a professor of marketing at the University of Akron and has been active in research, writing, and consulting in the health care marketing sector since the late 1970s. After several meetings to discuss the current problems of the dental industry, Simpson agreed to use the problem as one of the class projects for her marketing research course. In return, Akron Dental Services agreed to pay for all out-of-pocket expenses and to make a substantial contribution to the Marketing Department's scholarship fund.

Simpson tried to help the dentists "think marketing" and see the business aspects of providing dental services to customers in a retail environment. Of course, the dentists needed to continue providing excellent professional dental services, but Simpson also tried to help them in their personal interactions with patients and in their role as providers of a professional service within a retail environment. She also gave the dentists tips on how to make the patient's trip to the dentist more pleasant. Simpson tried to get the dentists to consider the patient's point of view as the recipient of the dental care. For example, they learned that fear was estimated to be the prohibitive factor in 30 to 40 percent of the people who don't go to the dentist.[2] Office atmosphere and professional image also were discussed at these meetings.

Next, Simpson assigned the problem to one of the class groups. After studying the problem, the group organized and conducted a survey of a random sample of 1,000 residents of the Akron, Ohio, SMSA to determine the importance of various factors relating to dental care marketing. A total of 353 people responded to the mail survey.

---

[1]Donna Boetig, "Dentists Polish Up Their Image," *The Saturday Evening Post* 259, no. 8 (November 1987): 28.

[2]Dr. Nancy Chu cited by Donna Boetig, "Dentists Polish Up Their Image," *The Saturday Evening Post* 259, no. 8 (November 1987): 28.

EXHIBIT 3-2
Results of the Surveys

Rank	Description of Retail Marketing Factors	Average Importance*	Average Satisfaction†
1	Quality of care	4.70	4.20
2	Personal attention	4.60	3.60
3	Easy-to-understand explanations of diagnosis, treatment, and progress	4.25	3.70
4	Amount of health information provided	4.04	4.25
5	Cost of services	3.84	4.00
6	Efficient staff	3.83	3.55
7	Availability of/ease of securing an appointment	3.70	4.12
8	Amount of time spent in waiting room	3.66	3.87
9	Friendly staff	3.62	4.04
10	Billing procedures/handling of insurance forms	3.41	3.50
11	Convenient location	3.15	3.75
12	Attractive office and facilities	2.91	4.50

*Scored on a five-point scale where 1 = not important, 2 = below-average importance, 3 = average importance, 4 = above-average importance, and 5 = most important.
†Served on a five-point scale where 1 = very dissatisfied, 2 = dissatisfied, 3 = neither dissatisfied nor satisfied, 4 = satisfied, and 5 = very satisfied.

In addition, 200 patients of Akron Dental Services were mailed questionnaires to determine their level of satisfaction with the same dental care marketing factors. Eighty-five patients completed and returned the form. They had no way of knowing that Akron Dental Services sponsored the research or that only these patients were polled to gauge satisfaction. Simpson hoped that this procedure would lead to more accurate reflections of patient satisfaction. The results of both surveys are shown in Exhibit 3-2.

Analytical Problem

Assume the role of the student group in Simpson's class that was assigned to this class project. Your assignment is to prepare a report for Akron Dental Services.

Having gathered the data (see Exhibit 3-2) and studied the case facts, now translate the data and case facts into useful information through interpretation. Your interpretation should consider tactics for (1) attracting new patients, (2) better serving existing patients, and (3) overcoming the excess dental capacity in the Akron area.

PART THREE
The Retail Environment

CASE 4 **SOFAST COMPANY:**
Evaluating Environmental Changes and the Impact on Retail Distribution

On a Monday morning in December 1980, when Jack Wilson, vice president of marketing at SoFast Company arrived at his corporate office as usual at 8:00 A.M., he found a marketing research report that he had been waiting for during the last few weeks. The report was submitted by InfoSearch, a consulting group in Chicago, which Williams had commissioned 6 months earlier to suggest some strategies the company could adopt to reverse the faltering sales and declining operating profits that had plagued it for the last 7 years.

Company Background

SoFast Company had occupied a predominant position in the home sewing machine industry for many generations. It was the industry's leader until the 1950s. It manufactured and assembled all the parts of its sewing machines in the United States and marketed these machines both in the United States and Europe. Not until after World War II did the company start to experience the pressure of foreign competition. Both the Japanese and the Italians began to invade the company's main markets by supplying low-cost, low-priced home sewing machines made in Taiwan and Korea, which were sold in the United States for practically half the price that SoFast Company charged for its similar sewing machine.

To add to the company's problems, the U.S. demand for sewing machines had declined by over 50 percent in the past 7 years, with more than half of that drop occurring in the last 2 years. More women in the United States took jobs outside of the home and as a result had less time for sewing. As their life-styles changed, women demanded more stylish clothing and allocated more dollars to their wardrobe than ever before. At the same time, ready-made clothing manufacturers successfully switched their supply sources to the Far East, enabling them to provide the American market with a good selection of ready-made clothing at reasonable prices. This trend further curtailed the incentive to sew at home. As a result, production in the whole U.S. industry had declined steadily after a peak in 1969.

This case was prepared by Nessim Hanna, Northern Illinois University. This case is hypothetical, presented merely to emphasize certain retailing principles. Any resemblance to existing companies is only accidental.

SoFast's Distribution Method

SoFast was unique in its distribution method. It sold and serviced its well-known sewing machines in exclusive company-owned centers found in virtually every small town in the United States, as well as in some European countries. Over the years, it added other complementary items to the line of sewing machines to provide shoppers with a reasonable selection of related products in the company's centers, as well as to capitalize on the centers' traffic. The complementary items included yard goods, sewing kits, yarn, patterns, and other types of sewing and decorating supplies and accessories.

The centers were placed in downtown locations, and each was run by a manager, assisted by a few sales clerks. The number of sales personnel varied with the size of the center, which in turn was a function of the size of the community served.

The company's objective in using direct distribution was to maintain the high-quality image and the reputation for superior service that had been its trademarks for many years. Wilson recalled when people used to say jokingly that every maiden dreamed of having two things in life, a good man and a SoFast sewing machine. He remembered when a household was not considered complete without a SoFast sewing machine.

The company, from its start, had followed a consumer-oriented philosophy, which meant that when a customer purchased a SoFast sewing machine, the transaction was considered to be the beginning, not the end, of a good relationship. The purchaser could sign up for beginning or advanced sewing classes, received periodic catalogs containing the latest styles and designs in clothing, and was granted fast and courteous service when needed.

SoFast's direct distribution eliminated the need for retailers as a link between the company and its customers. Two benefits arose from direct-distribution. First were the savings materializing as a result of eliminating retailers' markups, and the second was in allowing the company to control the quality of service offered to customers.

The drawback of this distribution method, however, was the heavy financial burden on the company. Maintaining the centers was a costly undertaking. Operating expenses included the fixed costs of the centers (such as rent, electricity, phone, insurance, and taxes); variable costs (such as wages, materials, and suppliers); and the various advertising and promotional costs needed to bring customers to the centers.

Competitors' Distribution Method

In contrast to SoFast's direct distribution method, foreign competitors selling sewing machines in the United States had a selective distribution policy. The Japanese sewing machine manufacturers, for example, had successfully distributed their sewing machines in the United States through a limited number of well-selected department stores where personalized selling was available. In such stores, the Japanese sewing machines were carried along with a range of other competing brands of sewing machines available for sale in the same department. The objective behind this distribution method was to provide as much exposure for the sewing machine as possible. Shoppers patronizing these large stores were exposed to the machines as part of the product offering of the store, whether or not they had ever thought of owning one. The distinctiveness of the Japanese sewing machine was further emphasized through in-store demonstrations performed by a group of trained field representatives maintained by the manufacturer. On selected weekends and/or on special occasions, a trained representative demonstrated to prospective buyers in each store the various stitches the Japanese sewing machine could perform.

In this type of distribution, however, service for the sewing machine is not provided at the point of purchase. Rather, the Japanese manufacturer maintained a central service facility to receive and service machines brought to the place of purchase for repair.

The Cost Crunch

The report in front of Wilson indicated that the production costs of SoFast sewing machines were rising steadily by approximately 5 percent per year, as a result of the unionized labor demands and the rise in material costs. The report also pointed out that the costs of running the company's centers was rising by approximately 10 percent each year as a result of the rising labor, services, and rental costs. The report also revealed that the ratio of sales per employee in each center averaged about twenty-five sewing machines annually—down from thirty-six sewing machines 2 years earlier.

The report questioned the wisdom of maintaining direct distribution. Observation of traffic patterns in most of the company's centers showed very few patrons. Shoppers who frequented the centers, the report indicated, were either already sold on the idea of specifically purchasing a SoFast sewing machine or were present owners of SoFast sewing machines who needed accessories or supplies. Few consumers considered the stores a place for "fun" shopping or for spending a pleasant time looking at merchandise or people, which may be reasons for shopping in large department stores or shopping centers.

The report went on to emphasize the need for SoFast to change with the times. In the past, the report added, the public may well have perceived the SoFast sewing machine as a "specialty item." As such, the exclusive sales and service centers were appropriate and effective. As life-styles changed, however, and as a new generation of working women appeared, the public no longer considered the SoFast sewing machine a specialty item but rather a "shopping good." Working women, even if interested in sewing, did not have preconceived notions about the SoFast brand. They did not seem to care as much about a sewing machine's particular brand as about its functions and price.

In addition, the report continued, considering the wide selection of available sewing machine brands on the market, the potential buyer was more likely to be willing to spend time and effort to compare available selections. Comparison is more logically accomplished in large department stores or shopping centers, which carry a wide variety of competing brands, and where shopping is more appealing and pleasant than in SoFast's confined centers, which carry only a single brand.

The Recommendations

In view of the preceding points, the report suggested three alternatives regarding the distribution method the company should follow:

1. SoFast should abandon direct distribution and use instead a selective distribution policy. The company, according to this alternative, should close down the exclusive centers it presently maintains and select instead a number of large and reputable stores to carry its sewing machines. The SoFast sewing machine would become part of the product offering of these department stores and would be sold along with the other competing brands that these large stores carried.

2. SoFast should close down the company's sales and service centers in all small towns and maintain only a few in larger towns. The centers maintained, however, should be moved away from the downtown sections and relocated in well-frequented shopping centers. The purpose behind this strategy was to accomplish wide exposure of SoFast sewing machines to the heavy traffic typical of shopping centers. This strategy also recognized the behavioral tendency of the retail consumer. The consumer typically likes to view a variety of competing brands, compares features and prices, and makes a selection without leaving the shopping center. With SoFast's owned stores relocated in shopping centers, shoppers could more conveniently compare SoFast's sewing machines with competing machines.

3. SoFast should discard the idea of owning and running its own centers and instead should "dealerize" these centers. The centers would be offered to parties interested in obtaining a franchising agreement with SoFast or in acting as exclusive dealers for the company's line of products. The company would still maintain the rights of a franchisor for control over the quality of service offered to customers.

As Wilson reviewed the details of the suggested alternatives, he thought of how difficult it would be to change a distribution system that the company had followed successfully for generations. He wondered what effect such a change would have on the present as well as potential customers of SoFast Company. What particularly bothered him about the proposed changes was the loss of control over the quality of service when the sewing machines were handled by independent dealers. This service quality had been the company's major trademark and main selling point for many generations.

Analytical Problem

Assume Wilson's role. He has been asked to submit a written report to the corporate president that analyzes the retailing options for the SoFast Company, given the recent changes in the retail employment. The report must recommend a specific retail plan of action with extensive justification for whatever decisions are made.

CASE 5 HOME STORES, INC.:
A Problem of Store Image Assessment

Home Stores, Inc. (HSI), was a regional retail chain store organization that operated six furniture–appliance stores in the state of Arkansas. One of these stores was located in Fayetteville. Despite the area's economic growth and HSI's respectable overall sales growth, sales for the Fayetteville HSI had declined over the past several years (see Exhibit 5–1). Early in 1986, Charlotte Johnson was appointed the new manager for the Fayetteville store. Upper management made infinitely clear to Johnson that the sales performance of the Fayetteville store *must* improve.

Johnson received a great deal of power to make many changes in the Fayetteville store. Indeed, each HSI store manager could develop local store policies and practices that varied greatly from one HSI location to another. These included many aspects of retail strategy such as merchandise assortment, pricing, and some promotional practices.

Ben Smith was the president of HSI at this time. He thought that sales at the Fayetteville HSI suffered because of a poor store image. It certainly was not as a result of a lack of growth in the market area. Exhibit 5–2 highlights some of the statistics that document the rapid growth and development of this trading area. Smith believed that both current and potential customers were somewhat confused about the Fayetteville retail outlet. This probably accounted for at least some of the problem with sales.

Smith felt that the Fayetteville store was unable to attract some potential buyers of furniture and appliances because they identified the store with various other merchandise, including hardware. The Fayetteville outlet was the only store in the chain that carried hardware items. But while the president had a "gut feeling" that

EXHIBIT 5–1
Sales for Home Stores, Inc.

Year	Sales ($000s)	
	Fayetteville Store	Corporation
1960	350	2,256
1970	905	5,652
1980	3,100	19,420
1985	2,400	21,315

This case was prepared by C. P. Rao and G. E. Kiser, University of Arkansas, and Jon M. Hawes, University of Akron. It was developed to provide a basis for class discussion, rather than to illustrate either effective or ineffective retail strategy. All names of individuals, firms, and some of the facts have been changed. This case was made possible by the cooperation of a retail organization, which remains anonymous. Copyright © 1988 by the authors.

EXHIBIT 5–2
Area Demographic Trends

Year	Fayetteville		Springdale		Washington County	
Population						
1960	20,600		10,500		56,300	
1970	31,400		17,300		78,800	
1980	37,000		24,000		101,300	
1985	36,600		26,000		107,600	
Total retail sales						
1960	$ 30,379,000		$ 21,578,000		$ 65,555,000	
1970	$ 76,798,000		$ 74,801,000		$171,581,000	
1980	$277,891,000		$184,058,000		$502,919,000	
1985	$367,560,000		$203,023,000		$623,247,000	
Retail sales of furniture, home furnishings, and appliance stores						
1960	$ 1,124,000		$ 450,000		$ 1,829,000	
1970	$ 3,638,000		$1,110,000		$ 5,809,000	
1980	$14,889,000		$4,574,000		$19,676,000	
1985	$13,582,000		$9,977,000		$24,675,000	
Effective buying income						
	Total EBI	BPI	Total EBI	BPI	Total EBI	BPI
1960	$ 38,356,000	.0118	$ 14,622,000	.0062	84,450,000	.0270
1970	$120,190,000	.0183	$ 53,570,000	.0118	$ 243,085,000	.0398
1980	$304,337,000	.0203	$186,918,000	.0130	$ 736,693,000	.0447
1985	$350,878,000	.0172	$258,515,000	.0112	$1,007,529,000	.0403

Source: *Sales & Marketing Management,* "Survey of Buying Power."
BPI, buying power index; total EBI, total effective buying income.

this was a major problem, he knew that corporate management lacked the adequate and appropriate information needed to scientifically pinpoint the problem. After obtaining that information, management could develop a systematic retail strategy to improve the situation. Both Smith and Johnson agreed that a clear understanding of overall store image was needed. Clarifying the strengths and weaknesses of the local store would help in developing an appropriate and creative retail strategy.

Within a month of her appointment as store manager in the Fayetteville location, Johnson concluded that the previous store manager, Fred Sawyer, had encouraged the projection of a "mom-and-pop" store image. Johnson also felt that many customers had come to believe that Sawyer had owned, as well as managed, the store during his 21 years as store manager. Many customers seemed to shop at the Fayetteville HSI because of their personal relationship with Sawyer. Although there could be some advantage in such a personal approach to retailing, Johnson knew that the lack of an effective corporate chain store image had deterred sales growth, especially in Fayetteville, where so many people were new to the community.

On the basis of her preliminary discussions with customers and store personnel, Johnson quickly agreed with Smith that a scientific study of the store's image would greatly help her to develop and implement policies for improving the store's sales performance. Additionally, Johnson agreed that an independent assessment of the HSI store in Fayetteville by someone not directly employed by the corporation would provide a more objective basis for the study. Consequently, with Smith's full support, Johnson sought the professional services of Market Research, Inc., a consulting firm, to conduct the image study.

After discussing the situation at length with the consultants, Johnson agreed that a store "image" study would be conducted. The research would be designed to achieve the following objectives:

1. Identify the relative importance of various store features that consumers consider when selecting or patronizing a furniture/appliance store.
2. Identify consumers' relative preferences for furniture/appliance stores in the Fayetteville area.
3. Identify consumers' evaluation of the HSI store in Fayetteville on the basis of those store features mentioned in item 1.
4. Collect data about the demographic characteristics of the respondents.

The consumer survey would use a structured questionnaire (Exhibit 5–3). The data would be gathered from a sample of present and past HSI customers, as well as from a more general list of local consumers. With this purpose, the consultants developed the following research plan:

1. Approximately one third of the respondents were selected from *present customers* who previously had patronized the Fayetteville HSI. These respondents were selected randomly from a file of sales tickets issued during the past 5 years.
2. The remaining two thirds of the consumers contacted were selected randomly from telephone directories covering the market area. Although Market Research, Inc., expected that most of these respondents were *potential customers* in the sense that they could patronize the Fayetteville HSI store, it was also expected that some of these respondents were already store patrons. In this case, they were replaced in the sample by the next listing in the telephone directory with no record of purchases from this store.
3. Approximately 20 percent of the sample members in each group were personally interviewed. Data from the remainder were collected through mailed questionnaires.
4. For considerations of time and cost, 150 present customers and 300 potential customers were contacted and their assistance requested.
5. Following the data-collection phase, the marketing consultants submitted a written report consisting of the following parts: (a) an independent, professional evaluation of the Fayetteville HSI by the marketing consultants and (b) a summary of the data gathered from the interviews.

EXHIBIT 5–3
Questionnaire

Please answer the following questions with a check mark and/or a brief remark to express your experience or opinions.

1. Have you purchased any of the following items in the last 6 months? Are you planning to buy the item in the next 6 months? (Please check as many as applicable)

Type of Item	Purchased During the Last 6 Months		Planning To Buy in the Next 6 Months		
	YES	NO	YES	NO	NOT SURE
Major appliances (refrigerator, washing machine, etc.)	____	____	____	____	____
TV, phonograph, tape recorder, etc.	____	____	____	____	____
Major furniture item(s) costing more than $200	____	____	____	____	____
Minor furniture item(s) costing less than $200	____	____	____	____	____

2. Below is a list of potentially desirable features in any furniture/appliance retail store. Please indicate how important these features are to you in selecting or patronizing such a store. For example, if you consider a feature highly important, circle the 7. On the other hand, if the feature describes a least important consideration, please circle 1. When your importance rating is in between for any statement, please circle the number—2, 3, 4, 5, or 6—that most closely expresses your opinion.

	Most Important						Least Important
Attractive decor and display	7	6	5	4	3	2	1
Accessibility of store	7	6	5	4	3	2	1
Informative advertising	7	6	5	4	3	2	1
Courteous store personnel	7	6	5	4	3	2	1
Easy credit	7	6	5	4	3	2	1
Competitive prices	7	6	5	4	3	2	1
Quality merchandise	7	6	5	4	3	2	1
Easy to find parking place	7	6	5	4	3	2	1
Wide selection of merchandise	7	6	5	4	3	2	1
Carry well-known brands	7	6	5	4	3	2	1
Store is well-known to our friends	7	6	5	4	3	2	1
Quick delivery service	7	6	5	4	3	2	1
The type of customers patronizing the store	7	6	5	4	3	2	1

EXHIBIT 5–3 *(continued)*

Convenient location	7	6	5	4	3	2	1
Store is generally well-known	7	6	5	4	3	2	1

3. Please mention as many furniture-appliance stores that you can recall, in the order of your preference. (If you like a store most, please mention it first, then the next preferred, and so on.)

1. _____   3. _____   5. _____

2. _____   4. _____   6. _____

4. What do you think of Home Stores, Inc., in Fayetteville? (Please write the word(s) that first come(s) to mind.)

HOME STORES, INC., mostly sells _____.

5. On the following list of features, how do you evaluate the Home Stores, Inc., in Fayetteville? If your evaluation is highly favorable, please circle 7. Alternately, if your evaluation is highly unfavorable, please circle 1. If your evaluation is in between, please circle the number—2, 3, 4, 5, or 6—that most closely expresses your evaluation.

	Highly Favorable						Highly Unfavorable
Attractive decor and display	7	6	5	4	3	2	1
Accessibility of store	7	6	5	4	3	2	1
Informative advertising	7	6	5	4	3	2	1
Courteous store personnel	7	6	5	4	3	2	1
Easy credit	7	6	5	4	3	2	1
Competitive prices	7	6	5	4	3	2	1
Quality merchandise	7	6	5	4	3	2	1
Easy to find parking place	7	6	5	4	3	2	1
Wide selection of merchandise	7	6	5	4	3	2	1
Carry well-known brands	7	6	5	4	3	2	1
Store is well-known to our friends	7	6	5	4	3	2	1
Quick delivery service	7	6	5	4	3	2	1
Type of customers patronizing the store	7	6	5	4	3	2	1
Convenient location	7	6	5	4	3	2	1
Store is generally well-known	7	6	5	4	3	2	1

Would you please provide the following information about yourself:

1. Please check your age group on the following:
   ____ Under 20 years   ____ 30–39 years   ____ 50–59 years
   ____ 20–29 years   ____ 40–49 years   ____ Over 60 years
2. Which of the following categories applies to your total family income:
   ____ Under $10,000   ____ $20,000–29,999   ____ $40,000–49,999
   ____ $10,000–19,999   ____ $30,000–39,999   ____ Over $50,000
3. Person completing the questionnaire: ____ Male ____ Female
4. Occupation of the head of the household: _____

The consultants completed the study within the specified time frame of 2 months. Highlights of the report follow.

Store Evaluation

The HSI retail outlet in Fayetteville is a relatively large furniture, appliance, and hardware store. The store carries a wide variety of brand names in furniture, such as Broyhill, Marflex, Woodward, DeSoto, and Twin Oaks. A limited selection of Westinghouse appliances is complemented by a good selection of television sets and stereos. There is also a small hardware department within the same large building.

The HSI store generally projects a "mom-and-pop" image and definitely does not give the impression of a chain store operated by a large, progressive corporation.

The professional decor that one would expect to find in a quality, full-line furniture and appliance store is lacking. The store does not appeal to visitors, and one can generally describe the atmospherics as "lifeless." On entering the store, the first impression is that of a wholesale outlet. Although the furniture department is not haphazardly laid out, it lacks originality and does not portray a realistic grouping of the items. There are no partitions between sets or individual pieces. When displaying furniture, attractive arrangement is extremely important, especially in the bedroom layouts, but this is very much missing here. Lighting is minimal and makes the decor even more drab. Although the store carries a line of tile and carpeting, there is none on the floor or on display.

The hardware department is not laid out well and appears "messy." In general, the quality of hardware lines is good, though not exceptional. In some merchandise lines such as small appliances, the store carries a good variety. This is not true of all merchandise lines, however.

The market areas for furniture and appliance merchandise consist of two major geographic segments: the city of Fayetteville and the surrounding areas. The regional economy has grown faster than other areas of the state. Despite this healthy environment, the local store is not keeping pace in sales. Although there are some problems with the store's interior and its arrangement, it carries quality furniture, televisions, stereos, and appliances at competitive prices. As an indication of deficient marketing effort, the store lacks adequate exposure to the target market. Thus, customer awareness of the Fayetteville HSI's existence and what it has to offer is very limited.

Prestige comes from customers recognizing the store's high-quality merchandise and excellent service. In this connection, the store suffers not only from a lack of exposure to the target market but its image is diffused and diluted by multiple lines of diverse merchandise. It is difficult to improve the prestige of the store as a primary furniture–appliance business while the store also tries to sell "nickel-and-dime" hardware items. For many potential customers, the esteem associated with a furniture store would be one of the main reasons for purchasing from that store. The customer demands a degree of distinctiveness when purchasing high-value items. But a store carrying and selling low-value and low-prestige items inflicts a damaging effect on the high-value and high-prestige items. In this sense, the hardware unit of the Fayetteville HSI outlet is quite incongruous with the store's main effort.

Survey Results

Some of the results of the questionnaire are reported in Exhibits 5–4 through 5–8. Remember that two groups of people were interviewed: (1) those who had pur-

EXHIBIT 5-4

Relative Importance of Various Furniture-Appliance Store Attributes*

	Most Important 7		6		5		4		3		2		Least Important 1	
	I	II	I	II	I	II	I	II	I	II	I	II	I	II
Attractive decor and display	23.1	7.3	10.3	16.4	20.5	16.4	25.6	30.9	7.7	5.5	0.0	5.5	12.9	18.2
Accessibility of store	25.6	25.5	20.5	16.4	25.6	20.0	10.3	23.7	10.3	5.5	0.0	3.6	7.7	5.4
Informative advertising	23.1	10.9	28.2	20.0	20.5	27.3	15.4	14.5	0.0	10.9	2.6	5.5	10.1	10.9
Courteous store personnel	69.2	60.0	15.4	10.9	12.8	16.4	0.0	7.2	0.0	1.8	0.0	0.0	2.6	3.6
Easy credit	5.1	7.3	12.8	15.4	30.8	10.9	15.4	9.1	7.7	10.9	5.1	9.1	23.1	38.2
Competitive prices	56.4	61.8	20.5	21.8	12.8	9.1	7.7	1.8	0.0	0.0	0.0	1.8	2.6	3.6
Quality merchandise	71.8	87.3	20.5	9.1	5.1	1.8	0.0	0.0	0.0	0.0	0.0	0.0	2.6	1.8
Easy to find parking place	30.8	27.3	17.9	7.3	25.6	20.0	12.8	32.7	7.7	3.6	2.6	5.5	2.6	3.6
Wide selection of merchandise	38.5	40.0	28.2	23.6	12.8	21.8	5.1	9.1	5.1	1.8	2.6	0.0	7.7	3.6
Carry well-known brands	35.9	34.5	25.6	18.2	12.8	18.2	7.7	21.8	7.7	3.6	5.1	0.0	5.1	3.6
Store is well-known to our friends	12.8	3.6	7.7	7.3	7.7	5.5	15.4	25.5	17.9	10.9	5.1	9.1	33.3	38.2
Quick delivery service	17.8	18.2	5.1	16.4	15.4	18.2	28.2	20.0	15.4	7.3	5.1	3.6	12.8	16.4
Type of customers patronizing the store	5.1	3.6	2.6	3.6	20.5	3.6	17.9	16.4	7.7	9.1	5.1	18.2	41.5	45.5
Convenient location	33.3	21.8	10.3	21.8	20.5	12.7	15.4	21.8	10.3	10.9	0.0	5.5	10.3	5.5
Store is generally well-known	12.8	14.5	12.8	5.5	15.3	25.5	33.3	16.4	7.7	12.7	2.6	3.6	15.4	21.8

*Respondent evaluation ratings were gathered on a seven-point scale—7 representing most important and 1 least important. Under each value of the evaluation scale, the percentages under I represent the Fayetteville HSI customer group (n = 78), and II the potential customer group (n = 110).

EXHIBIT 5–5
Mentions of the Number of Area Furniture-Appliance Stores that the Respondents Liked
(percentage of respondent group)

Respondent Group	Number of Area Furniture-Appliance Stores Mentioned				
	One (%)	Two (%)	Three (%)	Four (%)	Five (%)
HSI customer group (n = 78)	12.8	10.3	35.9	28.5	2.5
Potential customer group (n = 110)	36.4	14.5	21.8	27.3	0.0

See Exhibit 5–3, question 3.

EXHIBIT 5–6
Number and Order of Mentions of HSI Store as One of Respondents' Preferred
Furniture-Appliance Stores in the Area (percentage of respondent group)

Respondent Group	Total Number Of HSI Mentions (%)	Order of mentions				
		First (%)	Second (%)	Third (%)	Fourth (%)	Fifth (%)
HSI customer group (n = 78)	100	30	40	30	—	—
Potential customer group (n = 110)	38	—	9	21	8	—

See Exhibit 5–3, question 3.

EXHIBIT 5–7

Respondent Evaluation of the Fayetteville HSI on Various Furniture-Appliance Store Attributes*

| | High Favorable | | | | | | Respondents Reporting (%) | | | | High Unfavorable | | | |
| | 7 | | 6 | | 5 | | 4 | | 3 | | 2 | | 1 | |
	I	II	I	II	I	II	I	II	I	II	I	II	I	II
Attractive decor and display	30.8	7.3	17.9	3.6	23.1	12.7	17.9	10.9	5.1	5.5	2.6	0.0	2.6	60.0
Accessibility of store	33.3	10.9	23.1	9.1	20.5	12.7	15.4	5.5	5.1	3.6	0.0	1.8	2.6	56.4
Informative advertising	17.9	3.6	12.8	1.8	23.1	5.5	28.2	7.3	7.7	12.7	0.0	7.3	10.3	61.8
Courteous store personnel	38.5	5.5	25.6	13.6	17.9	17.3	15.4	19.1	0.0	11.8	0.0	11.8	2.6	20.9
Easy credit	30.8	1.8	25.6	1.8	15.4	1.8	12.8	10.9	0.0	3.6	2.6	3.6	12.8	76.4
Competitive prices	20.5	5.5	23.1	3.6	28.2	10.9	15.4	9.1	2.6	1.8	0.0	1.8	10.3	67.3
Quality merchandise	33.3	5.5	15.6	5.5	20.5	9.1	10.3	5.5	10.0	1.8	2.6	7.3	7.7	65.5
Easy to find parking place	53.8	12.7	17.9	10.9	15.4	7.3	2.6	3.6	5.1	1.8	2.6	3.6	2.6	60.0
Wide selection of merchandise	23.1	1.8	23.1	10.9	35.9	1.8	10.3	9.1	2.6	9.1	2.6	3.6	2.6	63.6
Carry well-known brands	25.6	3.6	33.3	5.5	23.1	9.1	12.8	10.9	2.6	3.6	0.0	1.8	2.6	65.5
Store is well-known to our friends	17.9	3.6	15.4	3.6	25.6	3.6	20.5	7.3	2.6	7.3	5.1	5.5	12.8	69.1
Quick delivery service	23.1	1.8	20.5	3.6	15.4	0.0	25.6	12.7	2.6	5.5	2.6	0.0	10.3	76.4
Type of customers patronizing the store	20.5	3.6	12.8	1.8	28.2	5.5	20.5	14.5	7.6	3.6	0.0	0.0	10.3	70.9
Convenient location	30.8	10.9	23.1	10.9	15.4	9.1	20.5	5.5	0.0	1.8	7.7	7.3	2.6	54.5
Store is generally well-known	33.3	10.9	20.5	5.5	23.1	5.5	15.4	9.1	0.0	3.6	2.6	1.8	5.1	63.6

*Respondent evaluation ratings were gathered on a seven-point scale—7 representing highly favorable and 1 highly unfavorable. Under each value of the evaluation scale, the percentages under I represent the Fayetteville HSI customer group (n = 78), and II the potential customer group (n = 110).

EXHIBIT 5–8
Sociodemographic Characteristics of Respondents

	HSI Store Customer Group (n = 78) (%)	Potential Customer Group (n = 110) (%)
Age		
Under 20 years	0.0	5.5
20–29 years	35.9	45.5
30–39 years	25.6	23.6
40–49 years	5.1	5.5
50–59 years	17.1	7.3
Over 60 years	15.5	12.6
Total family income		
Under $10,000	10.3	16.4
$10,000–$19,999	15.4	10.9
$20,000–$29,999	20.5	9.1
$30,000–$39,999	25.6	20.0
$40,000–$49,999	12.8	14.5
Over $50,000	7.7	12.7
No response	7.7	16.4
Sex		
Male	61.5	36.4
Female	38.5	63.6

chased products at the Fayetteville HSI within the past 5 years and (2) consumers randomly drawn from the telephone directory. The latter are identified as the "potential customer group."

Analytical Problem

Assume the role of Charlotte Johnson, the store manager of the Fayetteville HSI. Ben Smith, HSI president, has asked you to write a report for the HSI Board of Directors that addresses the following concerns:

1. How do you evaluate HSI management's analysis of the problem? What alternative approach, if any, would you take in such a preliminary diagnosis of the problem?
2. Critically evaluate the research plan designed by the marketing consultant group.
3. What is your analysis of the survey results submitted by the marketing consultants?
4. On the basis of such analysis and the information on the store evaluation of the marketing consultant's report, what conclusions would you draw as to the nature and dimensions of the image problem?
5. After completing the analysis, what would you recommend to improve the sales performance of the HSI retail outlet in Fayetteville?

HALPIN'S OPTICAL:
Responding to a Changing Environment

Background

Dr. Herman Halpin, a Townson, Ohio, optometrist, watched his secretary/assistant open the doors of Halpin's Optical as usual at 9:00 A.M. on July 15, but he suspected it would be a few minutes before any patients arrived. Now age 55, Halpin had been giving eye tests and selling lenses, frames, and contacts for nearly 25 years, working out of a 750-square-foot office, examining room, and small showroom located on the first floor of a professional building just outside of downtown.

For over two decades, Halpin had enjoyed a quiet, steady, and prosperous retail business that he operated with little need for fanfare or change. He felt that he enjoyed excellent relationships with his patients and that this was the main reason so many of them remained loyal over time. During the past several years, however, revenues had begun to flatten out, leading to an actual decline last year. In fact, 4 years ago, net sales of examination services, glasses, contacts, and other eye care products were $340,000, with profit before taxes of $81,000. Last year, however, after adjusting for inflation, net sales were only $280,000, with before-tax profit of $68,000. The drop in sales and income had been particularly steep recently, and Halpin was concerned about the future of his business.

Several reasons for this decline were evident. First, the surrounding neighborhood, which had always served as the primary source of Halpin's patients, was decaying. Many of the middle-class residents who once populated the area had moved farther out into the suburbs. Halpin had also noticed a distinct decline of late in the number of office workers whom he served from the nearby downtown. This puzzled him, because the downtown area had been revitalized in recent years and seemed teeming with young professionals.

But beyond local factors, Halpin suspected that he was also feeling the effect of two 1978 legal rulings that changed the way the entire optical industry did business. The first was a Federal Trade Commission decision forcing optometrists to provide patients with their prescriptions, greatly facilitating their ability to purchase glasses and contacts from other providers. The second was a court ruling allowing professionals such as lawyers and doctors to advertise. Combined, the two decisions opened up opportunities for aggressive and sophisticated retailing practices in the optical field and enhanced the growth of optical store chains such as Pearle Vision Centers, Lens Crafters, and the Eyeworks. The chains were capturing a rapidly growing share of the market, driven by the success of the new concept of huge "megaoptical" stores. As a result of the many changes in the environment, the nature of optical retailing and consumer perceptions of eyewear had been significantly altered.

Many of these new optical stores carried large overhead expenses, requiring a much higher sales volume than the old-style stores to make a profit. The increased sales requirement led in turn to a new array of marketing and merchandis-

This case was prepared by Dan Gilmore, The University of Akron.

ing strategies capable of increasing both store traffic and per-transaction sales to levels well above those achieved by individual practitioners like Halpin. A common element in these strategies was the stimulation of product demand through efforts to move the eyecare and eyewear industry out of the paramedical realm into a more fashion-oriented product market.

Freed from legal restraints on their ability to compete and seizing the opportunity for changing consumer attitudes toward eyewear, this new breed of optical retailer quickly raised the scope, sophistication, and competitiveness of eyewear retailing to an extent that traditional operators had never imagined would be necessary. One example of this revolution was Manhattan Eyeland, a store that occupied 20,000 square feet over two floors in a very high-rent area of New York City. It was distinguished by its ritzy interior, live piano player during store hours, battery of doctors and salespersons, and heavy advertising. Though the store was eventually closed because it did not generate enough sales to meet its extraordinary operating expenses, the concept did catch the attention of many in the industry.

Halpin's business was better than average that Friday. He personally escorted his last customer of the day, an elderly woman whom he had known for many years, to the door. "I'll have your glasses back from the lab and ready for you in 5 days," he said. "They've cut the delivery time by more than half since you were last here. Remember, it used to take 2 weeks."

Despite the good sales day, Halpin knew, as he locked up the office at 5:00 P.M., that he would spend a lot of time over the weekend thinking about what to do with his business. Certainly, the business had been good for him over the years. While he was proud of the care and service he provided for his patients, he realized that years ago he did not have to work all that hard to attract and retain them. They had always seemed satisfied, and his business had remained strong and profitable—at least until recently.

Current Situation

Halpin had an important decision to make. At a recent meeting of the local optical professionals association, he was approached by an old friend from school, Jim Keller, who was now a representative for The Eye Catcher chain of optical stores. He told Halpin that the chain was looking for potential investors to become owner–operators, or franchisees, of Eye Catcher franchise stores in the area. Management hoped to soon open two franchises in the Townson vicinity, with contractual arrangements with franchisees designed as follows:

1. The stores would be located in or near popular shopping malls.

2. Store size would be 5,000 to 7,500 square feet, and each store would contain a wide selection of frames, lenses, and contacts, plus a lab for grinding and fitting eyewear on site.

3. The franchises would have a "business format," providing not only the right to use the Eye Catcher name but also complete store layout and design strategies, initial and continued management training, accounting methods, merchandising programs, and other comprehensive managerial assistance and rules in running the business.

4. The initial franchise fee paid to the company was to be $50,000. Franchisees also were required to have or be able to obtain $150,000 of additional capital. Once in operation, they had to pay 7.5 percent of gross profit as a royalty fee, plus another 2 percent for advertising.

Keller had sent Halpin a disclosure statement, or prospectus, which franchisors are required by law to provide. The statement detailed a wide range of information on the company, its financial position, franchises, and many other topics of interest to investors. With some professional help, Halpin had reviewed the prospectus thoroughly and made other investigations, from which he concluded that The Eye Catcher chain was quite reputable, with most stores (but not all) generally turning a nice profit. Nevertheless, because he had always considered himself much more of a doctor than a businessman, he was somewhat uncertain of his ability to manage an operation the size of an Eye Catcher store, which would have as many as a dozen or more employees.

Though Halpin had the ability to raise the capital requirements, he also wondered whether such a large outlay would result in adequate profits and how hard he would have to work to earn them. Plus, the idea of turning over 9.5 percent of gross profits troubled him somewhat. His son, a recent college graduate in business administration, was skeptical of this aspect as well. "Why should you invest all that money and then give them nearly one tenth of your earnings?" his son asked. He realized there were problems with his father's business, but suggested moving to a new office in one of the modern professional buildings in the suburbs and improving some of the practice's business techniques and strategies. Halpin had also considered such a move in the past few years as his business had declined.

Over the weekend, Halpin reviewed the Eye Catcher prospectus once more. Keller had given him a month to think things over, but that was 2 weeks ago. Halpin was determined that by the end of the week he would decide whether to (1) go with the franchise opportunity, (2) move to a new location but remain independent, or (3) stay where he was and try to do a few things to stabilize his business. The one thing he knew for certain was that the once simple and stable retail optical industry now left him feeling topsy-turvy.

Analytical Problem

Assume the role of the dutiful son or daughter, and surprise your father by conducting the research and analysis necessary to answer the following questions and issues:

1. Discuss the current situation of Halpin's Optical. How have the legal decisions of 1978 cited in the case changed the nature of optical retailing? How would these changes affect Halpin's Optical and why? What problems do you see with your father's business?

2. Most of the new optical chains have in just a few short years developed sophisticated marketing and merchandising techniques that have changed

not only the stores themselves but consumer attitudes and perceptions toward eyewear. If you were a large optical retailer, what strategies could you devise for your store(s) to increase sales compared to traditional operators like your father?

3. Which alternative should you recommend to your father? What are the pros and cons of each option? Justify your recommendations, and write a report that would make your father proud.

AMERICAN SUPERMARKETS:
Assessing Consumer Consumption Behavior Patterns

Randi Jensen hoped to graduate at the end of the semester from the University of Santa Clara with a B.S.B.A. in Marketing. She specialized in retailing and hoped to work in the supermarket industry.

Jensen would soon be ready to begin her career. While she had worked part-time in a number of supermarkets over the past 6 years, she was now being considered for a full-time management trainee position at American Supermarkets. Jensen signed up for her first interview with the company through the university placement service. She prepared extensively for the interview and must have done a good job, because she was soon invited to meet a number of American's executives at the corporate headquarters.

Jensen was pleased with this series of interviews, too. After about a week, she received a package of information from American. The company appeared to be interested in hiring her for their management training program. The next step in the interview process was the preparation of a written report (see Exhibit 7–1).

Jensen was surprised at this request, but on reflection she thought she understood the company's objectives. American Supermarkets was a large organization with stores in many of the nation's largest metropolitan areas. Employees hired as management trainees were expected to move frequently—perhaps as often as five times during the first 4 years of employment. The firm's management held that it was important for the employee to understand that products were sold at quite different rates in various markets. Effective buying decisions and retail merchandising management demanded this insight. Also, written communication skills were important within large corporations. The report would provide the company with an opportunity to assess Jensen's communication skills.

Jensen was quite interested in the opportunity with American Supermarkets and wanted to further demonstrate her abilities in the report.

Analytical Problem

Assume Jensen's role and prepare the report for American Supermarkets. Keep in mind that the central issue is "why do sales vary so much across markets?" What additional sources and types of outside information (e.g., secondary information) might Jensen use to analyze and explain different consumption patterns?

This case was prepared by Jon M. Hawes, University of Akron.

EXHIBIT 7–1
Examination of Sales Patterns

Research firms specialize in the monitoring of sales patterns for products within particular markets. A. C. Nielsen and Selling Areas Marketings, Inc. (SAMI), each offer various types of sales analyses to our company for a fee.

The results of a SAMI sales analysis of relatively high-volume grocery products in six U.S. Standard Metropolitan Statistical Areas (SMSAs) are shown below. A sales index was computed for various product categories within each of the SMSAs, and some of the products that achieved disproportionately high per capita sales within each of the markets are reported.

The sales index is a measure of the relative sales per capita for each of the products. An index of 100 would indicate the average rate of sales for the product throughout the United States. Thus, an index of 200 for a product within a particular market would mean that the item sold at twice the national per capita rate within that market. To cite a specific example, note that "Sausage and franks, canned" had a sales index of 316 in Market 1. Thus, within Market 1, these products sold at 3.16 times the national per capita rate.

Carefully analyze the nature of the mix of disproportionately high-volume products within each of the six markets. Then, consider the nature of each of the six listed SMSAs. Try to match each of the markets with the appropriate SMSA. Provide a written explanation of your logic for each response on as many additional sheets of paper as necessary.

SMSA
Baltimore/Washington, D.C.   Detroit
Houston   Los Angeles
Miami/Fort Lauderdale   San Francisco/Oakland

SAMI Best-Sellers	Sales Index	SAMI Best-Sellers	Sales Index	SAMI Best-Sellers	Sales Index
Market 1		**Market 2**		**Market 3**	
Sausage and franks, canned	316	Cocktail mixes, dry	492	Bluing	206
Insect repellents	289	Lima beans, frozen	299	Miscellaneous sanitary	
Insecticides	288	Croutons	223	needs	174
Sandwich Spreads	258	Sterilized milk and milk		Bath additives	155
Meat dishes, canned	256	products	204	All-fabric bleach detergent	151
Lunch meats, canned	249	Buffing floor wax	202	Croutons	143
Meat spreads, canned	247	Frosting mix, single layer	197	Frosting mix, single layer	140
Rodenticides	242	Chocolate-covered creams	178	Chili sauce	137
Mexican food, frozen	241	Asparagus, frozen	170	Crackers	129
Blended fruit juice, canned		Miscellaneous snacks/dips	170	Packaged chocolate-	
and bottled	240	Corned beef, canned	155	covered fruits	127
Corn meal	235	Spinach, frozen	154		
Motor oil and additives	213				
SMSA: _____		SMSA: _____		SMSA: _____	
Market 4		**Market 5**		**Market 6**	
Mexican food, frozen	377	Fruit nectar, canned and		Refrigerated salad dressing	
Dried figs	334	bottled	427	and sauce	426
Fireplace logs	312	Refrigerated yogurt	260	Juices/drinks, concentrated	286
Refrigerated salad dressing	287	Diet canned vegetables	251	Frozen yogurt	250
Ripe olives	252	Coffee creamer, frozen	235	Cider, canned and bottled	222
Raspberries, frozen	222	Car wax and polish	230	Nonchocolate candy bars	221
Cider, canned and bottled	220	Dried prunes	222	Fireplace logs	220
Deluxe vegetables, frozen	214	Refrigerated herring	219	Upholstery cleaners	216
Southern vegetables, frozen	206	Prune juice, canned and		Cocktail mixes, dry and	
Chili, canned	202	bottled	217	bottled	212
Peppers	197	Refrigerated juice/drinks	214	Peppers	211
Dried apricots	195	Diet fruit, canned	211	Ripe olives	205
		Insecticide	211	Mexican food, frozen	198
		Cream cheese	204	Single-pack gum	189
SMSA: _____		SMSA: _____		SMSA _____	

Note: 100 = average market.

| CASE 8 | AXEHELM'S HARDWARE: |
| | Analyzing Financial Statements |

As Bill Severenson examined the afternoon mail, he was delighted to see his former roommate's name on the return address of a thick envelope, and he opened it immediately. He noted with some surprise a series of financial statements, but he turned his attention to the letter attached to them:

Dear Bill,

I figure it's about time to catch up on my continuing adventures. As I reported in my last letter, I sure wasn't having much luck with the job market. You were right. There isn't a large market for a history major with an interest in soft rock music.

About the middle of the summer, I had a hiatus in my search. I took time to visit my aunt and uncle in Kansas. I'm sure you remember them—they came to graduation.

While I was visiting, one of the clerks at the store was seriously injured in an automobile accident. Uncle Harry was in a bit of a bind and asked if I could give him a hand at the store for a couple of days. He had all the right reasons—they were all green. It was a good chance to make some money, because I admit I was really running short. I was getting adept at freeloading, but I can't say I really enjoyed it.

The upshot of all this is that I've become a permanent employee of Axehelm's Hardware, Inc. Uncle Harry has been quite good about showing me the ropes. I do enjoy the chance to meet people, and I think I've made a generally good impression on my Uncle and the populace of Eastphalia, Kansas.

We have a rather broad line of hardware. Uncle Harry has stressed quality and service. He has been quite successful, because he has the largest operation in these parts. There isn't much competition or service available within about a 10-mile radius. There are some general-purpose stores that handle some tools as part of a grocery line, but we are the place you go to get a broader line of hardware—if you think you can get it at a hardware store, you can get it here!

We carry an enormous inventory to properly service our customers. Even so, we still do a good deal of special ordering for our customers, when we do not have what they want. There's a big warehouse in K.C., where we can get a lot of stuff.

We also have some stuff that's been around since year one. Uncle Harry was telling me that he sold some barbed wire he'd had for years. Believe it or not, there

---

This case was prepared by John Works, The University of Akron.

are people who collect different types of barbed wire. My uncle ended up with a spool of one of the rarer types.

For the present, I'm going to be part of the life of the small town. It certainly is a far different life from that of the U.

More to the point, while I was talking to Uncle Harry the other day, he showed me the store's latest financial statements—fresh from his accountant. When he asked me what I thought of them, I told him I didn't have the vaguest idea of what they meant or if they were good or bad. I told him my rooming with you was as close as I got to analyzing financial statements. I told him you relish financial analysis and felt you wanted it for a life's work.

As we talked further, I asked him how he had learned to use the statements. He said he had quickly learned to look at the bottom line. If there wasn't some profit, it was time to reduce his take-home. He regaled me with stories of the Great Depression and his family's hand-to-mouth existence. More than once he got paid with a chicken or some other farm produce. I have the feeling he looks at the statements with a good deal of intuition that comes from a lifetime of learning what works and what does not.

We got to talking about the importance of intuition in running a business. I asked whether it wasn't pretty important to see whether you could use some more objective standards as well. But Uncle Harry argued, although not adamantly, that horse sense was one of the most important factors in the business. He argued, for example, that he had to temper his business with the times. When the farmers were slower in paying, as they are now, then he would expect to extend more credit. He knew some would walk away from the farm without paying, but most would pay up.

I told Uncle Harry that you'd argued that any one with a little practice should be able to analyze a business without being intimate with it. You said, I believe, there were a lot of standards that could be used to tell if the company was doing well or poorly. I think I am quoting you fairly.

I finally suggested we test this argument. I suggested I could send the statements along to you. I thought you would, for old times' sake, come up with some kind of a measure of the business. Since Uncle Harry thinks he's pretty progressive, he went along with the idea. I think he figures that if nothing else happens, perhaps I will learn something.

This is a long preamble, but I'd appreciate it, if you do have a little time, if you'd pass along what you think about the operations out here in Eastphalia. If you want to analyze companies, here is one that has managed to survive for a considerable period of time.

Best regards,
John

The financial statements that were included with the letter are shown as Exhibits 8–1 and 8–2. Bill accepted the challenge and procured from his company library the Robert Morris Associates reports for hardware companies. These are shown in Exhibit 8–3.

Analytical Problem

Assume the role of Bill Severenson, and prepare the report that John Axehelm needs.

EXHIBIT 8–1
Axehelm Hardware, Inc., 1980 to 1984, Income Statement

	1980	1981	1982	1983	1984
Revenues (Net)	2,547,313	2,881,443	3,014,711	3,156,070	3,293,675
Cost of sales	1,681,731	1,907,002	2,057,151	2,083,413	2,205,184
Other	2,136	4,236	3,744	3,888	4,102
Gross margin	863,446	970,205	953,816	1,068,769	1,084,389
Other costs and expenses (income)					
G & A expenses	537,293	616,847	651,833	667,307	667,134
Rent	34,714	36,829	39,002	37,041	38,725
Depreciation and amortization	22,925	24,976	27,431	28,674	28,997
Advertising & promotion	29,135	33,467	35,766	36,998	36,864
Officers' salaries	117,176	132,456	134,937	135,662	125,462
Other	31,927	35,611	38,007	34,561	35,467
Professional services	6,000	6,600	6,600	6,900	7,200
Total Costs and Expenses	779,170	886,786	933,576	947,143	939,849
EBIT	84,276	83,419	20,240	121,626	144,540
Net interest	14,239	18,497	16,547	14,356	15,216
EBT	70,037	64,922	3,693	107,270	129,324
Income taxes (% of EBIT)	16,715	13,253	555	29,884	38,699
Net income from continuing operations	53,322	51,669	3,138	77,386	90,625
Extraordinary items	137	413	0	(2,156)	457
Net income	53,459	52,082	3,138	75,230	91,082

EBIT, earnings before interest and taxes; EBT, earnings before taxes; G & A, general and administrative.

EXHIBIT 8–2
Axehelm Hardware, Inc., 1980 to 1984, Balance Sheet

	1980	1981	1982	1983	1984
Assets					
Cash and equivalents	79,042	91,208	87,203	89,765	87,314
Receivables	198,012	231,977	251,777	253,773	299,997
Inventories	668,421	723,999	762,073	793,233	821,867
Other current assets	13,351	16,228	14,356	17,345	16,795
Total current assets	958,826	1,063,412	1,115,409	1,154,116	1,225,973
Gross property, plant and equipment	438,226	481,211	502,314	518,937	561,663
Less accumulated depreciation	(215,936)	(235,876)	(241,006)	(244,356)	(251,698)
Net property, plant, and equipment	222,290	245,335	261,308	274,581	309,965
Other assets	7,134	7,034	7,136	7,006	7,272
Total long-term assets	229,424	252,369	268,444	281,587	317,237
Total assets	1,118,250	1,315,781	1,383,853	1,435,703	1,543,210
Liabilities and net worth					
Short-term debt	140,869	197,608	295,723	307,866	353,826
Accounts payable	246,841	291,883	288,645	272,089	271,828
Income taxes payable	7,138	4,734	231	11,300	15,621
Accruals	59,896	64,892	65,779	66,666	67,206
Other current liabilities	8,137	10,616	13,245	13,882	14,301
Total current liabilities	462,881	569,733	663,623	671,803	722,782
Long-term debt	38,600	35,600	32,600	29,600	26,600
Capitalized leases	14,956	17,803	16,847	13,287	12,894
Total long-term debt	53,556	53,403	49,447	42,887	39,494
Other long-term liabilities	0	0	0	0	89
Total long-term liabilities	53,556	53,403	49,447	42,887	39,583
Total liabilities	516,437	623,136	713,070	714,690	762,365
Common equity	25,000	25,000	25,000	25,000	25,000
Retained earnings	646,813	667,645	645,783	696,013	755,845
Total net worth	671,813	692,645	670,783	721,013	780,845
Total liabilities and net worth	1,188,250	1,315,781	1,383,853	1,435,703	1,543,210
Dividend per share	1	1	1	0	0
Number of shares outstanding	25,000	25,000	25,000	25,000	25,000

EXHIBIT 8–3
Axehelm Hardware: Selected Robert Morris Associates Ratios for Hardware Retailers

	1980	1981	1982	1983	1984
Current	2.2	2.2	2.1	2.2	2.1
Quick	0.5	0.5	0.4	0.5	0.5
Sales/receivables	18.9	19.3	21.3	20.8	21.6
Cost of goods sold/inventory	2.6	2.5	2.6	2.5	2.8
Sales /working capital	5.6	5.6	6.2	5.4	6.2
EBIT/interest	2.6	2.1	2.0	2.3	2.0
Cash flow/currently maturing long-term debt	1.9	1.4	1.3	2.0	2.1
Fixed/worth	0.3	0.3	0.3	0.3	0.3
Debt/worth	1.4	1.4	1.4	1.3	1.5
Profit before taxes/tangible net worth	15.7	13.1	9.1	11.4	13.0
Profit before taxes/total assets	6.0	4.9	3.7	5.1	4.9
Sales/net fixed assets	22.0	21.2	20.1	20.9	21.6
Sales/total assets	2.1	2.1	2.1	2.0	2.2
Depreciation, depletion, amortization/sales (%)	0.9	0.9	1.1	1.1	1.2
Officers' compensation/sales (%)	4.7	4.7	5.2	4.1	4.3
		Quartile Data, 1984			
Current		3.0	2.1	1.5	
Quick		0.8	0.5	0.2	
Sales/receivables		48.8	21.6	10.8	
Cost of goods sold/inventory		3.8	2.8	1.9	
Sales/working capital		3.9	6.2	10.8	
EBIT/interest		5.1	2.0	1.2	
Cash Flow/currently maturing long-term debt		5.2	2.1	1.0	
Fixed/worth		0.2	0.3	0.7	
Debt/worth		0.7	1.5	3.2	
Profit before taxes/tangible net worth		23.8	13.0	3.1	
Profit before taxes/total assets		10.0	4.9	1.0	
Sales/net fixed assets		41.4	21.6	11.4	
Sales/total assets		2.9	2.2	1.7	
Depreciation, depletion, amortization/sales (%)		0.8	1.2	1.7	
Officers' compensation/sales (%)		2.5	4.3	6.3	

EBIT, earnings before interest and taxes.

DIAMOND JIM'S:
Assessing Financial Strengths and Weaknesses

Background

Merchandise Amalgamated's recent acquisition of Diamond Jim's had thrown the jewelry store into a state of turmoil. Before the acquisition, Diamond Jim's had been an independent jewelry store owned and operated by Jim Weatherbee, who promptly retired after the transition period. As part of a retail conglomerate, the new management of Diamond Jim's was involved in preparing the jewelry store's first strategic plan. The planning staff at Merchandise Amalgamated had requested a situation analysis to negotiate Diamond Jim's strategic role in the Merchandise Amalgamated portfolio and to specify objectives. The next phase would be strategy formulation.

According to the strategic format, a situation analysis identifies internal and external (environmental) constraints that must be considered in making strategic choices for a strategic business unit (SBU). An overall assessment of the firm's strengths and weaknesses must be included in the analysis of internal constraints. Merchandise Amalgamated considered financial strength and performance to be necessary components of this assessment. Competitive comparisons were encouraged.

Current Situation

Allison Green, newly appointed assistant manager of Diamond Jim's, had assembled data from Jewelers of America, Inc., to compare the financial performance of Diamond Jim's to "high-performance" jewelry stores (see Exhibits 9–1 to 9–4). Her

EXHIBIT 9–1
Operating Statements for Diamond Jim's ($3.1 million sales per year) and a high-performance jeweler ($1.5 million to $5.0 million sales per year)

	Diamond Jim's (%)	High-Performance Jeweler (%)
Net sales	100.0	100.0
Cost of sales	51.1	44.0
Gross profit	48.9	56.0
Operating expenses		
Payroll	24.9	28.1
Occupancy	6.0	7.0
Promotion	4.8	6.1
All other	9.9	8.5
Total operating expenses	45.6	49.7
Net profit	3.3	6.3

This case was prepared by J. B. Wilkinson, The University of Akron.

EXHIBIT 9–2
Sales Analysis for Diamond Jim's and a High-Performance Jeweler ($1.5 million to $5.0 million sales per year)

	Sales (%)		Sales Increase/Decrease (%)	
	DJ	HPJ	DJ	HPJ
Total sales	100.0	100.0	+5.4	+28.0
Diamonds and colored stones	38.3	54.9	+8.2	+29.0
Watches	9.2	14.3	+7.0	+36.1
Karat gold and cultured pearls	18.5	29.6	+6.5	+25.5
All other merchandise and repairs	34.0	1.2	+4.5	—

DJ, Diamond Jim's; HPJ, high-performance jeweler.

assignment was to identify financial strengths and weaknesses of Diamond Jim's as well as to pinpoint performance problems. Although this type of analysis was only a small component of the situation analysis, it was thought to be an important consideration when formulating the retail strategy.

Analytical Problem

Assume the role of Allison Green and prepare a report that will satisfactorily complete her assignment. Consider the following issues:

1. What are the major operating problems of Diamond Jim's? What are its principal strengths and weaknesses?
2. What strategy changes do you recommend, based on your financial analysis?

EXHIBIT 9–3
Inventory Analysis for Diamond Jim's and a High-Performance Jeweler ($1.5 million to $5.0 million sales per year)

	Inventory Turnover (Times)		Gross Profit (% of Sales)	
	DJ	HPJ	DJ	HPJ
Total sales	2.00	2.00	48.9	56.0
Diamonds and colored stones	2.50	2.06	50.2	56.0
Watches	1.50	1.80	43.6	54.4
Karat gold and cultured pearls	1.09	2.02	52.5	56.5
All other merchandise and repairs	2.07	1.14	46.9	62.7

EXHIBIT 9–4
Glossary: Definition of Terms

Total sales	Total sales at retail less returns and allowances and sales taxes. Includes repair sales.
Gross profit	Percentage of sales dollar that remains after deducting cost of merchandise sold (FIFO basis). Reaching an adequate gross profit level is a matter of merchandise mix, initial markup percentages, markdowns, and competitive position, as well as management's attitude and smart buying.
Payroll	Includes all salaries paid; payroll taxes; worker's compensation insurance; and health, medical, and life insurance for employees. Excludes withdrawals by owners.
Occupancy	All rents paid and other leasing costs such as area maintenance. Includes all utility expenses (except telephone), taxes and insurance on building, as well as depreciation on furniture and fixtures. If company owns building, this category includes mortgage interest, taxes, upkeep, and depreciation.
Promotion	All expenses for advertising or promotion. Also includes costs for window and interior displays, direct mail, and special promotions.
All other	Expenses not included in above categories such as telephone, bad debts, credit and collection expense, EDP expense, donations, interest charges, professional services, and travel.
Inventory turnover	Computed by averaging starting and closing inventory figures (at cost) and dividing this figure into cost of sales. Indicates how often inventory at cost "turns" or is sold. Measure merchandise productivity.

EDP, electronic data processing; FIFO, first in, first out.

BOHLS' DEPARTMENT STORE:
Controlling Personal Selling Expenses

Mr. Conrad Fish, a personnel planner and selling cost controller for Bohls' Department Store, was sitting in his office pondering a problem. It was his job to work with merchandise department personnel, department managers and their assistants, to help them keep their selling staff costs in line. The problem with which he was faced involved the costume jewelry department. The department, a fair profit producer, had a very high personal selling cost percentage. While the national average for such departments was about 8.6 percent, this department was running over 12 percent on an annual basis.

Mr. Fish felt the problem might be in the department's minimum staffing roster to which it was committed on a week-in, week-out basis. [See Exhibit 10–1.] The purpose of this minimum staffing roster was to give the department a staff with which it could effectively handle the low volume periods of sales. [See Exhibit 10–2.] Staffs were expanded with extra and seasonal help during major sale events and holidays. In addition to volume, shoplifting problems and stockkeeping needs were considered in establishing each department's roster.

With respect to the costume jewelry department, Mr. Fish felt that the store was committed to too many hours in the minimum staffing roster. The department was just overstaffed during the low volume periods.

EXHIBIT 10–1
Costume Jewelry Department (310), Accessories Division (2)—Minimum Staffing Roster and Hours Worked

Name	Hours Worked per Day						Total Hours
	Monday	Tuesday	Wednesday	Thursday	Friday	Saturday	
Schmidt	12:40–9:10	9:40–6:10	12:40–9:10	9:40–6:10	OFF		40
James	9:40–6:10	9:40–6:10	9:40–6:10	12:40–9:10	OFF	9:40–6:10	40
Green	12:40–9:10	OFF	9:40–6:10	9:40–6:10	12:40–9:10	9:40–6:10	40
Carlson	9:40–6:10	9:40–6:10	12:40–9:10	OFF	12:40–9:10	9:40–6:10	40
Bliss	9:40–2:40	9:40–2:40	9:40–2:40	9:40–2:40	9:40–2:40	OFF	25
Wharton	4:10–9:10	4:10–9:10	OFF	4:10–9:10	4:10–9:10	11:30–4:30	25
Gormes	4:10–9:10	4:10–9:10	4:10–9:10	4:10–9:10	OFF	11:30–4:30	25
Boyle	9:40–2:40	4:10–9:10	4:10–9:10	4:10–9:10	9:40–2:40	OFF	25
Parton	11:30–4:30	OFF	9:40–6:10	12:40–9:10	9:40–6:10	9:40–6:10	37
Skivins*							
Courtney°							

*Department Manager.
°Assistant Department Manager.

This case is reprinted with permission from John S. Berens, *Contemporary Retailing: Cases from Today's Market Place*, 2d ed. (Danville, IL: The Interstate Printers & Publishers, Inc., 1985), 41–46.

EXHIBIT 10–2
Sales Distribution for Typical Low-Volume Week

Days	Department 310 Costume Jewelry ($)	Department 540 Books ($)	Store Hours
Monday	1,000	750	10:00–9:00
Tuesday	500	400	10:00–5:30
Wednesday	700	550	10:00–9:00
Thursday	900	700	10:00–9:00
Friday	700	650	10:00–9:00
Saturday	1,200	950	10:00–5:30
Sunday	—	—	Closed
Week	5,000	4,000	—

In an attempt to verify his suspicion, he got out the roster of the book department, which, like costume jewelry, was located on the first floor. [See Exhibit 10–3.] This department's annual personal selling cost was about 7.2 percent. Industry-wide, such departments ran an average of about 7.0 percent. He thought that by analyzing the two rosters he could come to some conclusion whether or not the personal selling costs of the costume jewelry department were out of line. After all, both were on the first floor, both carried items of relatively small unit value, and both departments lent themselves well to self-service. While the costume jewelry department had a greater annual volume, both departments did have similar average wage rates of about $3.75 per hour.

EXHIBIT 10–3
Book Department (540), Small-Wares Division—Department Minimum Staffing Roster and Hours Worked

Name	Monday	Tuesday	Wednesday	Thursday	Friday	Saturday	Total Hours
Flippo	12:40–9:10	OFF	9:40–6:10	12:40–9:10	9:40–6:10	9:40–6:10	40
George	9:40–6:10	12:40–9:10	OFF	9:40–6:10	9:40–6:10	9:40–6:10	40
Mayton	9:40–2:40	OFF	9:40–6:10	OFF	4:10–9:10	11:30–4:30	23
Sprawls	9:40–2:40	9:40–2:40	OFF	9:40–2:40	OFF	11:30–4:30	20
Simpson	4:10–9:10	9:40–2:40	4:10–9:10	11:30–4:30	OFF	OFF	20
Dreyfus	4:10–9:10	OFF	4:10–9:10	OFF	4:10–9:10	OFF	15
Grace	OFF	4:10–9:10	OFF	4:10–9:10	OFF	1:40–6:10	15
Plover*							
Zither†							

*Department Manager. †Assistant Department Manager.

When he looked at the book department roster, he saw that the book department used over 100 fewer hours in its minimum roster than did the costume jewelry department. Something must be wrong. He left his office and went to the jewelry department manager's office. He confronted Mr. Skivins with his observation. Mr. Skivins quickly rejected Conrad's arguments, saying, "Look, Conrad, books are different from jewelry. Jewelry is smaller and is more easily shoplifted. This is even more of a problem when you consider that we're right in front of the main door, while the book department is tucked away in a corner at least 50 feet from any entrance. Also you must consider the merchandise. Jewelry is loose, and we have to do a lot of straightening of stock—and that takes time. Because our department consists of many islands of counters, we need someone in the middle of each in order to serve the customers adequately. Our staff just can't float like they do in books. Here, take a look at this floor plan and you'll see what I mean. [See Exhibit 10–4.] Now you want to cut my staff! I can't do what I should be doing with what I've got!"

EXHIBIT 10–4
Floor plan

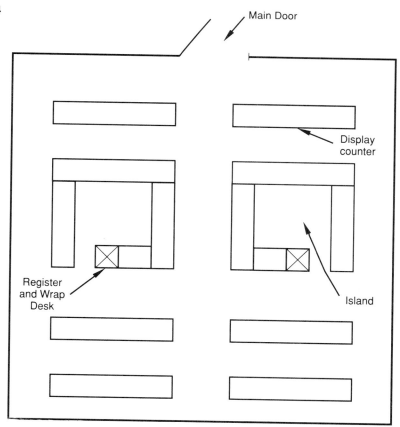

Mr. Fish countered with the fact that the jewelry department had over one and a half times as many hours per week to do a volume of only about one and a quarter times that of the book department. Mr. Skivins replied, "We're different! Can't you see that?"

Mr. Fish left, somewhat dejected. He thought he had a good case for a staff reduction. Maybe he had better take a look at the two departments again, do some more calculations, and then make an appointment to see Mr. Skivins again.

Analytical Problem

Assume the role of Mr. Fish and develop a written analysis designed to determine a possible need for staff reduction in the jewelry department.

CHRISTIAN'S RESTAURANT:
Evaluating a Business Investment Opportunity

Background

In the spring semester of 1984 four seniors at the University of Virginia were trying to decide whether they should invest in Christian's Restaurant, a small eating establishment located several miles from the university's campus in Charlottesville, Virginia.

The four students—Jeff Curry, Dean Salpini, Art Scibelli, and Gordon Shanks—were all business majors who had become involved with Christian's as the result of a management course they took entitled "Entrepreneurship." The objective of this course was to "set up a new company that is completely researched in all phases of the business (location, services, finance, etc.) and submit the written business plan for evaluation." The four students had decided to work together on the project at the beginning of the semester and had quickly begun investigating potential business ventures in the Charlottesville area.

The group's first idea centered on the opening of a seafood restaurant. Art believed that a restaurant offering the same product as a local chain of seafood houses near his home in northern Virginia could prove highly successful in Charlottesville. These restaurants offered fresh seafood for relatively moderate prices in a family-type atmosphere and also featured several "all you can eat" items. Art had gotten in touch with one of the owner-founders of the chain, Mr. Easby-Smyth, and the group had gone to northern Virginia to meet with him and discuss their idea.

The meeting with Easby-Smyth had produced two conclusions: Charlottesville was probably too small a market to support the size restaurant the group had originally considered, and the money involved would make the project unfeasible for the group. Easby-Smyth had informed them that the cost of building and outfitting a seafood house of 6,000 square feet would be approximately $300,000. The group had no desire to enter into an investment of this magnitude and were also aware of the great difficulty they were sure to encounter in trying to raise the capital for such a venture.

The students still felt a smaller seafood restaurant might be successful in Charlottesville and began searching for a suitable building for their restaurant. Ideally they hoped to find a restaurant that was selling out and could easily be converted for their purposes. Then news of the Happy Clam reached them.

The Happy Clam was a new seafood restaurant opening on Route 29 North, the main highway leading from Charlottesville. One visit to the new restaurant confirmed that not only was it in the general area in which the group had hoped to locate, but it was also selling the same basic product mix as they had hoped to offer. In addition, the restaurant's owner had already successfully opened an identical seafood house in nearby Fredericksburg, Virginia.

This case was prepared by Jeff Curry, Dean Salpini, Art Scibelli, and Gordon Shanks under the supervision of Professors Thomas L. Wheelen and Moustafa H. Abdelsamad. Copyright © 1984 by Thomas L. Wheelen and Moustafa H. Abdelsamad. Reprinted with the permission of the North American Case Research Association.

Up to this point, there had been no restaurant in the area similar to the one the students had considered. Now they were faced with a direct competitor of proven success in the seafood business. At this point, as the students reconsidered their strategy, Art visited a local realtor and found out about Christian's.

Christian's was a small restaurant specializing in sandwiches for lunch and specialty dishes for dinner [see dinner menu, Exhibit 11–1]. It was being sold as an ongoing business which would include the name Christian's. The students met with the realtor handling the sale, William Page, who arranged a meeting with Christian's owners.

EXHIBIT 11–1
Dinner Menu

SOUPS	WINES
French Onion $1.50	By the glass $1.25
Cream of Asparagus $1.25	1/2 liter $3.25
Vegetable $1.00	Full liter $5.75
Split Pea or Lentil $1.00	Champagne cocktail $1.25

ENTREES (served with salad and bread)

Beef Bazzare	$4.25
Marinated beef, onions and green peppers broiled and served on rice	
Broccoli Casserole	$3.25
Broccoli, tomatoes, onions, and eggs topped with cheese	
Lobster Scampi	$4.25
Langostinos broiled in herb butter and served on rice	
Syrian Chicken	$3.85
Marinated Chicken in pita bread with lettuce and tomatoes	
Sausage Lasagne	$4.25
An Italian dish that speaks for itself!	
Omelet Special	$3.95
Large dinner omelet filled with pepperoni and provolone cheese	
Crêpes	$3.75
Chicken Divan or Sauteed Mushrooms	

DESSERTS

Ginger Sherbet $.75
Homemade Pecan Pie $1.00
Cheesecake $1.25
Carrot Cake $1.25

Coffee or Tea $.35
Soft Drinks $.50
Beer $.75

Peter and Mary Tarpey, a young couple from the New York area, were the owners of Christian's along with a University of Virginia professor who acted as a silent partner. The students met with Page and the Tarpeys as scheduled on a Wednesday afternoon in Christian's to answer each others' questions and to discuss the possible purchase.

Mary Tarpey first showed the group a handwritten profit-and-loss statement for the period from June 13, 1983, to October 31, 1983 [see Exhibit 11–2]. She

EXHIBIT 11–2
Christian's Profit and Loss Statement
June 13, 1983 to October 31, 1983

Sales	$100,000.00
Cost of sales	
Beer and wine	2,688.30
Food	29,189.60
Total	31,877,90
Gross profit	68,122.10
Operating expenses	
Paper	1,079.88
Insurance	
Store	600.00
Car	150.00
Health	460.00
Workmen's compensation	950.00
Employment commission	360.00
Laundry, linen	483.25
Licenses	250.00
Sales tax (state)	4,000.00
Repairs maintenance	250.00
Rent	2,500.00
Rubbish removal—city	448.50
Salaries and wages	20,000.00
Payroll taxes	6,000.00
Utilities	4,000.00
Loan payment	1,150.00
Equipment payments	1,150.00
Life insurance	625.00
Car payment	1,095.00
Maintenance	950.00
Lease dishwasher	448.50
Advertising	2,750.00
Business association dues and expenses	450.00
Administrative salaries	5,000.00
Total	55,150.13
Income before taxes	12,971.97

This was a handwritten statement provided by the owners.

explained that some of the expenses were direct payments to the banks and were being written off as business expenses like car payments and a life insurance policy, and need not be incurred by a new owner. She also showed the students monthly sale figures for the period of January 1983 to October 1983, as verified by a local CPA firm [see Exhibit 11–3], as well as a list of assets owned by Christian's [see Exhibit 11–4].

The Tarpeys defined their target market as "young professionals." By this, they meant persons in the 18–35 age group who worked in the area and came to Christian's for the menu variety and quality of food. They stated that these people eat out about 22 times a month for lunch and dinner, and their strategy was to try to have them eat at Christian's five days a month. The Tarpeys also quoted the average lunch check as being $3.76 and the average dinner check amounting to $5.92.

The Tarpeys also answered questions concerning Christian's daily operations and suppliers. One of the important issues raised was that of a transition period. The group hoped to hire an experienced, full-time manager for the restaurant, and the Tarpeys agreed they would stay on for a period of two weeks or so to help train the manager and show him the cost control and portion control procedures they had used. In addition, the Tarpeys stated that the whole employee staff had expressed their willingness to stay with the restaurant after an ownership change. The group viewed these two factors as distinct assets.

Another important issue was the future plans of the Tarpeys. As it turned out, the Tarpeys would be opening a new restaurant in a shopping center being built three quarters of a mile from Christian's. Peter Tarpey explained that the restaurant was to be more dinner-oriented than Christian's. He described it as an "Irish cafe with French food" that would serve more expensive meals than Christian's and also serve liquor, which Christian's did not feature [although they did sell beer and wine]. Tarpey estimated that by his moving and opening a new restaurant, Christian's might lose at most 5 percent of its customers.

A second meeting was held with the Tarpeys at a later date, during which more of the group's questions were answered. The lease would have to be renegotiated by any new owner in August 1984, which would be substantially higher than the current rate. The students had questions about Christian's supplier's and asked to see the restaurant's books, but the Tarpeys wanted some sort of firm commitment on the group's part before giving out more information about Christian's.

The price being asked for Christian's was $57,750 and the students estimated they could put up about $17,500 of their own capital. Since the balance would have to be financed by a loan, Jeff visited several banks to discuss terms. One bank told him they loaned money for a restaurant only if it was going to be family owned and operated. At Sovran Bank, Jeff got a more positive response. The loan officer there stated the bank would loan up to 70 percent of the purchase price, fully collateralized. The interest rate would be 14 or 15 percent.

At this point the group decided to evaluate their objectives and "take stock" of the situation. They hoped to run the restaurant as absentee owners with the full-time manager handling daily operations. Art's immediate plans included law school

EXHIBIT 11–3

Monthly Sales Figures, January 1983 to October 1983

**BROWN AND JONES COMPANY CERTIFIED PUBLIC ACCOUNTANTS
CHARLOTTESVILLE, VIRGINIA 22906**

January 9, 1984

Peter Tarpey
Christian's, Inc.
1703 Allied Lane
Charlottesville, Virginia 22901

Dear Peter:

As per your request, enclosed are sales figures for Christian's, Inc., for the ten months ending October 1983 as filed on your monthly Virginia sales tax returns.

January 1983	$18,543.30
February 1983	19,085.43
March 1983	18,097.54
April 1983	19,984.20
May 1983	20,422.71
June 1983	21,836.37
July 1983	19,307.76
August 1983	22,231.69
September 1983	20,002.19
October 1983	20,588.86

If you need sales figures for November 1983 and December 1983, you will have to get these amounts from worksheets in your files. Let me know if I can be of further assistance.

Yours truly,

Thomas L. Brown
Certified Public Accountant

TLB/d
P.S. The sales figure for November 1983
is $19,300.00
TLB

EXHIBIT 11–4
Additional Information Provided by Thomas L. Brown,
September 27, 1983

Attached is a schedule of fixed assets owned by Christian's, Inc., and the estimated market value of each. Since a purchaser of these would have a cost basis for depreciation and useful life different from that of Christian's, Inc., this information is not provided.

21 Tables	$ 525
43 Chairs	430
2 Banquettes	100
6 Church pew benches	120
Small refrigerator	300
Walk-in box	1,500
Ice machine	100
NCR cash register	150
3 Toasters	225
Jordan box	250
Fogle refrigerator	1,200
Hobart slicer	1,000
Hobart microwave	1,000
Sandwich box	200
Stainless prep. table	100
Deep-fat fryer	75
Steam table	75
Stainless prep. table	125
3 butcher-block chef tables	300
Small Hobart slicer	200
3 Basin sinks	75
Universal freezer	100
Sears' freezer	75
Stereo system	150
Curtains	100
Pots, pans, flatware, china, glassware	600
Place mats, salt and pepper mills	100
New sign	2,000
Total fixed assets	$11,175

Should you desire additional information on this matter, please contact Peter Tarpey and the data will be forthcoming.

in September, although he was still unsure which law school he would attend. Dean planned to work in northern Virginia after graduation, and Jeff and Gordon would return to the University of Virginia in the fall to complete their degrees.

The students' families, from whom they hoped to borrow some of the initial equity capital, all had reservations about the venture. Most of the doubt centered on the policy of running the restaurant as absentee owners. The families also wondered if it was wise for the students to make such an investment at this time in their careers when their futures were so undecided.

By now it was March 24, and the students knew a decision had to be made soon. A call to William Page had confirmed the rumor that another party was seriously considering buying Christian's. The group called a meeting to decide their next move.

At the meeting, the students decided some sort of comprehensive analysis of the information they had gathered was necessary. With the analysis they felt they would be able to reach the best conclusion.

The group decided to break up the information into sections, with Jeff concentrating on the finance, Dean on the marketing, and Gordon and Art on the operations. When they got back together on March 31, one week away, to put all the results together, the decision would have to be made.

Market Analysis

Although Mr. Tarpey assured the group of the existence and loyalty of a definite market for Christian's, it was felt that a marketing survey would strengthen the group's understanding of this market. The survey was conducted among 88 people who were customers at competitive restaurants, using the survey form shown [in Exhibit 11–5]. The competition was determined from an assessment based on a number of factors including location, clientele, product offering, and Peter Tarpey's estimates. Christian's was not included, however, because the group felt their regular clientele might bias the result in favor of the restaurant.

The survey revealed that most people were aware of Christian's but were not attracted to it. In addition, only 7 percent of those who had eaten at Christian's did so at least five times a month, so their repeat business seemed to be lacking. Of those who ate there regularly, 60 percent seemed to prefer the lunch period, as opposed to the dinner period, which Peter Tarpey had claimed would occur. Analysis of the various factors involved with Christian's showed that location was the most significant problem, with 64 percent of respondents rating it below average. However, a study of traffic flow patterns in Charlottesville around the McIntyre Road area, where Christian's is located, revealed that 20 percent of the entire day's traffic passed Christian's between 11:00 and 2:00 P.M. Price and service seemed to be average and comparable to that of other restaurants in most respondents' minds.

The most significant factors in a person's decision to eat at Christian's were the menu variety and food quality. Most diners named specific food items as their main reason for coming. This also accounted for Christian's major form of advertising, which seemed to be word-of-mouth from satisfied customers. As far as changes in Christian's were concerned, most respondents favored adding seafood to the menu (81 percent), whereas the same percentage felt live entertainment would be a mistake.

One of the problems that might confront the group was the introduction of the Tarpeys' new restaurant down the street. Since the Tarpeys had already developed a loyal clientele, the group was afraid of losing them to the new restaurant, although Peter Tarpey assured them that only 5 percent of the market would be affected. According to the survey, the figure to determine those customers that

EXHIBIT 11–5
Marketing Survey

Hello, we are students doing a research study on Christian's restaurant. Could you please take a little time to help us to fill out our survey and help make Christian's a better place to eat. Thank you for your cooperation. The key results of the survey are summarized below:

1. Have you ever eaten at Christian's? YES <u>50%</u> NO <u>50%</u>
   If NO, have you heard of it? YES <u>59%</u> If NO, no further questions <u>41%</u>
   If YES, how often do you eat there? Less than 5 times a month <u>93%</u>
                                                   5 times a month <u>5%</u>
                                          More than 5 times a month <u>2%</u>
2. Which meal do you usually eat at Christian's? Lunch <u>59%</u>
                                                       Dinner <u>32%</u>
                                                       Both <u>9%</u>
3. How would you rate Christian's on these factors:

	Poor	Fair	Average	Above Average	Excellent
Location	29.5%	34%	32%	4.5%	
Food quality			23.3%	53.5%	23.3%
Price	4.5%	11%	61.5%	16%	7%
Service		14%	48%	33%	5%
Atmosphere	9%	11.4%	41%	34%	4.6%
Menu variety		5%	33%	45%	17%
Cleanliness	9.5%	9.5%	36%	33%	12%

4. What is the main reason(s) you eat at Christian's? *Answers varied but were mostly complimentary.*
5. How did you hear about Christian's? TV <u>2%</u>; Radio <u>12%</u>; Newspaper ads <u>10.6%</u>; Friends <u>58%</u>; Drove by <u>5.8%</u>; Other (please specify) <u>11.6%</u>
6. Would you like to see the following at Christian's?

	YES	NO
More vegetarian dishes	44%	56%
More seafood	81%	19%
More take-out variety	48%	52%
Live entertainment	19%	81%

7. An informal survey of age was conducted.

would be lost through a change in management was approximately 6.8 percent, a little higher than Tarpey's estimate.

    Although no survey questions directly addressed demographics, respondents were asked to place themselves in one of the three age brackets: 18–35, 35–50, and over 50. Customer age was thought to be important in the decision to purchase Christian's so that the target market could be firmly established. Overall, it was found that 60 percent of those interviewed were between 18 and 35 years of age, while 31 percent fell into the 35–50 bracket. Further analysis showed that 98 percent of those who presently eat at Christian's were within the 18–50 range. Diners over 50, therefore, figured to be an insignificant part of Christian's target market. Therefore Tarpey's claim of "young professionals" as his primary customers seems to have been supported by these age group data.

As can be seen [Exhibit 11–6], sales for eating and drinking establishments in 1982 were 10.5 percent above 1982, while total retail sales increased only 6.8 percent for the same period. Households also seemed to be forming at a faster rate than the total population was growing. In addition, the Virginia State Planning Office projections showed that the 20–35 year-old segment had showed disproportionate increase, which could explain the faster formation of households. These same figures also showed that the 25–39 year-old age group would increase 17 percent between 1980 and 1985. In Albemarle County, where Charlottesville is located, this increase would be almost 32 percent.

These growth figures were considered important because of the number of people who drive into Charlottesville's central business district (CBD) from the county who use McIntyre Road as a major artery. The CBD itself was also considered to be important, since a large part of Christian's clientele came from there. Over $2,000,000 had been privately invested in the downtown since 1982; thus the CBD appeared to be booming. Another important development was the county's move of their executive offices into Lane High School, located down the street from Christian's. This move would increase Christian's target market, since these people seemed to fit the characteristics of their clientele.

Advertising and Promoting

Christian's present advertising program was very sporadic with a yearly expenditure of only $2,750. Tarpey spoke of occasional spots on television that he had used, along with local radio stations and the major newspaper in Charlottesville. However, Dean and the other members of the group felt that the effectiveness of this program was lacking.

EXHIBIT 11–6
The Charlottesville Market*

Year	Retail sales ($ thousands)	Eating and drinking[†] sales ($ thousands)	Population (thousands)	Households[‡] (thousands)
1978	153,995	NA[§]	38.8	13.8
1979	176,731	NA	38.7	14.0
1980	224,588	NA	39	14.2
1981	235,679	17,882	39.1	14.7
1982	251,766	19,753	38.9	14.7

*Data provided by Virginia State Planning Service.

[†]Eating and drinking places: This is a broad classification that includes any establishment selling prepared food or drink. Caterers, lunch counters, and concession stands are included as well as restaurants.

[‡]Households: All people occupying a single housing unit whether related or not. Includes single persons living alone.

[§]NA; not available.

Operations

The students were aware of their lack of experience in the restaurant business, and since the daily operations of Christian's had gone smoothly in the past, they did not plan any significant changes upon taking over.

The entire employee staff had stated they would be willing to remain at Christian's after the ownership change, and Peter and Mary Tarpey agreed they would stay on for a transition period to "show the ropes" to the new manager.

The students had realized early in their involvement with Christian's that they would need to hire a full-time manager for the restaurant were they to purchase it. It was determined that they would want someone with experience in restaurant management from the Charlottesville area. Their realtor had informed them he knew of a man who fit this description and had expressed interest in the opportunity, but the group was unable to get in contact with him before the week ended.

The group planned on putting the manager in charge of general daily operations to include ordering, cost control, hiring, firing, scheduling, and any other operations-related duty. The students planned on doing the bookkeeping themselves. They planned to pay the manager a salary of approximately $12,000, plus a commission based on the bottom-line figure. This commission would be approximately 11 percent.

It was determined that the following employees would be needed to operate Christian's:

1 Manager @ $12,000 salary plus commission
3 cooks @ $5.00/hour
1 grillman @ $4.75/hour
2 countermen @ $4.25/hour
2 prep men @ $4.25/hour
2 dishwashers @ $4.25/hour
2 cashiers @ $4.25/hour
12 waitresses @ $1.50/hour plus tips.

Employees were to be allowed free drinks and half-price meals while working.

Under the students' ownership, Christian's would continue to buy its food supplies from institutional food distributors from Richmond, Va., who delivered to Charlottesville. In addition, they would obtain their beer from local distributors and their soft drinks from local bottling companies.

In the past, inventory had turned over approximately once a week. Normal credit terms of suppliers had been net 30 days.

The marketing survey had indicated that Christian's menu was one of its strongest points, so the group planned few changes. The lunch menu featured over 40 sandwiches along with omelets, salads, and chili. The dinner menu featured specialty dishes such as "Beef Bazzare" and "Syrian Chicken" [see Exhibit 11–1].

In the past, Christian's had varied its dinner menu daily. The students would plan to vary it weekly, and if one combination proved particularly popular, it would be used again at a different time.

Approximately 15 percent of Christian's gross sales came from beer sales. The restaurant carried mainly premium and foreign beers in keeping with its target market of young professionals.

Investment

Benefitting from knowledge obtained in a business law course the previous semester, the group decided to establish Christian's as a Subchapter S corporation. This business form was chosen because of the tax advantages and flexibility it would allow the group, since the business would be taxed as a partnership but would retain the limited liability of a corporation to protect the shareholders. Since income tax rates for individuals in this case are substantially lower than for a corporation, the group felt this form would offer the best return on their investment.

Lease

At the time of negotiations, Christian's was paying Allied Realty, the owner of the shopping plaza in which the restaurant was located, a base rent of $350.00 per month plus an additional percentage of gross sales (4 percent) not exceeding a total monthly rental of $500.00 per month. However, this lease would expire on August 1, 1984, and a new lease would have to be negotiated by the new purchaser.

The new rent terms would be considerably higher than those for previous owners and would consist of a minimum payment of $600.00 per month or 4 percent of sales, whichever is the higher, not exceeding $750.00 per month. Since Christian's historical monthly sales have averaged approximately $20,000.00, this would mean payments of $750.00 per month. There would be an additional requirement that if gross sales exceeded $60,000 in any quarter, the restaurant would pay 3 percent of sales exceeding this amount.

Fortunately, the group was informed by its realtor, Henry Brasswell, that it might be possible to negotiate a less expensive lease, so that average monthly payments would be between $650 and $700. Because the outcome of such negotiations was uncertain at the time, the group used $750 per month in developing *pro forma* statements for the business.

Income Statements

An examination of 1983 sales uncovered two major factors that had to be considered in developing *pro forma* income statements. First, the monthly sales figures supplied by the CPA firm indicated a seasonal fluctuation in sales [see Exhibit 11–7]. The effect of this on the cash flows of the restaurant and its ability to meet its debts had to be determined. Second, the revenue growth of this restaurant would be limited by its capacity. Jeff needed to establish how close to capacity the restaurant was currently operating. Lunch and dinner sales should be considered separately. Lunch projections would be based on 260 days a year (52 weeks × 5 days), and dinner would be based on the full 312 days the restaurant was open. The current owners had already estimated the average check at each meal. The restaurant seated 56 people.

Jeff then took the handwritten income statement provided by Mary Tarpey and attempted to adjust it to get an idea of the expenses the new management could face. Several of the prerequisites the Tarpeys enjoyed had been discussed during the meeting at Christian's. Excessive long-distance calls and the car payments could be eliminated. The new management would have to add the manager's salary and bonus. A 10 percent annual bonus on pretax profits would be offered to motivate

EXHIBIT 11–7
Seasonality Index 1983 Sales (100 = 19,945)

Month	Sales ($)	Actual Seasonality
January	18,543	93
February	19,085	96
March	18,097	91
April	19,984	100
May	20,423	102
June	21,836	109
July	19,304	97
August	22,231	111
September	20,002	100
October	20,589	103
November	19,300	97
December	18,948*	95*

*Assumed.

the manager to run a tight ship. These expenses had to be separated into variable- and fixed-expense categories to determine a break-even point. The new estimates were in line with those found in a book entitled *Restaurant Finance.*

Jeff was certain sales in the first year could be maintained at the current level with effective advertising. Forecasted sales for the second year were based on ex-

EXHIBIT 11–8
Pro Forma Income Statements for the Year Ended July 31

	Year ($ Thousands)			
	2	3	4	5
Net sales				
Lunch	120.0	120.0	120.0	120.0
Dinner	144.0	152.0	152.0	152.0
Total	264.0	272.0	272.0	272.0
Variable expenses (68%)	(180.0)	(185.0)	(185.0)	(185.0)
Operating margin (32%)	84.0	87.0	87.0	87.0
Fixed expenses	(40.8)	(40.9)	(42.4)	(42.4)
Earnings before interest	43.2	46.1	44.6	44.6
Interest	(3.9)	(2.9)	(1.9)	(1.0)
Earnings before bonus (EBB)	39.3	43.2	42.7	43.6
Bonus (0.10 × EBB)	3.9	4.3	4.3	4.4
Taxable earnings	35.4	38.9	38.9	39.2

panding lunch sales to capacity. Years three through five assumed the restaurant would operate at capacity for both lunch and dinner. Increased sales would be achieved through advertising.

The Bank Loan

With the income statements prepared, Jeff approached the Sovran Bank to discuss the terms of a loan [see Exhibits 11–8 and 11–9]. The bank was willing to set the monthly payments at a level the cash flows of the restaurants could meet as long as the maturity of the loan did not exceed ten years. It appeared that five years

EXHIBIT 11–9
Balance Sheet

	Year ($000s)					
	Initial	1	2	3	4	5
Assets						
Current assets						
Cash and securities	0.30	10.70	20.70	20.70	34.60	27.70
Inventory						
Beer and wine (0.04/month)	0.80	0.80	0.90	0.90	0.90	0.90
Food (0.36/month)	7.20	7.20	7.90	8.20	8.20	8.20
Total current assets	8.30	18.70	29.50	29.80	43.70	36.80
Fixed assets						
Accumulated	22.30	22.30	22.30	27.30	27.30	32.30
Depreciation	0.00	4.40	8.80	13.20	17.60	22.00
Net fixed assets	22.30	17.90	13.50	14.10	9.70	10.30
Intangibles						
Goodwill	35.20	35.20	35.20	35.20	35.20	35.20
Accumulated amortization	0.00	3.52	7.04	10.56	14.08	17.60
Net goodwill	35.20	31.68	28.16	24.64	21.12	17.60
Organizational costs	0.50	0.40	0.30	0.20	0.10	0.00
Total assets	66.30	68.68	71.46	68.74	74.62	64.70
Liabilities						
Current Liabilities						
Account payable	7.60	7.60	7.90	8.20	8.20	8.20
Note payable	1.00	0.00	0.00	0.00	0.00	0.00
Total current liabilities	8.60	7.60	7.90	8.20	8.20	8.20
Long-term note	40.25	32.20	24.10	16.10	8.00	0.00
Total liabilities	48.85	39.80	32.00	24.30	16.20	8.20
Equity						
Stock	17.50	17.50	17.50	17.50	17.50	17.50
Retained earnings	0.00	11.38	21.96	26.94	40.92	39.00
Total equity	17.50	28.88	39.46	44.44	58.42	56.50
Total liabilities and equity	66.35	68.68	71.46	68.74	74.62	64.70

would be an acceptable maturity. This would be monthly payments of approximately $1,000.

The bank would accept 50 percent of the book value (approximately the $11,175 listed as market value by the CPA firm) of the assets as collateral but demanded that the balance be fully collateralized also.

The loan officer was concerned that the purchase price was too high and that an excessive amount of goodwill would be involved in the new business. He was also concerned that none of the new owners had any experience operating a restaurant. With this in mind, he wanted to know more about the manager and the cook.

Evaluating the Purchase Price

Since several people had expressed concern over the price the owners were asking, the partners wanted to decide the proper value of the restaurant. They agreed this should be based on the present value of the income stream the restaurant could generate. In light of the fact that eight out of ten restaurants fail, the partners selected 25 percent as the hurdle rate that would be used to discount future earnings. The setup costs should not exceed the present value of the income stream. The partners wanted to include the eventual sales price or liquidation value of the restaurant at the end of five years in computing the present value, assuming various levels of sales would establish a proper price range. The setup costs included the $57,750 asking price and $500 organizational expense for legal and accounting fees. Since this was a going concern, they would not have to invest significant additional working capital.

Concluding Remarks

On March 31 at the final meeting to discuss the prospects of purchasing Christian's, the group members were fully aware of the implications such a decision would have. It was generally agreed that such an endeavor provided potential for optimum managerial skill and experience in the business world, though none of the group members was certain that this was the route he wanted to take. Faced with exams in the coming weeks, time pressure from the realtor, and the knowledge that at least one other party was interested in purchasing Christian's, the group set out to make a decision, which, for better or worse, would affect their immediate futures.

The students were informed by the present owners that they must reach a decision quickly since other purchasers were interested in the same business opportunity.

THE WOMEN'S CLUB, LTD.:
Managing an Organization's Assets for Revenue Growth

The Women's Club, Ltd. (TWCL), was the only women's club in the United States entirely owned and operated by its members. The club was designed to help women of all ages develop physically, socially, culturally, and creatively. On December 15, 1981, TWCL began operations; it was run through various committees, elected officials, and an elected board of directors.

Boise, Idaho, a city with a population of slightly over 100,000, was the home of TWCL. The state capital, Boise is a city with a very vocal and active Mormon minority. Although no large manufacturing plants are located in Boise, three national corporate headquarters are: Hewlett-Packard, Albertson's (grocery chain), and Morris-Knudson (construction company). The downtown area, like many other downtown areas across the country, struggles to compete with suburban shopping areas but still provides an adequate number of retail stores, restaurants, and theaters in a very picturesque setting.

The building and property that housed TWCL were purchased from Utah Mortgage for $885,000 and were recently appraised at $1.25 million. To raise capital for the downpayment, members purchased owner-certificates for $1,000 each. Within the first 2 months, 120 of these certificates were sold. During 1982, in accordance with the mortgage contract, TWCL made a series of balloon payments totaling $36,500 to reduce the principal (see Exhibit 12–1). As a result of a renegotiated contract in June of 1982, $30,799 in interest payments were due on March 15, 1983, as well. This brought the total balance due to $729,299.

To provide working capital, an investor group of three individuals was formed on December 15, 1981. Together, they loaned TWCL $17,000 at 12 percent interest and secured the loan with a second mortgage on the building and property. A fourth investor loaned $20,000 at 17 percent interest and secured the loan with the sig-

EXHIBIT 12–1
Mortgage Information

Purchase Price		$855,000
Down Payment	12/15/81	$120,000
Balloon Payment	3/14/82	$10,000
Balloon Payment	6/14/82	$5,000
Balloon Payment	7/14/82	$5,000
Balloon Payment	9/14/82	$1,500
Balloon Payment	10/14/82	$15,000
Principal Due	3/15/83	$698,500

This case was prepared by Bradley A. Dicks and Joseph W. Leonard, Miami University. It was developed to provide a basis for class discussion rather than to illustrate either effective or ineffective handling of organizational issues and practices.

natures of the four officers of TWCL. The entire loan plus interest was repaid on March 3, 1982.

During 1983 there were 210 owner-members who continued to show strong support when financial needs arose. For example, in May of 1982, over $9,000 was raised on one night; and on another occasion, $14,000 was raised within 1 week to meet the October balloon payment.

Financial Outlook

Exhibits 12–2 and 12–3 show TWCL's balance sheet and income statement, respectively.

In 1983, TWCL requested and secured a 15-year commercial real estate loan for $850,000. The loan was secured by a first mortgage on the land and building to refinance and provide working capital for the following:

Utah Mortgage
    Principal $698,500
    Interest at 18 percent $ 30,799
Investor Group
    Principal $ 17,000
    Interest $ 3,060
Operating Capital $100,641
                                        $850,000

The Women's Club, Ltd., planned to repay this loan from five income sources: (1) member dues, (2) initiation fees, (3) restaurant sales, (4) bar sales, and (5) physical department fees. Secondary sources of repayment were (1) the sale of owner certificates, (2) catering and banquet income, and (3) special events.

EXHIBIT 12–2
The Women's Club, Ltd., Balance Sheet (Year Ending December 31, 1982)

Current Assets	($)	Current Liabilities	($)
Cash	4,234	Accounts payable	10,317
Dues receivable	869	Prepaid dues	7,062
Membership contracts receivable	4,960	Taxes payable	17,869
Inventory	2,054	Deferred revenue, current	5,760
Prepaid expenses	1,841	Interest payable	7,805
Refundable deposits	3,259	Mortgages payable	736,918
Subtotal assets	17,217	Subtotal liabilities	785,731
Property and equipment		Deferred revenue, net	26,664
Land	226,575	Total liabilities	812,295
Building	628,425	Members' equity	
Office equipment	11,020	Memberships	166,697
Accumulated depreciation	(24,240)	Accumulated deficit	(120,092)
Total property and equipment	841,780	Total equity	46,602
Total assets	858,997	Total liabilities and equity	858,997

EXHIBIT 12–3
The Women's Club, Ltd., Income Statement and Accumulated Deficit (Year Ending December 31, 1982)

Income and Expenses	($)
Revenue	
Dues	196,911
Restaurant and bar	63,041
Catering and banquets	22,513
Special events	16,961
Other	6,392
Interest	2,846
	308,664
Expenses	
Interest	117,382
Payroll and payroll taxes	110,615
Restaurant and bar	31,455
Special events	14,048
Utilities	34,050
Repairs and maintenance	25,165
Depreciation	24,240
Licenses and taxes	16,962
Insurance	9,690
Office supplies	9,086
Advertising	4,192
Other	19,070
	415,955
Net income (loss)	107,291
Accumulated deficit, beginning of year	12,801
Accumulated deficit, end of year	120,092

The request for operating capital of $100,641 was to offset a projected $100,000 negative cash flow for the next 2 years (i.e., until there was enough growth in the membership to attain positive cash flows).

Competition

The Women's Club, Ltd. was unique in the programs offered its members and in the fact that it was the only club offering ownership to its members. Most of the competitors stressed physical fitness; only the YWCA offered additional programs such as social, cultural, and arts activities. None of the other clubs had a full dining room. A summary of the primary competition and the structure of their fees follows:

1. Eastgate Health Club—open to members only and offered 1-year memberships for $15.00 per month
2. Court House, Inc.
   a. Aerobic and dance classes only, $80.00 plus $25.00 per month
   b. Nautilus weight program only, $80.00 plus $27.00 per month

  c. Racquetball courts only, $160.00 plus $35.00 per month
  d. Programs 1 and 2, $80.00 plus $32.96 per month
  e. Programs 1, 2, and 3, $160.00 plus $48.41 per month.
3. Family Fitness Center—lifetime membership of $1,700.00 plus $400 per child
4. Lady Fitness—(women only), 1-year membership $189.00; 2-year membership, 289.00
5. YWCA—$15.00 annual membership dues entitled member to $10.00 discount on all classes and 30 cents (per hour) discount on child care

Exhibit 12–4 provides a comparative listing of the facilities, programs, and services offered by TWCL and the five primary competitors. Exhibit 12–5 further describes the facilities available at TWCL.

EXHIBIT 12–4
Offerings by TWCL and Competitors

	TWCL	Court House	Eastgate	Family Fitness	Lady Fitness	YWCA
Facilities						
Basketball and volleyball court				X		
Dining room	X					
Dressing room	X	X	X	X	X	X
Jacuzzi/whirlpool	X	X	X	X	X	
Jogging track				X		
Racquetball court		X		X		
Sauna/steamroom	X	X	X	X	X	
Showers	X	X	X	X	X	X
Swimming pool	X	X		X		
Tanning booths			X		X	
Weight equipment	X	X	X	X	X	
Fitness programs						
Floor aerobics	X	X	X	X	X	X
Jazzercise	X					
Slimnastics	X		X		X	X
Swim classes	X					
Private swim lessons	X					
Tai Chi	X					X
Weight loss/nutrition	X			X	X	
Yoga	X					
Other services						
Child care		X	X		X	X
Masseuse	X				X	
Towel service	X					
Social/cultural programs						
Arts and crafts	X					X
Speakers/seminars	X					X
Theaters/luncheons	X					X

EXHIBIT 12–5
The Facilities of TWCL

Dining room and kitchen
Open from 6:00 A.M. to 9:00 P.M., Monday through Friday, seats forty-four. Available to members and guests. Serves sandwiches, salads, soups, omelettes, juices, fruits, hot and cold beverages, wine, and beer. Main entree, which changes daily.

Indoor Swimming Pool
Pool is heated, 48 feet long, and has four lanes. Two enclosed showers are located near the pool. Classes include water exercise, beginning and intermediate swimming, private lessons; open time for lap swimming also is available.

Indoor jacuzzi
Seats ten people, heated to 101 degrees Farenheit.

Dry heat sauna
Accommodates up to sixteen adults.

Exercise equipment room
Five different pieces of equipment to exercise upper and lower body, two exercise bikes, one set of barbell weights, two jogging trampolines. Room is carpeted, with a mirrored wall.

Masseuse room
Massage therapy is available by appointment.

Dressing room
Contains 156 individual lockers with carpeted change areas; six private tiled showers with changing areas; two sinks and vanity areas, equipped with hair driers and curling irons; four restrooms.

Large meeting room/floor exercise room
A 35 x 66 feet hardwood floor auditorium. Large stage with curtains, drapes, lighting and sound system. Built-in oak storage cabinets. Used for theater, lectures, banquets, dances, special events and other physical fitness classes such aerobics, jazzercise, slimnastics, and others.

Small meeting room
An 18 x 22 feet carpeted room is used for small meetings, classes in stress management, French, bridge lessons, and other activities.

Arts and crafts room
Three circular work counters with four stools each and one pottery kiln. Classes include oil painting, water color, pottery, and stained glass.

Library
Built-in bookshelves, fireplace, four sofas. This quiet area is used for studying or for small meetings.

Lobby
Receptionist and cashier counter. Small waiting/greeting room.

Administrative areas
Offices for the manager, the bookkeeper, and catering manager.

Public restrooms
Storage rooms

Membership

Any woman 19 years of age or older could apply for membership. The classes of memberships follow:

1. Inactive Owner-Member—$1,100 certificate. This was an investment certificate; the holder owned one share in TWCL for each certificate. The holder had voting rights but could not use the facility or participate in any activities not open to the public.

2. Active Owner-Member—$1,100 certificate plus $40 monthly dues. This member owned one share in TWCL and had voting rights. The monthly dues entitled the holder to full use of the facilities and its activities. For events that required an additional fee, the Active Owner received a small discount.

3. Lifetime Owner-Member—$1,100 certificate plus $3,900 lump sum dues. This member had the same rights and privileges as the Active Owner but paid no monthly dues.

4. Program Member—$150 initiation fee plus $40 montly dues (with a minimum agreement of 6 months at a time). This member was entitled to full use of the facilities and participation in the activities.

5. Business Member—variable dues. Business organizations were allowed to purchase any one of the above four membership types, but the organizations had to designate the person who would use the facilities.

6. One-Month Program Member—$45. This was a use-only membership for 1 month. This member had no voting rights but did have full use of the facilities and its activities. After 1 month, the person had to decide whether to become an owner or a program member.

7. Weekend Program Member—$20. This was a use-only membership that allowed the person full use of the facilities on Saturday and Sunday only.

8. Weekly Program Member—This was a use-only membership that could be purchased by owners or program members for their guests. The person had full use of the facilities for 1 week.

Management

The Women's Club, Ltd., was owned by its members and operated through its board of directors, which consisted of nine elected women. The president of TWCL's was Mary Johnson; she provided expertise in management, personnel, and budgeting. Johnson was currently the office manager for the Central Engineering Department of the Morris-Knudsen Construction Company, where she had 12 years of experience in budgeting systems, personnel, and resource management. Johnson previously had spent 3 years with the Inter-mountain Glass Company and the prior 9 years with the Western Equipment Company.

The vice president was Joan Cochrane. She provided expertise in business and food service. For the past 10 years, she had been the co-owner of Precision Manufacturing Company; previously, she had owned the U-Stick Cannery for 5 years, and before that she had owned Kuna Drive-in for 5 years.

Joyce Sager, the treasurer, provided expertise in fiscal management, nutrition, public health, state government, personnel, and teaching. She had served for 7 years as the program director of a major nutrition program for the Idaho Department of Health and Welfare. In this capacity, Sager had administered a $5 million statewide program and oversaw nine local health agencies and fifty-six clinics. She previously had spent 2 years as a public health nutritionist with the Southwest District Health Department; she had been a dietition with St. Alphonsus Hospital and also a nutrition instructor at Boise State University. Sager's education included an M.S. in public health nutrition from the University of California-Berkeley and a B.S. in food and nutrition from the University of California-Davis.

The secretary of TWCL was Jeanette Pauli, who for the past 25 years had been the corporate secretary for the Title Insurance Company.

These four officers, along with the other five members of the board, hired the manager, who handled TWCL's day-to-day operations. The manager's primary responsibilities were assisting in annual budget preparation, planning promotional and public relations activities, and planning long-term club/member activities and programs. In addition, the manager had to enforce TWCL policies and rules and submit reports and other information to the board as required. To carry out these responsibilites, the manager had to work with the treasurer; supervise department heads, who in turn were responsible for hiring, training, and evaluating their respective staffs; and oversee advertising, fund-raising, and membership campaigns. In performing this last duty, she spent a considerable amount of time making public presentations, coordinating public relations activites, and closely monitoring membership recruitment.

The manager of TWCL was Ruth Dicks, who had considerable expertise in bookkeeping, marketing, sales, and office management. Before joining TWCL, she had spent 4 years as the owner of Brad Realty, Inc., a real estate business in Ohio, and 15 years as co-owner of Insurance Consultants, Inc., a casualty insurance agency with over $2 million in assets. Dicks was formerly the treasurer for TWCL and currently was on the Boise Chamber of Commerce.

In addition to the board of directors, TWCL had three key financial advisors: Marilyn Clapp, who currently was the manager of the Tax Collection Department of the local IRS branch office; Bonnie Johnson, a CPA; and Margorie Moon, the Idaho State Treasurer.

The unwritten organizational chart for TWCL is approximated in Exhibit 12–6.

Marketing and Sales

The target market for TWCL consisted of women living or working in Boise or the surrounding area. The primary marketing task since TWCL's founding had been to attract members. The most effective sales method for TWCL had been member referrals. Members invited women guests to use the facilities or to join in the activities. The manager then met with potential members on the premises and explained the types of membership available. When the potential members became familiar with TWCL, they frequently joined. The members were very proud of their club and did an excellent job of selling its benefits to potential members.

Recruitment of new members continued to be a vital activity for TWCL. Membership drives were held periodically throughout the year, and a committee for membership expansion met weekly to report on its activities. Dicks wanted to

EXHIBIT 12–6
Organizational Structure

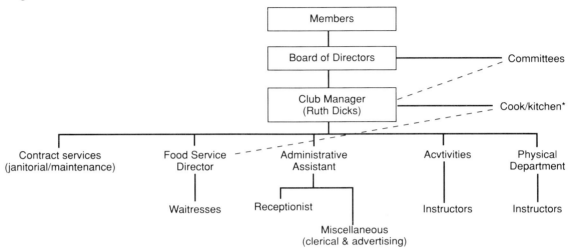

*Note: It is unclear where the cook/kitchen should appear in the organizational structure.

spend about half of her time on membership recruitment activities but could not do so because of other daily commitments.

Another recruiting method that TWCL used was newspaper advertising. The Club Manager developed these advertisements (see Exhibit 12–7) with the help of an advertising committee. Available funds (cash) were limited, and thus the number and size of ads were restricted. The organization had no formal advertising budget. The club also used flyers placed in local retail stores and businesses announcing new membership drives, holiday specials, and special upcoming events.

The club also tried to take advantage of other promotional activities. In 1981, TWCL gathered 6,000 names on a petition to influence a major department store to locate in downtown Boise. That effort generated a considerable amount of publicity, including several TV interviews with Dicks on the local news programs. The Women's Club, Ltd., attempted to participate in other newsworthy events and with other community-minded groups, such as by sponsoring the Boise Special Olympics. This activity gained favorable publicity and supported TWCL's goal of being community service minded.

TWCL Programs

The Womens Club, Ltd., had a wide range of events to develop each of its members physically, socially, intellectually, and culturally. The members' physical needs were met by classes in slimnastics, yoga, jazzercise, water aerobics, water exercises, and a body-contouring program. A popular offering was the "red-eye special," a body-

EXHIBIT 12–7
Recent Ads for TWCL

300 MAIN
The Women's Club Ltd.

A NEW LIFE STYLE FOR

$1.33
A DAY

- Pool
- Jacuzzi
- Tai Chi
- Water Exercise
- Sauna
- Slimnastics
- Aerobics
- Bridge

CLASSES

- painting
- pottery
- stained glass

FOR PENNIES MORE

- French classes
- Jazzercise
- Lectures
- Massage
- Great Books

Meet your friends for lunch or after work. Wine in our dining room.

345-0300   300 MAIN

LESS IS DEFINITELY MORE!
(Lose it at the Club)

SIX WEEKS of exercise & nutrition management tailored for you by our expert . . . Becky Swartz, M.S., R.D.
- Water exercise & aerobics in a gorgeous pool
- Jacuzzi & sauna for relaxation ● Diet breakfast & lunches available in our dining room.

FRIENDSHIP SPECIAL NOW — YOU & A FRIEND $100.00

The Women's Club, Ltd.
Boise's One of a Kind
300 Main   345-0300

YOU AND A FRIEND!
SHARE THE COST
JOIN FOR 1 MONTH
only
$50.00
Offer Expires November 30, 1983
The Women's Club, Ltd.
Boise's One of a Kind
300 Main
345-0300

The Women's Club, Ltd.
300 Main

Offers

CHRISTMAS GIFT CERTIFICATES
for that Special Woman

- $99 for INITIATION FEE and 1 MONTH'S Dues (on a six-month contract)
- $50 for five private SWIMMING LESSONS
- $20 for One Hour MASSAGE

Available At
The Women's Club Ltd
345-0300 — 300 MAIN

THE WOMEN'S CLUB
300 MAIN

Invites
YOU AND A FRIEND
to join for
$75 a month
in July & August
●●●
Share the cost
and the fun!

300 Main   345-0300

contouring and slimnastics session from 6:00 to 7:45 A.M., followed by a diet breakfast in the club restaurant. Social needs were met through many interest groups
such as the bridge club. Also, the restaurant featured a "TGIF" social event each
Friday. There were many cultural programs available such as classes in painting,
stained glass, flower arrangement, pottery, and water color. An especially significant
cultural activity was the "Woman in the Arts" event. Exhibit 12–8 shows the facilities
used in offering these numerous cultural, social, and physical activities. Recently,
TWCL launched the "300 Main" Lecture Series to educate both its members and
the general public on topics of wide interest and local significance. Exhibit 12–9
shows a physical education program schedule for a typical month.

   These widely varied social, professional, and cultural offerings attracted many
women to TWCL. The diverse membership included 210 owner members and 198
program members. While all ages and income levels were represented, the majority
of the membership ranged between 30 and 55 years of age and included business
and professional women, as well as young mothers and retired women.

Analytical Problem

The Women's Club, Ltd., began operations in December of 1981. Within a little over
a year, the organization was providing a wide range of services in an impressive
physical facility. As the financial data indicate, the future success of the organization
clearly depends on TWCL's ability to achieve the following:

1. Effectively manage its assets in the provision of useful services to members.
2. Develop a marketing plan to continue to build its resource base by (a)
   recruiting additional members, (b) increasing revenues generated through
   the provision of its current service operations, and (c) developing new
   revenue-generating activities.

   Assume the role of an outside consultant recently retained by TWCL. Prepare
a written report that will provide useful guidance on these issues so necessary for
TWCL's long-run success.

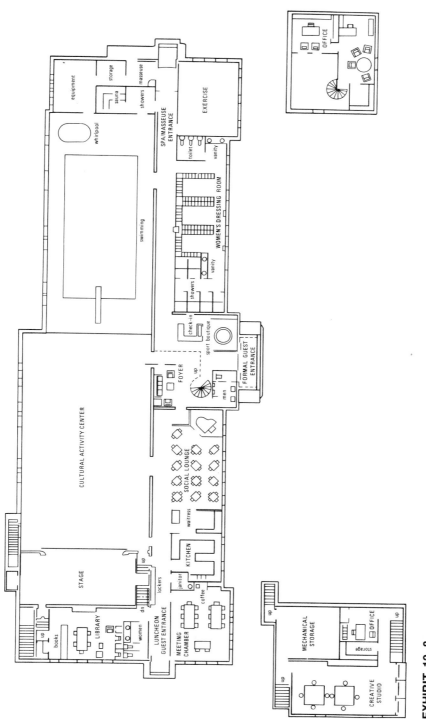

EXHIBIT 12–8

The Women's Club, Ltd., floor plan

EXHIBIT 12–9
Physical Education Program: November

Day	Time	Class	Instructor
Monday	6:00– 6:45 A.M.	Body contouring	Marilynn
	6:45– 7:45 A.M.	Slimnastics	Justine
	9:00–10:00 A.M.	Slimnastics	Karen
	9:30–10:30 A.M.	Yoga	Reekman
	10:30–11:00 A.M.	Water aerobics	Kris
	11:00–11:30 A.M.	Water exercise	Shannon
	12:00– 1:00 P.M.	Yoga	Debbie
	4:30– 6:15 P.M.	Lap swimming	
	5:30– 6:30 P.M.	Jazzercise	Debbie
Tuesday	6:45– 7:45 A.M.	Slimnastics	Justine
	9:00–10:00 A.M.	Slimnastics	Chris
	10:30–11:00 A.M.	Water aerobics	Marilynn
	11:00–11:30 A.M.	Water exercise	Shannon
	5:30– 6:30 P.M.	Water exercise	Marilynn
	5:30– 6:30 P.M.	Aerobics	Karen
Wednesday	6:00– 6:45 A.M.	Body contouring	Marilynn
	6:45– 7:45 A.M.	Slimnastics	Justine
	9:00–10:00 A.M.	Slimnastics	Karen
	10:30–11:00 A.M.	Water aerobics	Kris
	11:00–11:30 A.M.	Water exercise	Shannon
	12:00– 1:00 P.M.	Yoga	Debbie
	4:30– 6:15 P.M.	Lap swimming	
	6:30– 7:00 P.M.	Beginning swim lessons	Marilynn
	7:00– 7:30 P.M.	Intermediate swim lessons	Marilynn
	5:30– 6:30 P.M.	Jazzercise	Debbie
Thursday	6:45– 7:45 A.M.	Slimnastics	Shannon
	9:00–10:00 A.M.	Slimnastics	Karen
	10:30–11:00 A.M.	Water aerobics	Marilynn
	11:00–11:30 A.M.	Water exercises	Marilynn
	4:30– 6:15 P.M.	Lap swimming	
	5:30– 6:30 P.M.	Aerobics	Karen
	5:30– 6:30 P.M.	Water exercise	Marilynn
	5:30– 6:30 P.M.	Yoga	Reekman
	6:30– 7:30 P.M.	Water safety	Marilynn
Friday	6:45– 7:45 A.M.	Slimnastics	Justine
	9:00–10:00 A.M.	Slimnastics	Karen
	10:30–11:00 A.M.	Water aerobics	Kris
	11:00–11:30 A.M.	Water exercise	Shannon
Saturday	9:30–10:30 A.M.	Jazzercise	Debbie
	10:30–11:30 A.M.	Aerobics	Karen

CASE 13   GALUP-HARRIS:
Selecting High-Potential Retail Employees

Ron Galup was the executive director of Galup-Harris, a nationally known firm in the area of screening and selection of sales reps and other executives. Galup faced the task of reviewing hiring practices so that he could specifically recommend to his retail client firms which practices they should continue or discard. The task of screening applicants had increased in complexity as a result of federal regulations, particularly those of the Equal Employment Opportunity Commission (EEOC). Galup's greatest concern was in the area of psychological testing. He was aware of a study of 2,500 companies, conducted by the American Personnel Administration, which disclosed that a sizable percentage of the firms queried had phased out or reduced testing.

Galup also was aware of a Supreme Court case in which the Court ruled that Albemarle Paper Company was discriminating in its hiring. Albemarle had validated its testing for some jobs but had not validated the same tests for different jobs. Galup also knew that Flying Tiger Line, an air-freight firm, recently stopped giving its principal psychological test, the Wonderlic learning ability exam, because of the many uncertainties surrounding validation. Validation requirements also had caused a big midwestern manufacturer to discontinue using psychological tests as a hiring tool at its many diverse plant and office locations. That firm had decided to abandon its psychological examinations because the tests had not been validated by sex and race.

Retail firms faced these same regulations. Generally, professional validation of these tests is critical because a company should not use a test that in any way discriminates against a potential employee based on his or her race, color, religion, sex, national origin, or physical handicap. Professional validation of the tests therefore is necessary to ensure that they measure constructs critical to job success without being biased on any of these other criteria.

As a result of his many years of successful experience with psychological testing, Galup was not ready to join the bandwagon of dissenters and to recommend that his clients drop tests as a hiring tool. His first move was to call the EEOC office, where he talked with James Sharf, the commission's staff psychologist. Sharf was emphatic in stating that business was overreacting and misinterpreting the testing guidelines of EEOC. A common misconception on the part of personnel managers was that the fastest way to get into trouble with the EEOC was to test. Sharf, however, thought that the best way for companies to comply with the regulations was to conduct good validation studies on the tests they gave. To support his assertions, Sharf pointed to several blue-chip companies that had extensive and sophisticated personnel systems. These firms still find testing so valuable that they'd spent the time and the money to fully validate their tests. In particular, Sharf cited American Telephone and Telegraph Company and Exxon Corporation as companies with outstanding test validations.

This case was prepared by Steven J. Shaw, University of South Carolina.

Attitude Testing by Exxon

To learn more about the validation procedures at one of the companies Sharf had cited, Galup called an Exxon personnel officer who was familiar with its testing procedures. Most of this firm's testing is aptitude testing for entry-level jobs, in which candidates are trained in specialized skills. According to Paul Sparks, personnel/research coordinator for the oil giant, Exxon had begun testing in 1948 to reduce a high rate of failure in training programs, and the testing had greatly reduced employee turnover. Moreover, Exxon strictly adhered to a policy of continuously validating its tests. Exxon believed that although continuing validation studies cost money, the total expense was far less than the expense of starting from scratch in a massive crash-validation effort to comply with EEOC regulations. The cost of test validation was low when compared to the alternative of a large number of "bustouts" in training programs. Sparks estimated that it cost Exxon more than $8,000 to train one refinery worker, for example.

Sparks explained that the EEOC had received few discrimination complaints about Exxon's testing procedures. He cited one case, as an example, in which a black person claimed discrimination. Exxon, however, was quickly exonerated when the EEOC learned that this job had been given to another black person.

Drug Abuse Testing[1]

Drug abuse testing is another concern. Galup recognized that drug abuse is one of the nation's most serious problems. It is also an important factor as corporations seek to increase employee productivity. Experts have estimated that 10 to 23 percent of American workers use dangerous drugs while on the job. The cost of employee drug abuse has been estimated to cost American industry $33 billion per year. Obviously, from social and competitive perspectives, retailers are interested in reducing drug abuse among the work force.

Drug abuse testing is seen as a viable means for screening prospective employees and for discouraging drug use by current employees. Nearly one third of the Fortune 500 companies currently require prospective employees to pass this type of test. Several firms now market drug abuse tests and testing services. Several others are considering entry into this potentially lucrative market. In fact, a recent study indicated that the market potential for drug abuse testing has been increasing by 10 to 15 percent annually and could grow to become a $220 million industry by 1991.

Hoffmann-La Roche, Inc., for example, is one of many firms now selling drug abuse testing to corporate clients. They currently sell about $20 million per year in various drug-testing products. The company recently introduced a service known as Abuscreen and has begun promoting it as 99 percent accurate in testing for the presence of marijuana, LSD, amphetamines, cocaine, morphine, barbiturates, and methaqualone.

---

[1]Joe Agnew, "$220 Million Market Sales Seen by 1991 for Drug-Abuse Testing, *Marketing News* 20 (21 Nov. 1986): 1, and John Hoerr, "Privacy," *Business Week,* 28 March 1988, 61.

The high *reliability* of Hoffmann-La Roche's drug abuse testing is of great importance in marketing these services. The company's reputation, experience, and comprehensive services to potential customers are also important factors that have enabled Hoffmann-La Roche to sell its services to the 1984 Olympics, the U.S. Department of Defense, and many other organizations. Although price is a concern, most of the prospective corporate clients place more emphasis on quality of the drug abuse tests. Obviously, every precaution must be taken to minimize the number of false-positives, cases where an applicant's test indicates drug usage although he or she has not taken drugs. At the present time, however, no test is perfect.

Reference Checks

After his talks with the EEOC and Exxon officials, Galup was convinced that proven tests, properly administered, were still the most effective selection tools available to personnel managers. Galup had little faith in reference checks. From his experience, Galup believed that references could not be trusted because previous employers may have had unfounded personal biases against the applicant. Also, former bosses, Galup knew, were often unwilling to divulge the true reasons for an employee's discharge, even though the discharge might have been entirely justified. Conversely, applicants who truly did a rotten job might wind up with glowing recommendations simply because the previous employer either wanted to get rid of them or feared a lawsuit in the event the bad recommendation fell into the employee's hands. Several such suits had been won in court.

Personal Interviews

Although personal interviews can be used to explain job specifications and screen out misfits, Galup did not want his clients to rely heavily on them, because numerous studies have shown flagrant biases among interviewers. For instance, Galup read that tall men did markedly better in sales interviews because subconsciously interviewers generally equate height with potential sales success. Galup had also learned from another famous experiment that in a traditional face-to-face meeting, a group of businessmen could not consistently judge job applicants. The interviewers were twenty-three experienced men, mostly sales managers who regularly hired salespersons. Each individually talked to and rated the same twenty-four applicants. The results were almost as helter-skelter as if the names had been written on sheets of paper and churned up by an electric fan. No single applicant was ranked first by more than three of the twenty-three interviewers. As an example, one man was ranked first by one interviewer but sixteenth, nineteenth, and twenty-second by others.

Galup also learned that sociologists had conducted several studies that proved that flagrant biases exist among interviewers. One study assigned twelve people to interview 2,000 homeless men to find out what had put them on the skids. Among the interviewers were an ardent prohibitionist and a confirmed socialist. The prohibitionist found that the chief cause of the men's downfall was drink. The socialist determined that the chief cause was capitalism. The experiment proved that no interviewer can really see beyond his or her own prejudices.

Types of Tests to Recommend

Hundreds of tests were in use, and Galup's next task was to recommend specific types that his retail clients should use. In a letter he was drafting, Galup decided to recommend five types of tests: (1) intelligence tests, (2) personality inventories, (3) proficiency tests, (4) aptitude tests, and (5) attitude scales.

Intelligence Tests

Intelligence tests present, in varying combinations, tasks involving word meanings, verbal relationships, arithmetic reasoning, form classifications, spatial relationships, and other abstract symbolic material. Galup was leaning toward a test like the Wechsler Adult Intelligence Scale, which was designed to measure capacity to learn as opposed to past actual achievement.

Personality Inventories

Personality inventories frequently are referred to as social intelligence examinations. They are designed to measure an applicant's method of handling himself or herself in various social situations. Various socially sensitive situations might be described, and the applicant is asked to check which method he or she would use from a checklist of alternatives. Some of the tests try to measure the examinee's degree of extroversion or introversion by asking the person to check favorite hobbies and interests from a list that might include playing bridge, solitare, attending functions, and hunting or fishing alone.

Analytical Problem

1. If you were in Galup's position, which tests would you recommend to your retailer clients? Why? How and when should they be used?
2. Which of the tests would you be reluctant to recommend strongly? Why?
3. What role should personnel interviews play in selecting retail employees? Mention as many situations as you can where personal interviews might be very important in the hiring process.
4. What should be the place of reference checks in the selection process?
5. Can you suggest any other techniques that Galup might consider? For instance, could the polygraph or lie detector test be a useful screening device in situations where employees handle money?

PART FIVE

Retail Location and Facilities Management

CASE 14 **PRIME CUT STEAKHOUSES, INC.:**
Comparing Retail Locations

Prime Cut Steakhouses is a regional chain of steak house restaurants in what is often described as the family-priced steak house field. The Great Plains region of the United States serves as the primary market for the firm's eighty-four company-operated restaurants and its 120 franchised outlets. By using a marketing mix strategy consisting of standardized product offerings, quick service, uniform quality, convenient locations, and "family" prices, the firm has attracted a large segment of the Great Plains population.

Management Policies and Marketing Mix

The firm's product mix consists of a standard menu of prepared foods. The menu is restricted to a limited number of steak cuts, specials, and sandwiches, as well as a limited support menu of beverages, salads, side orders, and desserts. Product depth is limited to approximately four items per product line. The limited product mix is part of the firm's operational policy of maintaining strict centralized management control, which provides for operational efficiency as follows:

1. High-volume, low-cost procurement of foods, beverages, and restaurant items
2. Fewer product procurement costs and requirements because of the limited menu
3. Consistent product quality throughout the company-owned and franchised restaurants
4. Fewer preparation problems because of the limited menu
5. Lower advertising expense per restaurant, since all outlets benefit from the same campaign within the media's market area

The firm's pricing structure is designed to attract middle income ($25,000 to $50,000) families. Product-item pricing is based on a single price for a basic meal. The basic meal includes the meat (usually a steak), potato (french fries or baked),

---

This case was prepared by Dale M. Lewison, University of Akron.

and toast. Additional product items are priced separately. The base price plus the individual product-item pricing system is believed to be the most attractive to the widest range of potential consumers. The wide appeal is due to the consumer's desire to select only those items wanted. The firm's policy is to offer a quality product at a reasonable price. This policy has worked for Prime Cut, because it has been willing to accept a low unit-profit margin, believing that it could generate high sales volume while keeping overhead to a consumer-accepted minimum.

Management feels that their high sales volume is due to the fast-food, self-service policy. The basis of this approach is management's belief that a large segment of its customers have limited time, which is particularly true of the luncheon trade. Reasonable profits result from greater customer turnover in a limited space during limited trade hours and through lower operating overhead by eliminating table service personnel.

The firm's communication mix consists primarily of newspaper, radio, and television advertisements; however, personal selling and public relations also are employed informally and to a limited extent. The firm invests about 3 percent of its gross sales in promotional activities. General regional promotion costs for Prime Cut Steakhouse are 2 percent of gross sales, whereas individual store promotions account for 1 percent. Part of the firm's promotion costs are invested in special promotional programs, including (1) a free ice cream cone with each meal purchased; (2) discount coupons; (3) price specials; (4) newcomer programs, such as welcome wagon; and (5) gifts for new babies in the family. Management considers these "special promo" campaigns essential in creating new restaurant patronage and revitalizing former patronage as well as being important for promoting its family image.

The firm's distribution mix consists primarily of a central distribution center, which supplies all outlets (company and franchised) with most of the necessary operating inventory. The firm obtains some perishable items (such as meat, vegetables, and dairy products) directly from a prescribed list of vendors.

Management believes that one advantage Prime Cut has over conventional restaurants is the standardized architecture of its outlets. By using a standardized architectural style, sign, and interior layout, the firm has created wide consumer recognition of its outlets. Each restaurant is 90 by 60 feet with a seating capacity of 180 people. The interior layout is designed to maximize customer turnover during peak demand periods, while providing the consumer with a clean, uncluttered dining atmosphere.

The atmosphere of each of the firm's outlets can be described as a "Western" or an "authentic ranch-house style." This style, management feels, is consistent with the regional life-style.

The Firm's Operating Environment

On the national level, Prime Cut has several major chain competitors in the family-priced steak house field, which are Bonanza, Ponderosa, and Sizzler. Although Bonanza and Ponderosa are concentrated primarily in the East and Sizzler is basically in the far West, in several market areas, Prime Cut is in direct competition with the three national chains. In addition, numerous smaller regional chains as well as single, independent operations are in direct competition with Prime Cut. Furthermore, Prime Cut restaurants are located within trading areas that contain a variety of other well-known, nationally franchised restaurants. The competitive impact of fast-food operations such as Kentucky Fried Chicken, McDonald's, Roy Rogers Roast Beef, Pizza Hut, Denny's, and other chains is uncertain because the cumulative attraction versus competitive effects of these restaurants on the sales performances of Prime Cut outlets has not been determined.

Two peak demand periods (the noon and dinner hours) characterize the Prime Cut operation. Prime Cut must maximize sales during peak demand periods to maximize total daily sales. Daily sales maximization, however, is complicated by the differences in consumers for each of the two peak demand periods. Typically, the source areas of the noon-hour customers (11:00 A.M. to 2:00 P.M.) tend to differ from that of the dinner-hour customers (5:00 P.M. to 9:00 P.M.). Furthermore, these two peak-period customer groups differ substantially in demographic characteristics and patronage motives. Prime Cut management believes that these differences must be taken into account in developing the firm's marketing program.

Prime Cut Steakhouses: An Expansion Program

E. V. Smith, newly appointed Vice President of Real Estate and Development for Prime Cut, was faced with his first major company decision. Smith had to recommend to the firm's review board one of four site alternatives for immediate development. The decision was required by the end of the week to meet the firm's present expansion schedule of opening two additional outlets per month. Through Smith's long association with the fast-food industry and the commercial real estate business, he had considerable knowledge and experience in the problems of retail site evaluation and selection.

Smith's predecessor and the staff of the Real Estate and Development Department had selected the four available site alternatives from an original list of twelve alternatives. The list was narrowed down by an on-site inspection of the twelve alternatives. Reports indicated that land development and real estate costs were the principal criteria in selecting the four alternatives.

The northeastern area of Killian, Texas (standard metropolitan statistical area population 1.1 million), is the general trade area location of all four site alternatives. Killian is also the original market area for Prime Cut as well as the firm's corporate headquarters. The northwestern section of Killian had experienced tremendous growth in recent years. The development of several low-, medium-, and high-income residential areas and a corresponding commercial development had created a market that was not being served by one of the firm's eight existing Killian locations.

In an earlier discussion with Lindsey Barta, the firm's president, Smith got the distinct impression that filling the void in the Killian market was an objective that needed immediate attention. The general location and expansion strategy to which Prime Cut management adhered was market saturation. The policy involved "freezing out" the competition in a local market area by using a distributional pattern of outlets that created an intensive coverage of the market. Because the Killian market was the corporate headquarters for Prime Cut, this strategy acquired an even greater importance.

Contemplating the importance and the rush nature of the decision, Smith decided first to clarify the problem for himself. He felt that the major objective was to select the site alternative that offered the greatest sales potential. The current average monthly sales for the firm's existing outlets varied from $80,000 to $160,000. Reasoning that sales potential was primarily a function of locational attributes (all other marketing mix variables were standardized from one store to another), Smith believed the problem was to determine the site alternative that would best serve the type of consumer who patronized Prime Cut outlets. Realizing that the firm's outlets tended to draw different consumer groups at different peak hours, Smith decided to start the evaluation by considering a list of locational factors that had served him well in similar past decisions. Locational factors such as accessibility, cumulative attraction, compatibility, interception, store association, competition/saturation, and trade area demographics were, in Smith's experience, all spatial expressions of consumer preference in determining consumer store choice behavior.

Because of the time limitation, Smith felt that he had to base his decision primarily on the information in the two reports prepared by the staff of his predecessor. (See Exhibits 14–1 through 14–7.) Although the reports appeared to have been reasonably scientific in their preparation, certain omissions were obvious, such as the lack of demographic data. Smith felt that he must fill in the demographic and other missing data (at least subjectively) to arrive at the best possible decision within the next week.

Analytical Problem

Assume the role of E. V. Smith by completing the analysis of the four customer types and the four site alternatives. Write an internal report for Lindsey Barta, Prime Cut's President, outlining the relative advantages and disadvantages of the four site alternatives and making a specific recommendation of the site alternative most appropriate to both Prime Cut's mode of operation and the four customer types (see Exhibits 14–1 to 14–6) that characterize the steakhouse market. Justify and explain your recommendation.

Customer Type	Patronage Frequency	Average Percentage*	Percentage Range*
Passerby, drop-in trade	At least once	21.6	15–25
In-vicinity, drop-in trade	At least once a year	12.1	10–20
Occasional return trade	At least once a month	23.6	15–30
Steady return trade	At least once a week	42.7	35–50

*Percentage of all customers for all existing outlets.

EXHIBIT 14–1
Customer Type Based on Frequency of Patronage

Customer Type and Patronage Reason	Good-Quality Food			Fast Service			Convenient Location			Menu Selection			Reasonable Prices			Store Atmosphere			Other		
	1*	2†	3‡	1	2	3	1	2	3	1	2	3	1	2	3	1	2	3	1	2	3
Passerby, drop-in trade	9	12	17	16	17	22	40	29	12	21	23	26	12	18	22	1	1	0	1	0	1
In-vicinity, drop-in trade	16	15	12	16	28	23	30	26	17	20	20	16	15	20	28	2	1	2	1	0	2
Occasional return trade	20	22	20	18	15	20	18	19	20	18	20	15	21	21	25	4	3	0	1	0	0
Steady return trade	25	26	10	15	14	22	15	10	37	23	20	10	20	23	18	2	6	3	0	1	0

*1 = First choice †2 = Second choice
‡3 = Third choice

EXHIBIT 14–2
Customer Reasons for Patronage (Percentages)

Customer and Origin Type	Home			Work			Shop*			Visit†			R and E			Miscellaneous			Total		
	P	S	T	P	S	T	P	S	T	P	S	T	P	S	T	P	S	T	P	S	T
Passerby, drop-in trade	0	2	11	1	7	23	0	18	12	1	1	2	1	2	4	0	7	8	3	27	60
In-vicinity, drop-in trade	0	8	4	14	10	1	30	10	0	6	0	0	8	1	0	8	0	0	66	29	5
Occasional return trade	5	12	1	20	12	0	21	8	1	4	1	0	5	0	0	9	1	0	64	34	2
Steady return trade	11	2	0	40	16	1	14	13	1	2	1	0	3	2	0	4	0	0	74	24	2

P, primary trading area (0 to 0.99 miles); R and E, recreation and entertainment; S, secondary trading area (1 to 2.99 miles); T, tertiary trading area (3 miles or more).
*Individuals on commercial shopping trips (goods or services).
†Individuals on personal visits.

EXHIBIT 14–3
Noon-Hour Origin Characteristics (Percentages)

Customer and Origin Type	Home			Work			Shop*			Visit†			R and E			Miscellaneous			Total		
	P	S	T	P	S	T	P	S	T	P	S	T	P	S	T	P	S	T	P	S	T
Passerby, drop-in trade	0	1	12	1	10	25	0	8	18	0	2	3	1	3	6	1	3	6	3	27	70
In-vicinity, drop-in trade	0	2	7	1	3	8	31	17	3	7	2	1	6	0	0	12	0	0	57	24	19
Occasional return trade	3	14	0	16	20	1	22	5	0	4	1	1	5	2	0	6	0	0	56	42	2
Steady return trade	12	2	1	40	13	2	15	13	0	2	0	0	6	0	0	4	0	0	79	18	3

P, primary trading area (0 to 0.99 miles); R and E, recreation and entertainment; S, secondary trading area (1 to 2.99 miles); T, tertiary trading area (3 miles or more).
*Individuals on commercial shopping trips (goods or services).
†Individuals on personal visits.

EXHIBIT 14–4
Noon-Hour Destination Characteristics (Percentages)

EXHIBIT 14–5
Dinner-Hour Origin Characteristics (Percentages)

Customer and Origin Type	Home			Work			Shop*			Visit†			R and E			Miscellaneous			Total		
	P	S	T	P	S	T	P	S	T	P	S	T	P	S	T	P	S	T	P	S	T
Passerby, drop-in trade	0	6	20	1	7	19	1	7	17	0	2	4	1	4	6	1	2	2	4	28	68
In-vicinity, drop-in trade	0	14	12	1	5	9	15	16	0	3	6	1	4	4	0	5	5	0	28	50	22
Occasional return trade	30	13	1	15	15	0	8	7	1	3	1	0	2	2	0	2	0	0	60	38	2
Steady return trade	34	8	0	27	10	3	10	2	0	2	0	0	1	1	0	2	0	0	76	21	3

P, primary trading area (0 to 0.99 miles); R and E, recreation and entertainment; S, secondary trading area (1 to 2.99 miles); T, tertiary trading area (3 miles or more).
*Individuals on commercial shopping trips (goods or services).
†Individuals on personal visits.

EXHIBIT 14–6
Dinner-Hour Destination Characteristics (Percentages)

Customer and Origin Type	Home			Work			Shop*			Visit†			R and E			Miscellaneous			Total		
	P	S	T	P	S	T	P	S	T	P	S	T	P	S	T	P	S	T	P	S	T
Passerby, drop-in trade	0	8	43	0	3	6	1	2	12	1	3	3	0	7	6	0	3	2	2	26	72
In-vicinity, drop-in trade	2	4	29	5	3	4	10	4	7	1	4	6	1	7	8	1	3	1	20	25	55
Occasional return trade	24	18	4	7	4	1	12	6	0	3	1	0	9	2	0	8	1	0	63	32	5
Steady return trade	48	6	1	8	1	1	12	0	0	6	0	0	10	2	1	4	0	0	88	9	3

P, primary trading area (0 to 0.99 miles); R and E, recreation and entertainment; S, secondary trading area (1 to 2.99 miles); T, tertiary trading area (3 miles or more).
*Individuals on commercial shopping trips (goods or services).
†Individuals on personal visits.

Location Characteristics*	Site Alternative			
	Hawkins (1)	Main (2)	Route 6 (3)	Fourth (4)
Residential characteristics				
Number of single-dwelling units	1,714	2,341	905	3,172
Number of multiple-dwelling units	670	64	1,248	102
Number of transient-dwelling units	20	0	50	0
Owner-occupied units (%)	42	58	24	67
Nonresidential characteristics				
Total number of retailing units	94	100	81	57
Convenience goods retailers (%)	64	48	61	71
Shopping goods retailers (%)	30	42	31	29
Specialty goods retailers (%)	6	10	2	0
Total number of service units	128	134	311	54
Personal service units	24	26	19	35
Business service units	6	8	24	0
Automotive service units (%)	10	9	4	11
Recreation entertainment units (%)	18	10	15	15
Legal, financial, medical service units (%)	16	18	24	7
Governmental service units (%)	17	10	10	5
Educational service units (%)	5	9	1	10
Religious service units (%)	5	8	1	16
Miscellaneous service units (%)	3	2	2	1
Total number of wholesale units	7	7	21	0
Total number of manufacturing units	1	0	2	0
Population characteristics				
Total population	13,000	15,000	14,000	10,900
Mean family income	21,200	22,800	24,100	23,200
Low-income population: 7,000 (%)	24	8	10	28
High-income population: 20,000 (%)	2	12	24	32
Nonwhite population (%)	31	8	8	0
Elderly population: over 62 (%)	18	6	4	8
Teenage population: under 18 (%)	20	35	6	44

Site characteristics

Site size: Front footage	80	140	110	100
Site size: Total square footage	16,000	19,600	22,000	15,000
Site block position	corner	interior	interior	interior
Type of location	free standing	free standing	free standing	free standing
Number of entrances/exits	4	2	2	4
Footage of entrances/exits	100	140	100	120
Facing street: Number of traffic lanes	4	4	6	4
Facing street: Turn on-off lanes	no	yes	yes	no
Facing street: Medians	crossable	crossable	uncrossable	crossable
Facing street: Speed limit	35	40	45	35
Facing street: Average daily traffic volume	19,791	20,213	28,428	14,005
Side street: Number of traffic lanes	2	NA	NA	4
Side street: Turn on-off lane	no	NA	NA	no
Side street: Medians	crossable	NA	NA	crossable
Side street: Speed limit	35	NA	NA	35
Side street: Average daily traffic volume	4,952	NA	NA	6,200

Real estate characteristics

Percentage of gross sales	5.25	5.75	5.75	4.75

Competitive characteristics

Number of "like" establishments	2	1	2	0
Number of specialty sandwich units	6	7	8	2
Number of specialty nonsandwich units	7	9	10	2
Number of variety sandwich units	6	6	4	1
Number of variety nonsandwich units	9	10	12	2

NA, not applicable.

*Location characteristics are for the primary trading area only.

EXHIBIT 14–7
Locational Survey Report

SHORTSTOP RESTAURANTS:
Evaluating Retail Site Accessibility

Shortstop Restaurants enjoyed considerable success in the fast-food business during the decade of the eighties. In fact, during the last 10 years, the firm's expansion program had taken the firm from a local chain of four restaurants to a successful regional operation of sixty-four fast-food outlets. While expanding operations into five southeastern states, the firm had yet to experience a single failure. Being able to say that the firm had "never had a failure" was a matter of personal pride to Gary Bauer, the founder and president of Shortstop Restaurants, Inc. The lack of a failure was also an excellent selling point in the firm's attempts to attract potential investors—an important consideration in achieving the firm's growth objective of opening ten new restaurants each year for the next 5 years.

The Firm and Its Marketing Mix

Shortstop's success was predicated on offering the fast-food customer the best in both time and place convenience. For Shortstop Restaurants, the key marketing mix ingredients were offering a variety of well-prepared food items at very convenient locations supported by quick service. By targeting its marketing efforts toward the mobile, outdoor life-styles of the Southern consumer and by appealing to the working-wife family, the firm hoped to continue expanding on its past successes and to meet its future growth objectives.

The Product Mix

The firm's product mix consisted of a specialized menu of prepared foods featuring a limited selection of sandwiches and related complementary items. The menu was restricted to food items that could be prepared (1) quickly and efficiently, (2) with uniform product quality, (3) for carry-out service, and (4) in a variety of ways for the largest product selection possible.

The breakfast menu (served from 6 A.M. to 10 A.M.) offered a selection of two sandwiches: (1) the "Yankee" (a poached egg with Canadian bacon and Wisconsin cheese served on an English muffin) and (2) the "Rebel" (a poached egg with Southern pork sausage served on a homemade biscuit). Breakfast complements included hot apple or cheese danish; hash-browned potato patty, juices (orange, tomato, and grape); milk; and coffee. The breakfast menu was quite successful and accounted for 26 percent of total sales for the typical Shortstop Restaurant.

The lunch and dinner menu (served from 10 A.M. to 11 P.M.) consisted of a selection of three different-size hamburgers, a chicken sandwich, a ham sandwich, a fish sandwich, and a Coney hot dog. Each sandwich was made to order from a selection of standard condiments (e.g., pickles, onions, tomatoes). Lunch and dinner complements included french fries, onion rings, cole slaw, green salad bowl, deep-fried pies, soft-serve sundaes or cones, and a wide assortment of beverages (soft drinks, tea, coffee, milk, and shakes). In addition, each of the sandwiches

This case was prepared by Dale M. Lewison, University of Akron, and Bill C. Tadlock, University of Arkansas, Little Rock.

could be ordered as a platter with a choice of french fries or onion rings and cole slaw or salad bowl.

The Service Mix

Shortstop Restaurants offered its customers the choice of self-service in-store eating or drive-up window service. Originally, the drive-up service was added to the service mix to distinguish the firm's operations from those of its competitors. The drive-up window service, however, had clearly become the single most important factor in explaining Shortstop's success. Although the exact percentage varied among restaurants, drive-up window sales accounted for approximately 47 percent of the total sales volume for the typical Shortstop Restaurant. A recent survey of the firm's regular customers identified the convenience of the drive-up window service as being the most important patronage reason for 36 percent of the survey's respondents. The importance of drive-up window sales in the fast food business was further evidenced by the large number of McDonald's and Burger King restaurants that had been remodeled to include this service.

The Pricing Mix

Competitive parity was the Shortstop's primary pricing tactic. With the exception of a daily price special, the firm strove to maintain prices that were comparable with the local prices of such nationally franchised prepared food retailers as McDonald's, Wendy's, and Burger King. For the price-conscious consumer, the sandwich platters represented a notable savings over the sum of the individual prices for each item—a 10 to 15 percent savings.

The Promotion Mix

Supported by 4 percent of the gross sales budget, the firm's promotional mix involved a variety of advertising media and sales promotion devices. First, Shortstop used heavy radio advertising during the morning and evening rush-hour. Management believed these audiences were most susceptible to the convenience appeals and messages featured in the firm's advertisements. Second, to build awareness of the firm and its operations, a local television advertising blitz was employed in selected markets periodically. Shortstop also extensively used local newspaper advertising, which often was tied to various sales promotions such as discount coupons and premiums (e.g., free glasses with a purchase of a large soft drink). To reinforce the promotional mix and to promote customer recognition, Shortstop's facilities (store and signs) were highly standardized.

The Firm's Location Strategy

From the beginning, Shortstop's management felt that the crucial element in explaining their success was their attention to carefully selected locations. Although management devoted a considerable amount of money and effort to identifying and evaluating potentially viable trading areas, the key feature in Shortstop's location strategy was site accessibility. In the words of the firm's founder, "the single most important physical site attribute is direct site accessibility; an inaccessible site is of little value to us in the fast-food business, even if it is located within a potentially high sales volume trading area." In the firm's view, the site accessibility factor encompassed the four basic accessing activities of (1) approaching, (2) entering, (3) traversing, and (4) exiting a site. Any evaluation of site accessibility must consider the ease with which the consumer could accomplish each of these four tasks. If the potential consumer encountered any major difficulty in any one of the four tasks, the site's accessibility was notably negatively affected. Management developed a site accessibility checklist to ensure close attention to the site accessibility problem, to guide the firm's site accessibility evaluation process, and to evaluate all site alternatives (Exhibit 15–1). This checklist identified the principal factors Shortstop management wanted to consider when evaluating site accessibility.

The Firm's Expansion Program

For the last 3 years, Cheryl Stone, Store Operations Manager for Shortstop Restaurants, Inc., had conducted the firm's expansion program. Part of that responsibility included identifying and evaluating new locations. Based on the sales performance records of existing restaurants, Stone became a firm believer in the necessity of good site accessibility. Sales records showed a direct correlation between high levels of site accessibility and above-average sales performances. Having become a student of the art and science of selecting profitable locations, Stone recognized long ago that site accessibility had both physical and psychological dimensions. Physical site accessibility involves the tangible attributes of a site and its surrounding area and how those tangible factors interact either to enhance or to hinder potential customers as they approach, enter, traverse, and exit a site. The psychological dimensions of accessibility are those related to the potential customer's perception of the ease of site access. From past experience, Stone had learned that the customer's perception of a site's accessibility was as important as the site's actual physical accessibility. If a consumer believed that a site was difficult, dangerous, or inconvenient to access, then a psychological barrier had been created equal to any physical barrier.

For the 1990s expansion program to be as successful as the expansion in the 1980s, Stone would have to ensure satisfaction of the time and place convenience needs of the firm's targeted consumers. To meet the convenience needs of the typical Shortstop consumer, Stone realized that she had to find new locations that were both physically and psychologically accessible.

The Waynesville Site

Currently under consideration for a new Shortstop Restaurant was a site in Waynesville, Mississippi (population 186,000). The site was located at the intersection of Ross Boulevard and Green Avenue. The results of the trading area analysis for the Waynesville site were very favorable. The site's trading area appeared to contain both the number and type of consumers necessary to support a Shortstop Restaurant. Before Stone could make a recommendation on the site, the firm's field survey team had to complete the analysis of the site accessibility information. The team's report contained the following information: (1) a general land use and major traffic arteries map of Waynesville (Exhibit 15–2); (2) a traffic control map of the proposed trading area (Exhibit 15–3); (3) a 24-hour traffic count by direction and traffic lane (Exhibit 15–4); (4) a 24-hour traffic count by time period (Exhibit 15–5); (5) a com-

EXHIBIT 15–1
Site Accessibility Checklist

I. Traffic factors
  A. Traffic arteries
    1. Number of traffic arteries adjacent to site
    2. Number of traffic lanes associated with each of the site's traffic arteries
    3. Designated directional flow of each traffic artery
    4. Number, location, and configuration of intersections
    5. Type and configuration of medians
    6. Presence or absence of protected traffic lanes
  B. Traffic flow
    1. Total volume of traffic on each of the adjacent traffic arteries
    2. Directional variations in the volume of traffic flow (northbound, southbound, eastbound and westbound flows)
    3. Temporal variations in the volume of traffic flow (seasonal, monthly, weekly, and daily variations)
    4. Spatial variations in the volume of traffic flow in terms of traffic lanes (inside, middle, and outside lanes)
    5. Composition of the traffic flow in terms of its trip behavior (work trips, shopping trips, pleasure or recreation trips, and through trips)
  C. Traffic controls
    1. Speed limit of each of the adjacent traffic arteries
    2. Number, type, and location of traffic lights
    3. Number, type, and location of stop signs
    4. Number, type, and location of traffic rule signs (U-turn, left-turn, and no parking signs)
    5. Number, type, and location of traffic guidance lines (lane dividers, turning arrows and through arrows)
II. Site factors
  A. Site layout
    1. Size of site (square footage)
    2. Shape of site (square, rectangular, triangular, and odd)
    3. Elevation of site (at, above, or below street level)
    4. Boundaries of site (front footage, number and character of entrances and exits)
  B. Site location
    1. Side of street (left- or right-hand side)
    2. Part of block (corner or interior location)
  C. Site position
    1. Interceptor qualities—the ability of the site to intercept customers as they travel between identifiable origins and destinations
    2. Intervening opportunities—the ability of the site to serve as an intervening shopping opportunity between the location of competitors

EXHIBIT 15–2
General Land Use and Major Traffic Arteries Map

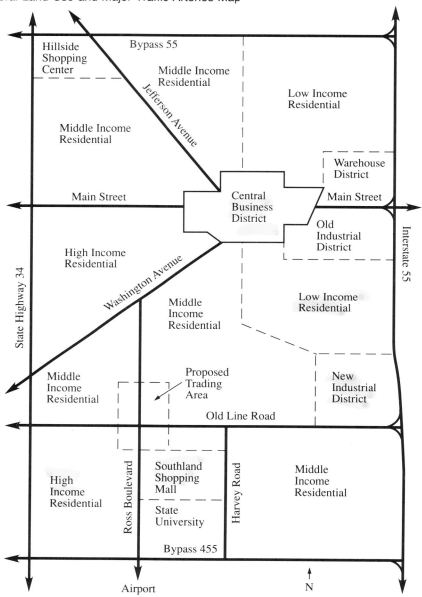

EXHIBIT 15–3
Traffic Control Map of Proposed Trading Area

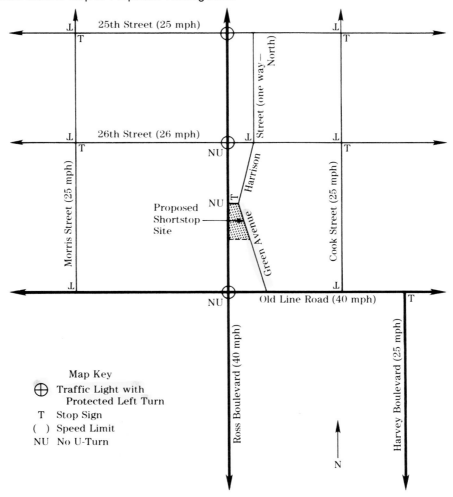

petitor location map of the proposed trading area (Exhibit 15–6); and (6) a site layout map of the Ross–Green site (Exhibit 15–7).

Analytical Problem

Assume the role of Cheryl Stone and prepare a written analysis of the accessibility of the Ross–Green site using the information provided in the field survey team's report. Make a specific recommendation as to whether the Ross–Green site should be selected as a future location for the Shortstop Restaurant.

EXHIBIT 15–4
Twenty-four–Hour Traffic Count by Direction and Traffic Lane

Southbound on Ross Boulevard	
Left lane	3,370
Middle lane	4,120
Right lane	3,710
Total	11,200
Northbound on Ross Boulevard	
Left lane	3,490
Middle lane	4,470
Right lane	4,400
Total	12,400
Southbound on Green Avenue, total	80
Northbound on Green Avenue, total	1,190

EXHIBIT 15–5
Twenty-four–Hour Traffic Count by Time Period (Weekdays)

Time Period	Ross Boulevard	Green Avenue
1 A.M. to 3 A.M.	300	30
3 A.M. to 5 A.M.	300	40
5 A.M. to 7 A.M.	1,100	110
7 A.M. to 9 A.M.	3,800	200
9 A.M. to 11 A.M.	2,200	120
11 A.M. to 1 P.M.	3,600	220
1 P.M. to 3 P.M.	2,400	115
3 P.M. to 5 P.M.	2,100	75
5 P.M. to 7 P.M.	8,400	210
7 P.M. to 9 P.M.	2,000	70
9 P.M. to 11 P.M.	800	55
11 P.M. to 1 A.M.	600	25
Total	27,600	1,270

EXHIBIT 15–6
Competitor Location Map of Proposed Trading Area

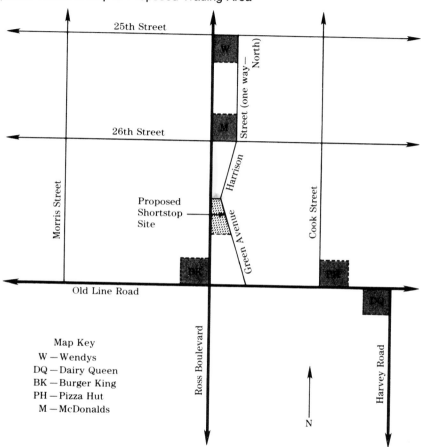

Map Key
W — Wendys
DQ — Dairy Queen
BK — Burger King
PH — Pizza Hut
M — McDonalds

EXHIBIT 15–7
Layout of the Ross–Green Site

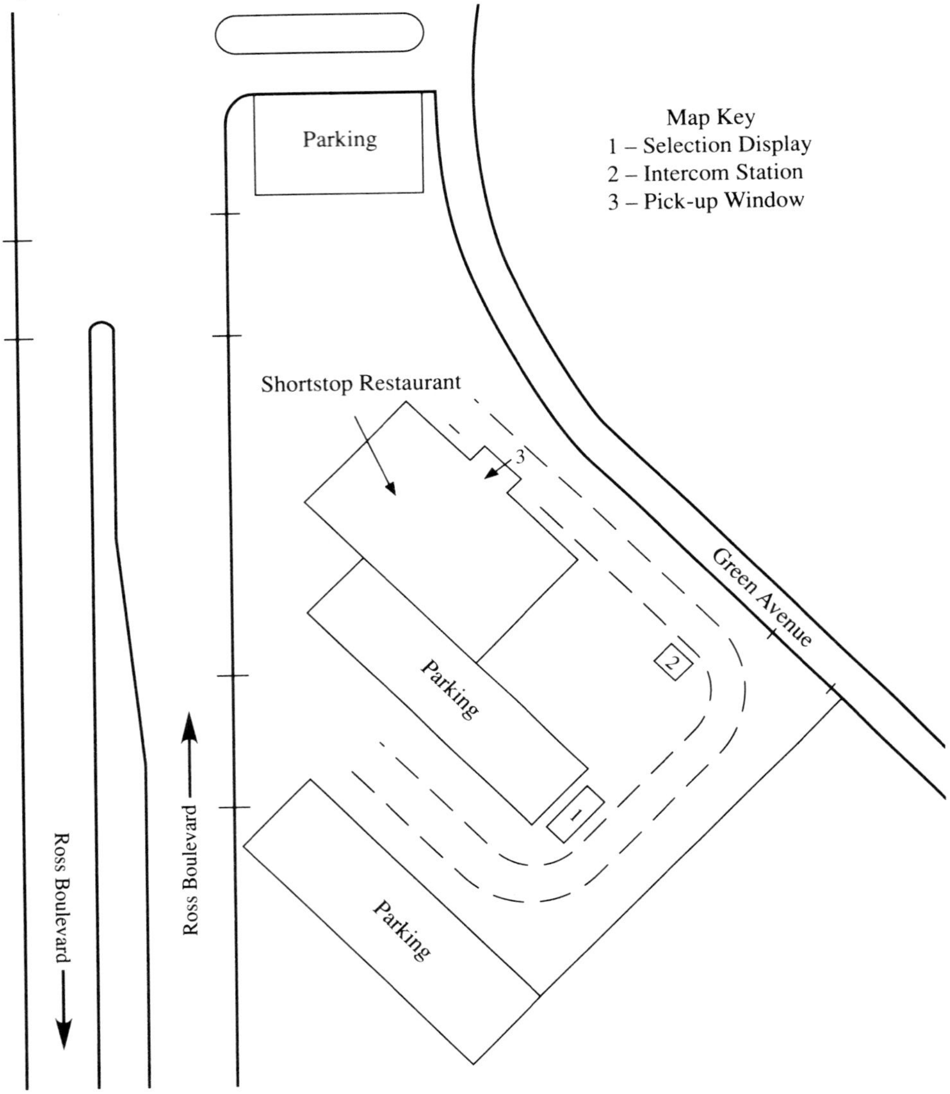

Map Key
1 – Selection Display
2 – Intercom Station
3 – Pick-up Window

Parking

Parking

Parking

Shortstop Restaurant

Green Avenue

Ross Boulevard

Ross Boulevard

DIAMOND JIM'S:
Evaluating Store Layouts and Physical Facilities

Allison Green, manager of Diamond Jim's, was deeply concerned about her upcoming meeting with top-level staff planners in Merchandise Amalgamated. She was considered a very successful manager and also had been the first assistant manager of Diamond Jim's when Merchandise Amalgamated acquired the jewelry store just over 4 years ago. But she was uneasy about her role and competence in the decision situation that would be the focus of the meeting: choice of a new location and store facility.

Background

Merchandise Amalgamated's acquisition of Diamond Jim's was its first foray into the jewelry store business. Previously, the retail conglomerate had concentrated its developments and acquisitions within two major lines of business: department stores and specialty clothing stores. Since the acquisition of Diamond Jim's, though, Merchandise Amalgamated had acquired fifteen additional jewelry stores within a three-state area. Most of these stores had been modestly successful independent businesses.

Over the past 5 years, all sixteen jewelry stores had been incorporated into Merchandise Amalgamated's strategic planning process. In addition, the corporate staff responsible for marketing and merchandising studies had conducted numerous research studies designed to identify opportunities and problems for these jewelry stores. The immediate result of these efforts was encouraging. All sixteen stores had improved their financial performance significantly, and over half had achieved a performance level that compared favorable to "high-performance" jewelry stores in their geographic areas.

In the opinion of staff planners, those stores that had failed to achieve the status of "high-performance" jewelry store did have the potential to do so if investments in new locations and facilities could be made. Diamond Jim's was such a store. Its central city location and older facility hindered further improvement in the store's financial performance. In addition, shoppers often complained about the store's cluttered and unattractive layout (Exhibit 16–1).

After looking at the various investment opportunities across the company, staff planners had recently recommended investment in a new location and facility for Diamond Jim's. Within 6 months, the in-house real estate group had identified two possible locations in a new upscale, suburban shopping mall serving above-median-income shoppers. Preliminary store layouts were prepared for each location. Green was currently reviewing each layout (Exhibits 16–2 and 16–3). She fully expected to be asked for her opinion of the best layout. According to staff planners, the new location and store facility should reflect the following:

1. Appeal to an upscale shopper. Specific targets include fashion-conscious women, working women between the ages of 25 and 35, and affluent businessmen who buy men's jewelry.

This case was prepared by J. B. Wilkinson, University of Akron.

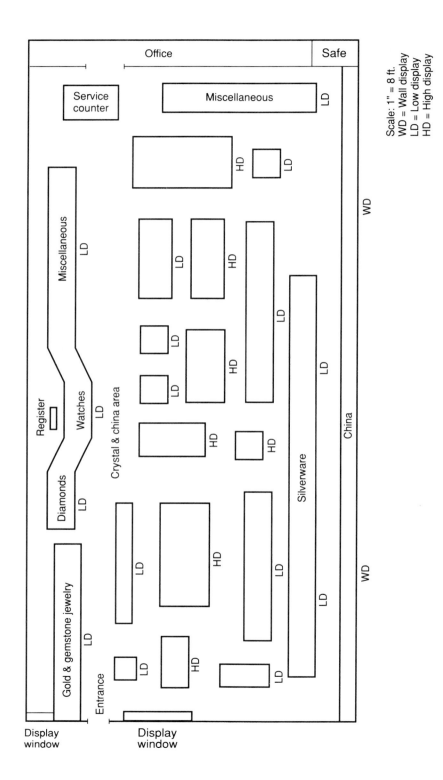

Scale: 1" = 8 ft.
WD = Wall display
LD = Low display
HD = High display

EXHIBIT 16–1
Diamond Jim's Current Store Layout

110

EXHIBIT 16–2
Proposed Store Layout A

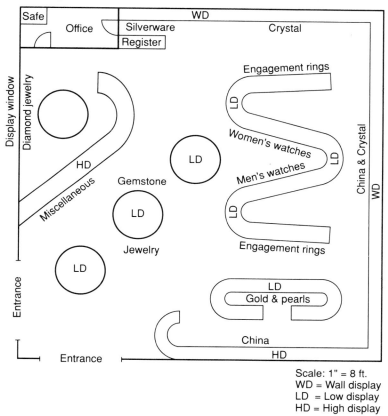

Scale: 1" = 8 ft.
WD = Wall display
LD = Low display
HD = High display

2. Emphasize gold jewelry, pearls, and colored stones. Primary objective is to reduce dependence on sales of diamonds, which are tied to infrequent events such as engagements and anniversaries, and to increase sales of everyday gold or fashion jewelry, such as cocktail rings, earrings, bracelets, and so on.

Store Layout A is a corner location in the mall with an open storefront to two mall aisles (Exhibit 16–2). Three stand-up cases are positioned down the main aisles. At the back of the store is a long, low, "snaked" sit-down case for watches and engagement rings. Off to the side is an oval sit-down case for gold and pearls. Behind one of the higher case elements at the store's perimeter is a "Diamond Room." The 7-feet-high showcase separates the special area from the rest of the store and provides a private space to show diamonds and more expensive jewelry at a 30-inch round table with three chairs. To maximize exposure to merchandise, 7-feet-high cases wrap around the perimeter walls.

EXHIBIT 16–3
Proposed Store Layout B

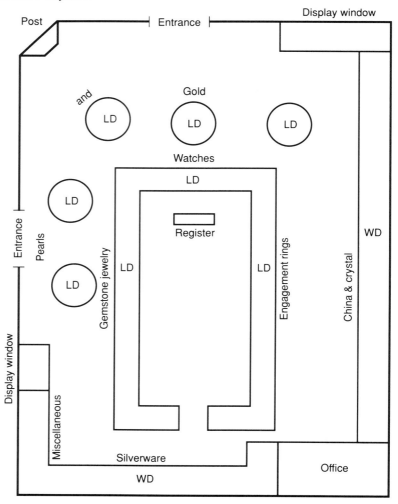

SCALE: 1" = 8ft.
WD = Wall display
LD = Low display
HD = High display

Store Layout B is a different corner location in the same mall with an open entrance to two mall aisles (Exhibit 16–3). Entering customers pass stand-up cases for gold and pearls to reach the large U-shaped, glass-enclosed showcase. High display cases for china, crystal, silverware, and giftware line the walls.

Analytical Problem

1. How should Allison Green evaluate each of the two proposed store layouts?
2. What are the strengths and weaknesses of the current layout and each of the proposed layouts? Which one would you recommend? Why?
3. How could each of the proposed layouts be improved?

CASE 17 BUTTERFIELD'S:
Creating and Adjusting Merchandise Assortments

Retail management constantly faces decisions regarding adjustments to its dynamic operating environment. Changing consumer and retail structure patterns create a continuing need for reevaluation of market positions and merchandising strategies. The director of stores for Butterfield's, a large soft goods specialty retailer, and his staff faced a series of product-mix decisions as a result of the planned introduction of a large regional shopping mall into the firm's local retail market and the opening of an additional Butterfield's outlet within the new mall. A recently completed impact study conducted at the local state university intensified the need for decisions.

The Market: Tri-City Area

Centrally located within the state, the Tri-City Area reaped the economic and political benefits associated with that position. The pleasant physical environment (climate, terrain, and vegetation) of the state's uplands area provided highly desirable "quality of life" factors that contributed greatly to the population and economic growth of the area. As the central focal point of the state, the Tri-City Area had evolved into the cultural, political, and economic hub of the state.

The Tri-City Area's current population of 313,200 was expected to continue its steady growth rate of the last decade, as a result of a strong and balanced economy. The area's economic base was reasonably well balanced between primary and secondary production, distribution, and service sectors of the economy. Tri-City enjoyed the benefits of a stable state and federal employment sector as well as the presence of a major state university and a large federal military base.

The demographic characteristics of Tri-City's population are shown in Exhibits 17–1 to 17–3. The six demographic variables presented are (1) total population, (2) racial composition, (3) median family income, (4) age composition, (5) occupation status, and (6) employment status. Exhibit 17–4 is a map of census tracts.

This case was prepared by Dale M. Lewison and Jon M. Hawes, University of Akron, and Wilke English, University of Texas at El Paso.

| Census Tract | Total Population | | Racial Composition | | | |
| | | | White (%) | | Black (%) | |
	1980	1988	1980	1988	1980	1988
1	1,050	900	26	18	74	82
2	2,800	2,100	18	18	82	82
3	5,400	4,300	32	30	68	70
4	6,100	6,200	34	14	66	86
5	4,900	4,950	38	36	62	64
6*	—	—	—	—	—	—
7	6,400	6,950	64	68	36	32
8	5,700	5,700	72	72	28	28
9	5,350	5,400	70	70	30	30
10	4,750	4,700	72	71	28	29
11	6,200	6,300	35	34	65	66
12	5,750	5,700	81	80	19	20
13	4,900	4,900	77	77	23	23
14	5,100	5,000	83	81	17	19
15	6,450	6,350	74	70	26	30
16	6,100	6,700	52	46	48	54
17	5,200	5,300	50	39	50	61
18	7,400	7,300	21	7	79	93
19	6,700	6,900	58	58	42	42
20	4,100	4,100	64	62	36	38
21	5,350	5,250	94	94	6	6
22	6,100	6,050	63	62	37	38
23	5,100	5,250	97	97	3	3
24	3,000	3,400	69	68	31	32
25	3,100	3,300	70	70	30	30
26	2,200	2,900	74	73	26	27
27	3,900	4,700	84	84	26	26
28	1,900	3,400	83	82	17	18
29	1,200	5,100	84	90	16	10
30	1,700	3,900	87	89	13	11
31	2,100	6,300	95	98	5	2

Tract						
32	2,600	4,900	92	96	8	4
33	3,700	5,650	94	94	6	6
34	3,650	5,100	88	88	12	12
35	1,200	2,900	74	75	26	25
36	800	7,000	50	95	50	5
37	200	800	100	100	0	0
38	1,700	3,700	98	99	2	1
39	2,300	5,250	99	99	1	1
40	1,800	6,100	100	100	0	0
41	1,250	2,700	98	99	2	1
42	1,600	8,200	96	99	4	1
43	1,000	4,800	90	96	10	4
44	1,200	6,400	94	99	6	1
45	800	5,100	98	99	2	1
46	1,400	5,400	92	99	8	1
47	1,300	4,900	94	99	6	1
48	1,300	3,900	81	87	19	13
49	1,200	4,100	87	97	13	3
50	1,700	3,700	96	98	4	2
51	1,100	4,400	96	99	4	1
52	1,400	7,100	99	99	1	1
53	1,100	6,100	100	100	0	0
54	300	4,100	100	100	0	0
55	1,300	8,000	96	99	4	1
56	2,100	7,000	97	99	3	1
57	800	6,000	99	99	1	1
58	1,100	4,000	100	100	0	0
59	1,600	8,700	100	100	0	0
60	900	6,900	99	100	1	0
61	1,700	4,700	96	100	4	0
62	1,900	6,300	99	100	1	0
Total	181,900	313,200				

*Census tract 6 is the University of South Carolina, consisting of 16,000 full-time students. Approximately one third of the student body resides in campus housing in census tract 6.

EXHIBIT 17–1

Population Characteristics: Total Population and Racial Composition

Census Tract	Median Family Income		Age Composition			
			Under 18 (%)		Over 65 (%)	
	1980	1988	1980	1988	1980	1988
1	$19,500	19,900	22	16	12	28
2	19,750	20,150	26	21	10	29
3	20,100	20,450	20	20	8	12
4	20,700	21,100	21	16	7	10
5	20,500	21,350	16	12	9	14
6*	—	—	—	—	—	—
7	21,900	21,300	28	16	12	8
8	20,500	21,000	26	21	15	15
9	21,600	23,100	21	20	14	16
10	23,100	22,400	19	10	12	26
11	22,300	23,100	18	13	10	18
12	22,400	24,300	23	23	11	13
13	22,000	24,100	21	21	9	9
14	22,100	25,700	22	26	7	7
15	22,700	24,600	20	23	6	10
16	22,000	22,900	18	20	6	14
17	21,700	22,400	16	17	7	19
18	20,100	21,100	17	22	6	10
19	20,900	21,700	14	14	7	14
20	20,700	21,900	17	16	8	17
21	21,200	23,300	19	19	10	10
22	21,500	22,900	16	18	7	8
23	21,800	24,100	24	24	4	3
24	20,900	23,300	23	22	3	5
25	21,100	23,100	21	22	3	4
26	21,300	23,200	20	21	5	5
27	22,100	24,600	18	19	3	3
28	22,200	24,400	19	20	4	5
29	22,000	25,200	18	19	4	3
30	21,800	24,600	17	17	5	5
31	22,300	25,300	16	16	4	4

32	22,000	25,400	14	18	6	5
33	22,400	25,500	16	19	2	2
34	22,000	24,300	19	21	2	4
35	21,800	23,900	21	21	1	4
36	20,800	23,900	20	21	4	3
37	21,100	23,800	20	24	6	1
38	21,400	24,300	19	21	1	1
39	21,300	24,400	18	22	2	1
40	21,400	24,700	18	23	3	1
41	21,500	25,000	14	20	2	2
42	21,900	26,200	13	20	2	0
43	22,000	25,100	14	18	3	2
44	21,800	26,300	15	18	3	
45	22,500	27,900	14	19	2	0
46	22,000	26,900	15	18	1	1
47	23,100	29,500	10	16	0	0
48	23,300	30,200	14	18	1	1
49	21,200	24,900	20	20	2	2
50	21,800	24,700	21	20	2	3
51	22,100	25,000	20	20	3	3
52	21,900	25,800	21	21	2	1
53	21,400	26,700	16	23	2	0
54	21,800	29,300	10	21	4	1
55	21,000	31,800	11	19	3	0
56	21,400	31,200	12	18	4	1
57	22,100	30,900	13	18	5	2
58	22,100	31,000	11	17	5	3
59	22,800	33,200	14	19	5	1
60	22,700	36,000	14	16	4	0
61	21,900	34,100	12	20	8	2
62	22,700	35,300	11	17	6	1

*Census tract 6 is the state university, consisting of 16,000 full-time students. Approximately one third of the student body resides in campus housing in census tract 6.

EXHIBIT 17–2
Population Characteristics: Median Family Income and Age Composition

| Census Tract | Occupation (Head of Household) | | | | Employment Status (Head of Household): Unemployed (%) | |
| | Blue Collar (%) | | White Collar (%) | | | |
	1980	1988	1980	1988	1980	1988
1	64	88	36	12	18	21
2	66	90	34	10	12	14
3	70	88	30	12	10	10
4	50	74	50	26	8	12
5	58	70	42	30	10	10
6*	—	—	—	—	—	—
7	34	58	66	42	7	6
8	52	56	48	44	6	4
9	53	63	47	37	5	5
10	49	59	51	41	3	3
11	46	63	54	37	3	4
12	70	70	30	30	4	2
13	60	65	40	35	4	3
14	34	40	66	60	4	3
15	33	48	67	52	1	1
16	74	80	26	20	2	5
17	90	91	10	9	4	5
18	83	92	17	8	4	8
19	75	79	25	21	5	4
20	68	70	32	30	4	4
21	75	78	25	23	4	3
22	70	70	30	30	4	4
23	68	72	32	28	2	2
24	58	52	42	48	3	2
25	50	52	50	48	3	3
26	40	36	60	64	3	4
27	38	32	62	68	2	1
28	42	42	58	58	2	1
29	22	20	78	80	2	1
30	30	26	70	74	2	2
31	12	10	88	90	1	0

32	20	20	80	80	1	1
33	18	17	82	83	0	0
34	34	36	66	64	2	1
35	48	50	52	50	2	2
36	37	35	63	65	4	1
37	55	60	45	40	1	1
38	70	75	30	25	0	0
39	80	78	20	22	0	1
40	78	82	22	18	0	0
41	60	61	40	39	1	1
42	60	32	40	68	0	0
43	24	22	76	78	3	1
44	30	30	70	70	1	1
45	35	30	70	65	0	1
46	30	25	70	75	2	0
47	22	21	78	79	1	1
48	39	37	61	63	3	1
49	42	43	58	57	2	1
50	58	57	42	43	1	1
51	59	67	41	33	1	0
52	70	70	30	30	3	4
53	80	82	20	18	3	3
54	74	70	26	30	3	5
55	52	24	48	76	2	0
56	27	27	73	73	2	2
57	25	27	75	73	2	3
58	27	16	73	84	2	1
59	21	10	79	90	0	0
60	18	17	82	83	0	0
61	23	20	77	80	0	0
62	14	12	86	88	0	0

*Census tract 6 is the state university, consisting of 16,000 full-time students. Approximately one third of the student body resides in campus housing in census tract 6.

EXHIBIT 17–3
Population Characteristics: Occupation and Employment Status

EXHIBIT 17–4
Census Tract Map

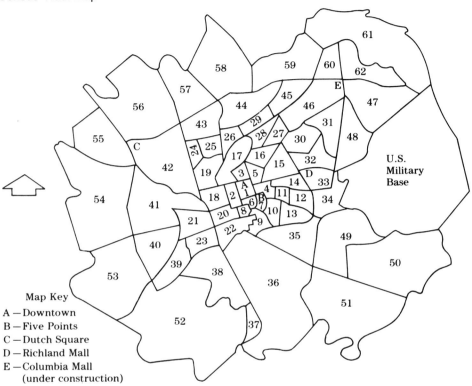

Map Key
A — Downtown
B — Five Points
C — Dutch Square
D — Richland Mall
E — Columbia Mall
   (under construction)

The Retail Structure of the Tri-City Area

The retailing structure of the Tri-City Area consisted of the following clusterings: (1) regional shopping clusters, (2) community and neighborhood shopping centers, and (3) free-standing string developments along major traffic arteries. As a result of the limited sales potential of the localized trading areas of the latter two clusterings, Butterfield's Department Store had limited its locations to clusterings having regional attraction. Four regional shopping clusters exist in the Tri-City area: (1) downtown, (2) Tri-City Center, (3) Summit Mall, and (4) Crossroads Shopping Center. Currently, Butterfield's operates a store in each of the four clusters. Although the size (square footage of selling space) of each store varied, the percentage of the selling space devoted to a given product line remained constant. The location of each major cluster is shown in Exhibit 17–4.

Downtown Cluster

The largest shopping cluster was the downtown area with 102 retailing establishments. Three "full-line" department stores, including J. C. Penney, T. S. Banks, and

Robertson's, provided the principal retail attraction for the downtown area. Several quality softgoods retailers with local and regional reputations also served as an important attraction force for the area; they included Harrison's, The Updated, Rudolphs, Twenty-One, and Butterfield's. In addition, the downtown area had the largest concentration of furniture and appliance stores, as well as many other specialty stores. Consumers' willingness to spend considerable time, money, and effort in making price and quality comparisons relative to these hard and specialty goods provided the downtown with additional attraction power. In general, the tenant mix of retailers in the downtown area was quite conducive to consumer trip generation and comparison shopping.

The downtown had several positional strengths from a retailing perspective: (1) centrality to the entire city's population; (2) close proximity to the federal, state, and local governmental office complex; (3) close proximity to the city's major complex of business offices; and (4) close proximity to the university. Additional positional qualities included the adjacent location of the area's sports and convention complex and its associated hotel complex. The completion of the new Main Street pedestrian mall should greatly enhance the downtown area's shopping atmosphere.

The downtown area was not without its retailing weaknesses. External and internal accessibility to and within the area was extremely limited. The accessibility problem was further complicated by a lack of sufficient parking in the immediate area. Although the new pedestrian mall should improve the shopping atmosphere, it could well represent a further deterioration in the accessibility and parking problems. Shopper security, especially during the evening and weekends, created additional problems. Muggings, robberies, and auto vandalism had a serious adverse effect on consumers' willingness to shop in the downtown area. This security had resulted in a 6:00 P.M. closing for most stores except during the annual holiday seasons and special events. With the slow but steady increase in the number of low-status retailers in and around the downtown area, the consumer security problem easily could worsen.

The general shopping atmosphere of the downtown area also placed certain limitations on consumer attraction. Even with the new pedestrian mall, many of the buildings were old and needed extensive repair. The numerous vacant buildings took their psychological toll on consumer purchase motivation. Some of the major department stores were rumored to plan to adjust their pricing points downward and to carry a lower quality of goods to appeal to the lower-income consumer living in the surrounding residential areas.

Finally, the "cost of doing business" in the downtown area was the highest in the city. High rent, extra security, and high storage rates all added to this cost. In addition, with very defined daily peak shopping periods (noon hour, coffee hours, and postworkday), labor costs were necessarily higher to meet those peak demand periods.

Tri-City Center

The Tri-City Center and its adjacent area was the second largest retailing cluster in the area. When completed in 1980, the mall consisted of forty-eight retailing establishments. In 4 years, the cluster had grown to its present size of eighty-nine retailing establishments. The tenant mix of the cluster consisted of (1) one full-line department store; (2) three large discount stores; (3) two catalog showrooms; and (4) five major softgoods retailers, Harrison's, The Updated, Rudolph's, Twenty-One, and Butterfield's. In addition, the mall contained the usual mix of specialty, shopping, and convenience goods retailers.

Located in the state's fastest growing upper-middle-class suburban area, Tri-City Center had been extremely successful. Sales per square foot were among the highest in the area. Lack of competition was the reason most often cited for the cluster's success. With good external accessibility, the mall area attracted from the entire metro area, as well as numerous surrounding communities. The recent addition of several office complexes should also enhance the cluster's drawing power.

Retailing weaknesses were relatively few, but two are noteworthy. First, with the rapid expansion of the last 4 years, the internal accessibility within the shopping cluster had been severely retarded. Long-term effects were certain to be felt as consumers sought more convenient and accessible shopping opportunities. The second weakness concerned the tenant mix. With only one major full-line department store, the mall lacked the sufficient "store name" drawing power of major full-line department store retailers, making it vulnerable to competition from malls that had "full-line anchors."

Summit Mall

Tri-City's third-largest shopping cluster with regional drawing power was Summit Mall. Located within a well-established, middle-class section of Tri-City, this mall obtained the bulk of its customers from local eastside neighborhoods. Forty-eight retail establishments were located within the mall and the surrounding area. Robertson's Department Store, The Updated, Rudolph's, and Butterfield's provided the nucleus of the regional drawing power. A limited number of specialty shops also aided in drawing consumers from outside the local markets. Excluding surrounding neighborhoods, Summit Mall usually ranked as either the third or fourth shopping cluster choice for most of the area's shoppers.

The principal limitations on interregional consumer drawing power were (1) extremely poor external and internal accessibility; (2) poor tenant mix (many of the establishments were convenience retailers, which conflicted with the shopping and specialty retailers in terms of traffic and parking congestion and the type of consumer affected); and (3) insufficient number of full-line department stores, other establishments, and activities capable of drawing consumers from considerable distances. There were rumors that Robertson's was considering relocating.

Crossroads Shopping Center

Excluding the downtown area, the Crossroads Shopping Center was the oldest shopping cluster in the Tri-City area. Consisting of approximately three-dozen shopping, specialty, and convenience goods retailers, the Center's ability to attract regional consumers was based on two factors. First, Tri-City's only Sears store was located adjacent to the cluster. In Tri-City, Sears alone could draw consumers from considerable distances. Second, historically, all of Tri-City's old-line specialty and shopping goods retailers (The Updated, Rudolph's, Harrison's, Twenty-One, and Butterfield's) had branch locations within the Center.

Located adjacent to Tri-City's most exclusive residential area (University Heights), Crossroads was once the exclusive shopping district of the upper-income consumer. With the migration to the suburbs in the 1950s and 1960s, University Heights subsequently evolved into a low-income multidwelling residential area populated with State University students and minority groups. The conversion of many of the single-family dwellings into multiple-family dwellings hastened the area's physical deterioration. Recently, however, restoration of the area and its dwellings had become a passion for many young, middle-class professionals. Its close proximity to State University made it a highly desirable residential area for the University administration, faculty, and staff.

The advantages associated with the cluster's adjacency to the University and the downtown area were far outweighed by the disadvantages of the reduced external and internal accessibility and increased competition. In terms of the Tri-City metro area, Crossroads was by far the least accessible. Internal traffic congestion and the lack of parking facilities were limitations, but congestion would probably be reduced with the imminent closing of Sears. In addition, there were plans to refurbish the center's many older buildings.

Highland Square Mall

The opening of the new Highland Square Mall, scheduled for the fall, would signal a new era in retailing for the greater Tri-City Area. Located in the northeastern section of Tri-City, the two-store, 1.5 million-square-foot development would contain 145 retailing establishments. Success of the venture was almost certain, given the consumer drawing power associated with noted shopping center "department store anchors" such as T. S. Banks, J. C. Penney, Sears, and Robertson's. The mall's opening would profoundly change the retailing structure of the Tri-City metropolitan area. Speculation abounded as to the effects of the new mall. To the Tri-City area consumer, it offered new and exciting shopping opportunities. To the existing and would-be Tri-City area retailer, it represented a business opportunity and/or a source of potential competition.

A recent study completed by the Business Research Division of the State University examined the potential impact of the Highland Square Mall on existing major shopping clusters. Four shopping clusters (Downtown, Tri-City Center, Summit, and Crossroads) and seven product categories (clothing, foot-wear, apparel accessories, furniture and appliances, household accessories, recreational and entertainment, and personal) were included in the study. Using a probability model, the study estimated the probability of a consumer in a given census tract traveling to a particular shopping cluster for a given product category. To ascertain the new mall's impact, a "before and after" research design was employed. The conclusions of the study follow:

> Of the seven product categories considered, the new mall should assume the dominant market share position in the five areas of clothing, footwear, household accessories, recreation and entertainment, and personal products. In addition, Highland

Square Mall's market share in apparel accessories should be second only to the Downtown area. Only in the furniture and appliance product category is the new mall's market share expected to be limited. If the market share positions projected here are assumed to be valid, then the Highland Square Mall may be expected to become the dominant force in the retailing activities of the Tri-City area. Further, these projections would indicate that the impact of the Highland Square Mall would not be evenly distributed. Substantial differences, given these conditions, would occur between product categories and shopping clusters. For most of the four existing clusters, substantial decreases in market share would be expected for most product categories. Overall, most of the existing clusters would experience their largest market share decreases in clothing and footwear product categories.

The entrance of the mall into the retailing structure of the Tri-City area poses several difficult problems for existing and potential retailers. Initially, decisions regarding locational strategies will need to be made. Later, as the effects of the new mall become apparent, marketing strategies relative to product, promotion, and price will require adjustment.

The impact of the Highland Square Mall already was felt. In the area surrounding the mall, several firms announced that they had purchased land and planned to build within the next year. Among these were two major discount-department stores, a major catalog showroom, a developer specializing in small (ten- to fifteen-store) specialty shopping clusters, and a firm that specialized in four-screen theaters. In addition, there were rumors that two major department stores had purchased adjacent properties.

The new Highland Square Mall would comprise two levels completely enclosed and, therefore, climatically controlled. Sunken gardens and a lower-level walkway had been designed to provide customers with an excellent shopping atmosphere. The planned activities for the garden and walkways included concerts, exhibits, shows, and displays.

Tenants of the mall included most of the major local retailers, as well as many nationally known retailers. The developers attempted to control the tenant mix in terms of product, price, and promotional mix. Hopefully, the tenant mix would be such that it would attract consumers from many income categories ranging from upper-lower- to upper-upper-income groups.

The Firm: Butterfield's

Butterfield's, a leading soft goods merchandiser in the Tri-City area for over eighty years, was first established by Robert Butterfield in 1889. Over the years, the name Butterfield's had become synonymous with quality and style. Appealing to the upper 40 percent of the market, Butterfield's product, pricing, and promotional strategy was directed toward consumers whose principal purchase motives were high quality, high style, and excellent service. For the last two decades, Butterfield's merchandising strategy had been to offer high-quality merchandise in a limited number of product lines at various pricing points. Sales departments, product lines, sales areas, pricing ranges, and annual sales are shown for each store in Exhibits 17–5 through 17–8. This standardized mix had proven to be quite successful for the last 20 years. Intra-urban population shifts, however, had created considerable sales

Sales by Department	Price Range ($)	Sales Area (sq. ft.)	1988 Sales ($)	1987 Sales ($)	1986 Sales ($)	1988 Gross Margin (% of Sales)	1988 Operating Expenses (% of Sales)
Men's department							
Suits	100–400	1,500	321,000	220,000	191,750		
Sportswear	15–100	3,800	345,000	222,750	188,500		
Accessories	10–100	1,500	243,000	178,750	136,500		
Total	10–400	6,800	909,000	621,500	516,750	44.1	40.3
Women's department							
Moderate dresses	25–100	6,350	417,000	371,250	347,750		
Moderate sportswear	15–100	3,050	252,000	222,750	227,500		
Better dresses	50–800	5,750	75,000	178,750	315,250		
Better sportswear	30–900	2,250	33,000	167,750	312,000		
Lingerie	10–90	3,350	90,000	88,000	123,500		
Cosmetics	1–50	3,000	333,000	327,250	357,500		
Accessories	1–100	3,500	285,000	231,000	256,750		
Total	1–900	27,250	1,485,000	1,586,750	1,940,250	46.2	41.5
Junior's department							
Sportswear	15–100	2,250	183,000	173,250	217,750		
Dresses	20–100	2,250	69,000	74,250	94,250		
Coats	20–200	500	33,000	27,500	32,500		
Total	15–200	5,000	285,000	275,000	344,500	45.8	41.7
Children's department							
Boys	10–100	2,250	24,000	35,750	100,750		
Girls	10–100	2,250	12,000	30,250	94,250		
Infants	3–40	1,100	18,000	49,500	123,500		
Total	3–100	5,600	54,000	115,500	318,500	46.5	41.8
Gifts-linen department							
Total	5–500	5,350	267,000	151,250	130,000		
Total sales	1–900	50,000	3,000,000	2,750,000	3,250,000	47.4	42.0

EXHIBIT 17-5
Sales Operations by Department: Downtown Store

Sales by Department	Price Range ($)	Sales Area (sq. ft.)	1988 Sales ($)	1987 Sales ($)	1986 Sales ($)	1988 Gross Margin (% of Sales)	1988 Operating Expenses (% of Sales)
Men's department							
Suits	100–400	1,000	125,000	130,000	191,750		
Sportswear	15–100	2,500	213,800	190,000	127,000		
Accessories	10–100	1,000	150,100	155,000	126,000		
Total	10–400	4,500	489,000	475,000	386,000	47.1	38.3
Women's department							
Moderate dresses	25–100	4,200	377,100	380,000	401,000		
Moderate sportswear	15–100	2,000	210,100	185,000	129,000		
Better dresses	50–800	3,800	299,800	315,000	377,000		
Better sportswear	30–900	1,500	171,100	165,000	119,000		
Lingerie	10–90	2,200	116,900	120,000	90,000		
Cosmetics	1–50	2,000	379,500	367,000	316,000		
Accessories	1–100	2,300	281,500	289,000	230,000		
Total	1–900	18,000	1,836,000	1,821,000	1,662,000	48.2	38.6
Junior's department							
Sportswear	15–100	1,500	414,300	374,000	301,000		
Dresses	20–100	1,500	134,900	153,000	167,000		
Coats	20–200	300	45,000	46,000	36,000		
Total	15–200	3,300	594,200	573,000	504,000	47.8	39.7
Children's department							
Boys	10–100	1,500	87,900	60,000	52,000		
Girls	10–100	1,500	104,000	77,000	66,000		
Infants	3–40	700	84,900	82,000	53,000		
Total	3–100	3,700	276,800	219,000	171,000	48.5	38.8
Gifts-linen department							
Total	5–500	3,500	209,600	208,000	180,000	49.4	40.3
Total sales	1–900	33,000	3,405,600	3,295,000	2,903,000		

EXHIBIT 17–6
Sales Operations by Department: Tri-City Center

Sales by Department	Price Range ($)	Sales Area (sq. ft.)	1988 Sales ($)	1987 Sales ($)	1986 Sales ($)	1988 Gross Margin (% of Sales)	1988 Operating Expenses (% of Sales)
Men's department							
Suits	100–400	1,000	69,000	78,750	82,080		
Sportswear	15–100	2,500	94,300	114,750	118,560		
Accessories	10–100	1,000	94,300	114,750	118,560		
Total	10–400	4,500	257,600	308,250	319,200	45.1	38.0
Women's department							
Moderate dresses	25–100	4,200	282,900	297,000	321,480		
Moderate sportswear	15–100	2,000	200,100	155,250	114,000		
Better dresses	50–800	3,800	115,000	137,250	143,640		
Better sportswear	30–900	1,500	135,700	114,750	70,680		
Lingerie	10–90	2,200	73,600	69,750	57,000		
Cosmetics	1–50	2,000	232,300	229,500	280,440		
Accessories	1–100	2,300	186,300	186,750	214,320		
Total	1–900	18,000	1,225,900	1,190,250	1,201,560	47.2	38.4
Junior's department							
Sportswear	15–100	1,500	257,600	234,000	228,000		
Dresses	20–100	1,500	94,300	92,250	91,200		
Coats	20–200	300	29,900	22,500	22,800		
Total	15–200	3,300	381,800	348,750	342,000	46.8	39.2
Children's department							
Boys	10–100	1,500	71,300	63,000	61,560		
Girls	10–100	1,500	73,600	67,500	63,840		
Infants	3–40	700	69,000	45,000	41,040		
Total	3–100	3,700	213,900	175,500	166,440	47.5	38.8
Gifts-linen department							
Total	5–500	3,500	220,800	227,250	250,800		
Total sales	1–900	33,000	2,300,000	2,250,000	2,280,000	48.4	39.9

EXHIBIT 17–7
Sales Operations by Department: Summit Mall

Sales by Department	Price Range ($)	Sales Area (sq. ft.)	1988 Sales ($)	1987 Sales ($)	1986 Sales ($)	1988 Gross Margin (% of Sales)	1988 Operating Expenses (% of Sales)
Men's department							
Suits	100–400	1,200	53,200	58,500	66,600		
Sportswear	15–100	3,040	109,200	105,000	86,400		
Accessories	10–100	1,200	72,800	70,500	66,600		
Total	10–400	5,440	235,200	234,000	219,600	41.1	37.5
Women's department							
Moderate dresses	25–100	5,080	114,800	160,500	219,600		
Moderate sportswear	15–100	2,440	114,800	120,000	95,400		
Better dresses	50–800	4,600	29,400	55,500	95,400		
Better sportswear	30–900	1,800	75,600	61,500	66,600		
Lingerie	10–90	2,680	35,000	39,000	48,600		
Cosmetics	1–50	2,400	123,200	120,000	198,000		
Accessories	1–100	2,800	95,200	90,000	118,800		
Total	1–900	21,800	588,000	646,500	842,400	45.2	38.0
Junior's department							
Sportswear	15–100	1,800	260,400	255,000	253,800		
Dresses	20–100	1,800	128,800	120,000	104,400		
Coats	20–200	400	43,400	48,000	46,800		
Total	15–200	4,000	432,600	423,000	405,000	42.8	38.8
Children's department							
Boys	10–100	1,800	14,000	30,000	86,400		
Girls	10–100	1,800	22,400	43,500	95,400		
Infants	3–40	880	11,200	33,000	66,600		
Total	3–100	4,480	47,600	106,500	248,400	42.5	38.1
Gifts-Linen department							
Total	5–500	4,280	96,600	90,000	86,600	44.4	38.9
Sales total	1–900	40,000	1,400,000	1,500,000	1,850,000		

EXHIBIT 17–8
Sales Operations by Department: Crossroads

variations among Butterfield's stores. These variations were more pronounced when reviewed in terms of sales per square foot. Perhaps some changes in the standardized mix were needed. Gross margin characteristics and operating expenses by department for each store also are shown in Exhibits 17–5 through 17–8.

Butterfield's management had secured a highly desirable corner location on the first level of the new mall. The location consisted of approximately 35,000 square feet of space; the firm's management believed that it had obtained one of the most desirable locations within the mall. The question now was how to use the location and the space most productively.

Analytical Problem

Lisa Reeves, Butterfield's Assistant Merchandise Manager, was assigned the task of analyzing the impact of the new mall and store on Butterfield's existing Tri-City operations. She also had been asked to recommend any changes that might be needed in Butterfield's merchandise strategies (product and price mixes) as a result of the new mall and store. In preparation, Reeves itemized the following questions to guide her investigation:

1. What are the potential positive and negative impact factors of the new mall and the new store on Butterfield's downtown, Tri-City Center, Summit Mall, and Crossroads locations?
2. Should any of Butterfield's existing locations be abandoned? Why or why not?
3. What, if any, adjustments are required in Butterfield's merchandising strategy (product and price mixes)? Will these adjustments vary by store location? How?
4. What merchandising adjustments are required in Butterfield's merchandising strategy for the new store in the Highland Square Mall?

Assume the role of Lisa Reeves and develop a report that will completely cover the basic concerns outlined in the preceding questions.

CASE 18   BENJAMIN'S BRIEFS:
Evaluating Merchandise Management Practices

Pulling off the interstate, Brad Benjamin hoped that traffic wouldn't be too bad at that time of day. The motel wasn't far from the highway, but there were always plenty of pedestrians and bicycles around the Lakeshore University Campus. Warm, sunny weather created tricky driving but good sales for area retailers.

Benjamin, the entrepreneurial driving force behind Benjamin's Briefs, had established his business in the Fall of 1986 by purchasing sportswear at inventory liquidation sales and reselling the merchandise directly to college students. From Benjamin's perspective, students were a lucrative market for several reasons. They were generally price-sensitive. They were willing to go out of their way for a savings and had flexible time available for shopping. They were fashion conscious and constantly needed clothing. Because Benjamin was dealing with his peers, he could track and predict market acceptance quite well.

Benjamin had started the business as a "one man show"; all of the tasks in his business were performed alone. So, as a student, he found it necessary to make trade-offs between his business and his studies. At present, Benjamin conducted 3-day sales, which were usually based in motels near any one of five college campuses within easy driving distance. Now that he was about to graduate, the destiny of his business had to be determined. What should he do? Should he continue "as is," expand geographically, or open retail stores in select (permanent) locations?

Background

It all started, seemingly by accident, several years ago. Benjamin was attending Midwest University, which is located in a college town (Carlene, Oklahoma). Typical of college towns, Carlene had attracted a fairly good number and variety of retail outlets. Nevertheless, Benjamin shopped more often at home in the "big city" to take advantage of both the more timely fashions and prevalence of discount merchandise. Although his parents were willing to underwrite his educational expenses, his discretionary funds were somewhat limited. So to cut down on expenses for leisure clothes, Benjamin had done his best to take full advantage of the bargains found at stock liquidation, bankruptcy, and end-of-season sales. This "buck-stretching" tactic had several unforeseen benefits.

Whenever Benjamin went on one of his personal shopping sprees, he often returned to school with more clothing than he really needed. Since his roommates and other friends had expressed an interest in his clothes and had questioned him about his shopping, Benjamin thought about selling the extra clothing to them. After thinking about it for a while, he concluded that it wasn't a bad idea. Even before he could make the offer, his friends were encouraging him to "share" some of his bargains with them.

This case was prepared by Doug Hausknecht, University of Akron; Patricia A. Robinson, Tennessee Tech University; and Alan Dick, SUNY-Buffalo. Although this case is based on an actual situation and study, names and data have been changed to preserve confidentiality.

Benjamin consented to sell his friends the overstock. Most of the clothing was large and medium-sized sportswear items such as sweatshirts, T-shirts, shorts, and the like. Since all of his friends were built and weighed about the same, sizes were not a real concern, and loosely fitting tops and bottoms were in style.

It wasn't long before selling his extras at cost evolved into taking orders for future shopping sprees. Benjamin's discretionary income began to increase very rapidly. Even after adding a modest markup, he could still supply his friends with garments at prices significantly lower than those of comparable items from local merchants. As the word spread among his friends, the customer base and sales volume grew rapidly. Consequently, to fulfill his customers' needs, Benjamin began to schedule regular trips to his home town to scavenge the market for low-priced sportswear items. He always looked for the best items and values he could find for himself and his associates, while trying to expand his merchandise offering.

"I don't quite remember exactly when it all got started, but I do remember how I became interested in this whole affair of running my own business," Benjamin explained. "As I recall, I just happened to be at a clothing close-out sale kind of late and noticed that the people in charge were practically ready to throw the stuff out. A lot of it was mismatched items, seconds, and irregulars—stuff I wouldn't wear when I was trying to look good. But it was OK for knocking around the apartment, playing basketball, and going to class. The stuff was so cheap that I bought as much as I could fit in the car, even without any specific orders. I figured that even if I could not use it, I could sell it. Even if I only sold a fourth of the stuff, I'd make my money back and turn a comfortable profit for the time invested." He paused, then reflected, "I guess it was at that point when I saw myself as a true merchant. It was the first time I had ever seriously thought about acquiring an inventory and selling on a cash-and-carry basis."

The bulk purchase Benjamin made changed the character of his operation. Previously, he had taken orders for merchandise from his friends and associates—sometimes after receiving only vague size and style preferences. After filling their orders, he prepared delivery bundles for each customer. They took what he could find and settled any differences between what they had initially deposited and the final price of the goods on delivery.

The new inventory required a different handling process. The items had to be sorted into categories before making them available for sale to potential buyers. Benjamin's apartment served as the showcase for his sportswear line. But, already cramped by its warehousing function, the apartment had little display space. When one of his roommates moved out, Benjamin allowed "the business" to flow over into the extra bedroom. He figured that the increased sales volume would more than pay for the rent.

Sales for the impulsively purchased merchandise were better than Benjamin had expected. People, many of whom he didn't even know, had heard about his operation and came by to purchase goods. He charged less than half the going retail price for most items (as best as he could estimate). As he remembered, "It almost seemed as if they were addicted to buying and were unable to get enough. I guess I eventually sold all of the first shipment, although I don't know just how long it took. The stuff was moving so fast and so well that I bought more to add to it." Benjamin, glowing with his memories, stated, "It seemed incredibly easy to make money that way."

Suddenly, it was spring, and the semester was over. Most students left the campus for home. The fast pace of Benjamin's business dropped virtually to zero during the period. For the first time, Benjamin became a bit worried about his business. He realized that his customers had left him with some cash and a relatively large inventory. At that point, things didn't look too promising.

The dead time (the seasonal effects of summer in college towns) that at first seemed to be a liability had its benefits. The business, although haphazardly operated, had grown rapidly. The excitement of prior selling activities had calmed down, and the slow pace of the summer allowed time for Benjamin to reassess his operation and to do some planning.

Time for a Change

"If I didn't learn anything else, the one thing that I learned in the business school was to make decisions by identifying opportunities and choosing from among specific alternatives. When I began operating my business, I had two concerns: how much money I would make and where I would buy merchandise. I had no intentions of doing this for the rest of my life. But opportunity to make a few bucks on the side interested me."

Never having expected things to grow so large so quickly, Benjamin had been very casual about his operation's organizational structure and record keeping. With the exception of monthly sales figures, he had never documented cost of goods, expenses, or gross revenue. "This is literally a cash-and-carry business," Benjamin explained.

Assets for the business at that time totaled about $3,000 in cash and half a room of inventory. With only a short time remaining in school, Benjamin faced some crucial decisions about his future. For the most part, he had enjoyed the hustle and bustle of running his small business but wasn't sure if the time invested had paid off very well. Going on buying trips nearly every weekend, performing inventory-management functions, and being open to every drop-in customer made studying difficult, and socializing was nearly impossible.

After having seriously thought about his business, Benjamin realized that some changes had to be made. He concluded that he had at least four options available to him. These included, but were not limited to the following:

1. Liquidate the remaining inventory and end the business.
2. Continue the operation as before but with a reduction in inventory and established operating hours.
3. Hire employees and delegate to them some of the tasks of running the business.
4. Structure the business as a legitimate retail operation.

Before selecting one of these alternatives, he evaluated various business structural arrangements: retail stores, mail order, telemarketing, and flea markets—to name a few. However, one weekend during the summer, Benjamin accompanied his girlfriend to an audio-component clearance sale at the Sneakers' Motel in his home town. He recalled watching and studying the people as they roamed the tables, picking through the merchandise on display. "They seemed to be deciding right then and there as to whether the 'deal' was good or not," he noted. "Brands that I have never seen or heard of before were selling like hot cakes. That was the moment I became very interested in the workings of motel clearance sales." Curious about the logistics of such sales, Benjamin asked to speak to the person in charge. From their conversation, Benjamin's business was headed for change.

The Beginning of Benjamin's Briefs

With what he had learned about small motel exhibition sales, Benjamin decided to structure his operation during the fall season as a legal entity and to keep the current operation going until the new business, "Benjamin's Briefs," was established. The format that had evolved for his new operation, based on his talks with the audio entrepreneur and other small retail business owners, was fairly simple: motel clearance sales. When he'd accumulated sufficient inventory, he'd rent a central location and organize a sale. If things went well, and sufficient inventory was on hand, the concept could be easily expanded to nearby cities.

Benjamin's father applied his legal background and other business connections in helping to organize the sole proprietorship. Benjamin obtained all the necessary operating business licenses, insurance, bonding, certifications, and tax certificates. He lined up friends at nearby universities to assist in organizing sales at those locations. In addition, he hired some employees to help run the business. To get the motel sales rolling, the only other items that still had to be obtained were temporary sale permits. The process of obtaining a sales permit was relatively simple but had to be done before each event. Although the city of each branch location had slightly different requirements for obtaining a temporary sales permit, the cost would never exceed $50 for 3 days.

Benjamin, his roommate, and his girlfriend had each agreed that they would handle the workload for all sales in Carlene. Promotional activities for the first sale were via word-of-mouth, classified ads in the campus paper, and flyers. For all sales, Benjamin was to prepare the advertising himself, although his branch managers were responsible for placing his ads in campus and local papers. The promotional format he had established for all the sales involved running a quarter-page display ad that would be placed the week before the sale in the relevant campus newspaper. This would be followed by classified ads in the campus and local newspaper each day of the sale. In addition, depending on the sale's location, display ads sometimes would be used. Everyone involved in working the sales was expected to distribute and post flyers and handbills wherever students were likely to be found.

The original plan was that sales would be conducted at one of the five branch locations every 3 to 4 weeks. Within a 4- to 6-month period, a motel sale would have been conducted in each of the branch locations. By October, "Benjamin's Briefs" was a going concern and ready for its first motel sale, which had been planned for a motel near Midwest University. Having assembled a large inventory of brand-name and off-brand merchandise, Benjamin needed only to decide on the most opportune time and location for each sale. Finding a motel that would provide adequate accommodation for both pedestrians and vehicular traffic (easily accessible rooms and parking) proved to be difficult.

Eventually, Zebra Inn, a motel near the university, was found and designated as the site for local sales. The first sale was held in the suite at Zebra Inn during the first week of October. As illustrated in Exhibit 18–1, the sale was a success. Sales volume, as when Benjamin first started his operation, continued to increase in subsequent sales. As a result, Benjamin had to devote increasing amounts of unanticipated time to the business. All four "branch" locations were quickly geared up, and sales were held there as well.

Buying for Benjamin's Briefs

Benjamin became very concerned about the stability and survival of his business because of difficulties in buying his merchandise, so he expanded his buying options. He scavenged the market south of Carlene, Oklahoma, and found numerous

EXHIBIT 18–1
Selected Sales Results (Direct operating income and costs)

University	Midwest University, October 8–10	Midwest February 4–6
Gross receipts	3,754	10,780
Cost of goods		
Shirts	NA	1,380
Shorts	NA	376
Sweats	NA	3,440
Other	NA	2,103
Total	1,928*	7,299
Gross profit on sales	1,826	3,481
Operating expenses		
Rent	235†	420‡
Transportation	120	165
Wages§	200	300
Administrative ‖	300	500
Advertising	150	747
Legal fees	25	25
Insurance	50	100
Other	223	317
Total	1,203	2,574
Net income from sale (before income taxes)	523	907

NA, not available.
*The total was estimated from stock shrinkage; records were not available by type of merchandise.
†Room at Zebra Inn.
‡Banquet room (Carlene, Oklahoma).
§Paid to clerks at sales.
‖ Distribution to partners.

Texan manufacturers and wholesalers who would sell directly to him. They varied by size and merchandise offering but provided him with the opportunity to expand and upgrade his merchandise while maintaining a low price orientation. Consequently, Benjamin switched some of his merchandise sources but still considered special bankruptcy and stock liquidation auctions as alternatives for bulk-quantity buys whenever the deals were attractive.

Collecting enough merchandise to stock a sale didn't require a lot of buying trips. "Every so often I rented a van, got together a big wad of cash to spend, and headed down south to purchase different types of merchandise. When making a trip I would usually go down the evening before and visit the large manufacturers just before closing. Buying from the small firms, on the other hand, wasn't a big problem. Most of the firms had a pretty good idea of the type of merchandise that I was looking for, so we never spent much time chatting about items in their line. Usually, when the small guys had extra merchandise to sell, they would set it aside, and eventually call me up to confirm whether I wanted to look at it. Quite often we didn't worry about whether I would buy the stuff but what I would pay for it. I knew my markets pretty well and what the merchandise would sell for. If we agreed on prices, I'd load the van, and go off to the next stop."

The nature of business relationships varied according to the size of the supplier. At the small factories, he was "Mr. Benjamin," who dealt directly with the owners or senior managers. To those businesses, Mr. Benjamin was the solution to their inventory management problems: overruns, cancelled orders, dye lot errors, and the like. Large manufacturers, some of whom supplied major department store chains, may not have been fully aware that this distribution channel existed. Sales and price negotiations with Benjamin seldom went beyond the loading dock or the warehouse foreman. Nevertheless, in addition to offering Benjamin unsold first-quality merchandise, the large manufacturers also needed to liquidate defects and seconds. Company policy among these institutions often dictated that inferior merchandise could not be distributed for sale with the manufacturer's labels affixed, but did not always dictate disposition methods. "You could get this stuff, sometimes even with labels intact, if you knew who to ask," Benjamin recalled.

For some of the items purchased, costs were less than those he had paid for comparable merchandise at closeout and bankruptcy sales. Much of the stock, however, did not provide any additional savings. Benjamin did not think his inventory turnover was high enough to support the risk of placing orders large enough to acquire preferential pricing (manufacturer's discounts of any kind).

Midwest University Sale

A typical sale was conducted the second weekend of February near Benjamin's own campus. The sale schedule was Thursday through Saturday, from 9:00 A.M. to 8:00 P.M. Benjamin handled all the arrangements for the sale including site selection. But, because of scheduling difficulties and a disagreement with the motel manager at the Zebra Inn, where the sales had been held previously, Benjamin chose to relocate. He contracted for the use of the banquet room in a less expensive motel located approximately 1 1/2 miles from the south edge of Midwest University. That motel was on a sidestreet off the main north–south road that passed through the city, an area that was not frequently visited by students.

Weekend rental rates for the banquet room were relatively inexpensive, $140 a day. With a few exceptions, the room was ideally situated for the sale. Its doors opened into a foyer that led outside, making it quite easy for Benjamin's patrons to enter and exit the building. However, the lighting was a serious problem; the relatively dim lighting made the merchandise appear less colorful and less attractive.

To publicize the sale, Benjamin had been persuaded by WQQZ, an AM radio station in the area, to try their advertising. He wasn't quite sure if that was a good idea, but he purchased some spots anyway—seventy-five 30-second spots over 5 days for $487.50.

To ensure that prospective buyers would find their way to the sale once they had arrived at the motel, he placed hand-lettered signs pointing the way to the banquet room in the parking lot at strategic locations. Despite the dim lighting, the sale proceeded at an active pace. Customers milled about, seemingly examining each item. Although fairly busy, the patrons did not crowd one another and usually remained courteous.

Before the sale, Benjamin had assembled quite a collection of merchandise. He had at least four styles of the several items: T-shirts, surfer shirts, athletic shorts, sweatpants, sweatshirts, and the inevitable socks. In addition to the sportswear merchandise, there were sweaters, pullover shirts, beach towels, jackets, and a few warm-up suits. Behind the "counter" were displayed an assortment of toiletries: colognes, perfumes, and hair-grooming kits. An example of the model stock plan Benjamin used to buy his sweatshirt line is shown in Exhibit 18–2.

At the beginning of each sale day, the clothing items were arranged by classification on the tables in the banquet room. By midmorning, the stacks were toppled, by noon the individual stacks were indistinguishable, and by the end of the day merchandise was scattered all over. Sizes, styles, and types of clothing became intermingled without regard to the tables' original order.

At one point during the sale, about fifteen to twenty customers could be seen picking through the merchandise. None of them appeared to be over age twenty-five, and about two thirds were women. "Business was pretty steady," Benjamin said. "When we were closer to campus, we experienced big rushes. Students would hurry to the Zebra Inn between and after classes to take advantage of the sales. Now they come and go all day."

Asked to characterize the clientele, Benjamin described his primary customers as couples, sorority members, and backyard jocks. Of these, he noted that only the jocks came to the sales alone. He was also aware of the fact that very few of his customers used the screened-off area set aside as the "fitting rooms." "Big and loose was the in thing; so, the bigger, the better," he explained.

But price, first and foremost, appeared to be the driving force behind customers' decisions to purchase. Initially, they examined the merchandise for bargains. Then they evaluated the items for their appropriateness for various occasions. Only then was the fit assessed. This process accounted for the migration of the merchandise from table to table with the customer, only to be abandoned later in favor of a more attractive bargain.

EXHIBIT 18–2
Model Stock Plan: Benjamin's Briefs

Branch:	Midwest University	Item:	Long-sleeve sweatshirts
Branch No.:	0001	Retail Price:	$8.00
Season: Fall–Winter		Buyer:	Brad Benjamin
Spring–Summer	1988		

Classification	Size	Quantity for Model Stock		Color Selections											
				Plain		Stripe		Scenic		Character					
		%	#	%	#	%	#	%	#	%	#	%	#	%	#
Designer	X-large		10		2		2		3		3				
% ____	Large		13		4		4		3		2				
# ___33___	Medium		10		1		1		4		4				
Total National															
Brands	X-large		14		4		3		5		2				
% ____	Large		18		4		5		5		4				
# ___56___	Medium		24		5		5		7		7				
Total Irregulars															
% ____	X-large		30		10		8		6		6				
	Large		34		11		9		9		5				
# ___80___	Medium		16		5		4		4		3				
Total															
Planned grand total		169		46		41		46		36					

To handle all the sales transactions, a hand-cranked adding machine with a cash drawer replaced the old pen, paper, and tin box used previously. Most of the customers paid cash for their purchases; only about 20 percent offered checks. Almost everyone who came to the sale made purchases in the low $20 range.

After the sale, Benjamin revealed that the sale was fairly typical, although the young entrepreneur was troubled by a major problem that he did not identify previously. "My biggest problem was theft. Right in my presence, my pockets were being picked by customers, motel employees, and even my own employees. I must tighten security." Benjamin had noted, on several occasions, evidence suggesting that motel employees had tampered with his inventory; but he had never confronted anyone. As he mentioned, lack of security and inventory control had both contributed to the problem.

Rough counts of the stock were made before and after the sale, but only by major price categories. Specific items were never accounted for, which made keeping track of pilferage during and after the sale nearly impossible. Benjamin suspected his merchandise losses came in spurts—more so during the last days of the sale. He suspected that customers probably walked away without paying for items. "I believe that most of the customers who stole acted on their own, but some may have been given 'gifts' by friends behind the counter. It was very possible for the clerks to steal directly—cash and merchandise."

When it was all over, despite the discrepancy between the amount of merchandise sold and cash-on-hand, things didn't look too bad (Exhibit 18–1). Although revenues had increased from prior sales, complaints had increased, too. Customers who attended the sale complained to Benjamin about the difficulty of finding the location. Guests of the motel complained to the manager about the "noisy, loitering students." The latter complaints made the conduct of future sales at this location unlikely.

Assessing the Situation

By this point, Benjamin had learned quite a bit about being a merchant. Sales had grown and evolved—branching out to four other nearby college campuses: Center State University, Lakeshore University, Butler College, and Channels University. Sales and profits had grown to a point that made Benjamin feel quite comfortable about his operations (Exhibit 18–3). As noted, Exhibit 18–3 illustrates the advancement Benjamin's Briefs had made since the days when he took orders to purchase clothing for his friends. His buying power had increased substantially, and he had learned the importance of planning and cost control.

With graduation approaching, Benjamin was still trying to determine the best strategy regarding his future. Before making a final decision, he thought that it was important to know more about the potential market. So he consulted his marketing research professor for advice and assistance in examining the situation. After offering some general guidance on entrepreneurship and market potential, the professor referred Benjamin to two marketing graduate students who might be willing to do some consulting.

"I'm twenty-two now and my goal is to make a million dollars by the time I'm thirty," was Benjamin's summary comment to the consultants. "I just want to

EXHIBIT 18-3

Benjamin's Briefs: Income Statement for the Periods Ending November 30, 1987, and May 31, 1988

	Six Months Ending November 30, 1987*	Twelve Months Ending May 31, 1988†
Net sales	8,930	92,840
Cost of goods		
Beginning inventory	600	600
Net purchases	4,975	35,130
Goods available for sale	5,575	35,730
Ending inventory	1,245	4,130
Cost of goods sold	4,330	31,600
Gross margin on sales	4,600	61,240
Operating expenses		
Rent (sales locations)	535	7,600
Rent (office/warehouse)	750	2,100
Transportation	480	6,275
Wages	500	5,400
Administrative	700	4,800
Advertising	450	12,940
Office expenses	100	475
Legal fees	125	600
Insurance	175	1,300
Miscellaneous expenses	60	463
Total operating expenses	3,575	41,953
Net income (before income taxes)	725	19,287
Tax allocations	150	5,800
Net income	575	13,487

*Includes results of three sales.

†Includes results of ten sales.

know from you how to build my business to that level. I'm thinking about opening a store but don't know if that's the answer."

The consultants agreed to hear him out and promised to provide whatever assistance they could. They also indicated that he would have to purchase future discussions or research at their normal fees. Benjamin summarized the situation to date and highlighted some of the problems he saw with the business. "It's bad enough that my clerks were probably stealing—it's not much and I don't really mind. My biggest problem is that all of my friends who help me out with the sales in other towns are also graduating. They'll be moving on, and I won't have anyone who I can trust to run things anymore. They could probably recommend several successors, but they are the ones who hired the clerks who stole from me in the first place. I have got to get my personnel under control.

"Convinced that locking up the merchandise was the only way to prevent hotel employee pilferage, I tried padlocking the banquet room at the last sale, but I was fined for fire code violations." To date, Benjamin had purchased a couple of trunks to use as inventory cases. Stuffing and locking them each night was one approach to prevent theft at the sale site, but it did little for the appearance of the merchandise. Another approach that might handle both the theft and inventory management problems was presented by a cash register salesman. He was promoting a register capable of maintaining inventory records and recording sales within product categories. Benjamin told the consultants that if he stayed in the business, he would seriously consider getting such a cash register to assist him in monitoring daily stock movement. He also felt that his employees would perceive the presence and use of a sophisticated cash register as a theft-prevention device.

Benjamin continued his discussion with the consultants by explaining other inventory management concerns that he had regarding product acquisition and merchandise assortment. "The initial focus of my business was on sportswear. Now the merchandise I sell includes all types of clothing. Sometimes I have even had opportunities to handle high-margin items that were not directly related to traditional softline items—toiletries, for example. As the business grew, my product mix became somewhat complex. I had a horrible time arranging the merchandise on the motel tables."

At that point, the consultants asked about displays that could be used to better separate the merchandise by size, quality, and styles. They suggested that racks and hangers would provide a more complete display and discourage customers from mixing up the items. This would also make a positive impact on the image of his business. Since the racks and hangers would have to be packed and moved along with the merchandise from sale-to-sale, Benjamin expressed concern about logistics.

After hearing his story, the consultants suggested that a retail outlet could be the solution to many of his problems. Benjamin, on the other hand, felt that the start-up costs for a small storefront, operated as a sole proprietorship, would be prohibitive. The consultants attempted to explain some of the benefits that would result from such an operation. They indicated that the business would generate regular employment opportunities that would enable hiring more responsible retail employees. Security measures could be introduced and enforced, and inventories could be properly stored, displayed, and counted as often as was necessary.

Both Benjamin and his consultants were familiar with the rise of retail chains that specialized in irregulars, seconds, and discontinued fashion apparel. Several such stores had limited selections of athletic wear, but none of them seemed to have a major emphasis in this product category. Although more information on the growth and operation of such establishments would, no doubt, be helpful, both parties agreed that pursuit of this research was not a fruitful use of the consultants' time.

Discussions followed over a 2-week period, concluding in a decision that research should be conducted on a small scale, given Benjamin's limited time and financial resources. Of primary concern was customers' perceptions of clearance sales held in retail stores versus motel sales. That is, Benjamin wanted to know whether the change from a motel to a storefront location would alienate his current customers. Whether or not the data indicated that a change in location was advisable, the merchandise mix that best meets customers' needs must be identified.

The proposal his consultants made was to survey current customers at the next Midwest University sale, with a focus on six specific areas of interest: customer characteristics, segmentation, media habits, shopping habits, perceptions of Benjamin's Briefs, and preferences for services and other ancillaries.

With Benjamin's approval, a questionnaire, disguised as to its source and purpose, was designed and administered at the last Midwest University sale of the semester. The survey was distributed randomly to the customers as they arrived at the sale. This technique resulted in the return of 205 usable questionnaires over a 3-day period. An attempt to cross-classify survey forms and each respondent's purchases failed as a result of recording errors.

Survey Results

The survey results are reported in Exhibit 18–4. The consultants' report provides some interpretation of these data, but Benjamin was on his own to determine the appropriate managerial decisions. One possibility was to collect additional information—but what kind and how?

EXHIBIT 18–4
Selected Survey Results

	Percentage
I. Demographics	
A. Sex	Percentage
Male	53.15
Female	46.85
B. Age	Percentage
Eighteen or less	16.01
Nineteen	20.80
Twenty	17.86
Twenty-one	16.33
Twenty-two	15.73
Twenty-three or greater	13.27
C. University class	Percentage
Freshman	14.4
Sophomore	18.9
Junior	18.9
Senior	20.3
Graduate student	4.2
No response	23.3
D. Employment	Percentage
Sales	2.85
Management and professional	1.90
Secretary and clerical	4.30
Other	14.33
None	34.21
No response	42.40

EXHIBIT 18-4
(Continued)

E.	Personal Income	Percentage
	less than $3,000	51.06
	$3,000–$4,999	14.89
	$5,000–$6,999	7.33
	$7,000–$8,999	4.55
	$9,000 +	7.26
	No response	14.91
F.	Transportation (usual)	Percentage
	Automobile	58.56
	Bicycle	13.51
	Bus	0.00
	Walk	11.80
	Other	0.90
	No response	15.23
G.	Transportation (to sale)	Percentage
	Automobile	68.09
	Bicycle	12.51
	Bus	0.00
	Walk	8.40
	Other	3.01
	No response	7.99

II. Media habits (at least "occasionally use," based on rating scale)

A.	Newspapers	Percentage
	Citipaper	32.4
	University Nuus	63.4
B.	Radio	Percentage
	AM1* (WQQZ)	12.0
	AM2	4.3
	FM1	42.3
	FM2	25.1
	FM3	9.4
	FM4	0.3

*Used for radio advertising

C.	Television	Percentage
	Network affiliate	92.7
	PBS affiliate	32.3

D. How did you hear about today's sale? (Numbers add to more than 100% as a result of multiple responses.)

	Percentage
Citipaper	5.81
University Nuus	41.44
Radio commercial	17.30
TV commercial	0.00
Sign/billboard	3.73
Poster/flyers	17.18
Happened by and stopped in	1.06
Heard from friend	32.30
Others	1.06

EXHIBIT 18–4
(Continued)

III. Shopping Habits
   A. Rate the likelihood of your shopping for clothing/sporting goods in the following: (1 = not at all likely, 7 = almost certain):

	Mean
Motel	5.30
Warehouse showroom	5.33
Roadside setup	2.69
Discount store	5.38
Mail order	3.08

   B. Have you been to a sale of this type before?

	Percentage
Yes	52.13
No	47.87

   C. How important is each of the following in purchasing clothing/sporting goods? (1 = not at all important; 7 = very important)

	Mean
Price	6.31
Selection	5.91
Attractive displays	2.93
High-quality goods	5.82
Brand-name goods	5.01
Sponsor reputation	3.91
Friendly salespeople	3.37
Good quality for the money	6.33
First-rate merchandise	5.63

IV. Customer perceptions of company
   A. Today's sale is being conducted by

	Percentage
An organization going out of business	2.40
A professional liquidator	14.70
A wholesaler	9.63
The motel	11.11
Other	2.93
Don't know	52.03
No response	7.20

   B. Type of goods being sold:

	Percentage
Brand name/top quality	34.04
Brand name/seconds or irregulars	37.23
Off brand/top quality	8.51
Off brand/seconds or irregulars	4.26
Don't know	2.13
No response	13.83

   C. Please rate today's sale on each of the following (1 = very poor; 7 = excellent).

EXHIBIT 18–4
(Continued)

	Mean
Price	5.37
Selection	4.23
Attractive displays	3.55
High-quality goods	4.88
Brand-name goods	4.74
Sponsor reputation	4.22
Friendly salespeople	4.96
Good quality for the money	5.36
First-rate merchandise	4.72

V. Other preferences

A. What kinds of sales would you prefer to see in a motel setting (versus other distribution methods)? (Numbers add to more than 100% as a result of multiple responses.)

	Percentage
Closeout sporting goods	50.00
New sporting goods	40.27
Used sporting goods	3.60
Second-quality sporting goods	17.12

B. How important is the following (1 = not at all important; 7 = very important):

	Mean
Ability to pay by check	5.47
Ability to pay by credit card	4.29

C. Average size of sale

	Mean
Cash transactions	$18.14
Check transactions	$27.62

The consultants reported that attempts to find segments within the customer respondents were fruitless. No categorization that was attempted yielded any significant differences. The data therefore were reported across the entire sample. The profile of the sample was consistent with a university student population. Not surprisingly, the respondents favorably evaluated motel sales in general and the one being patronized, in particular. Questions concerning other merchandise sold in motels revealed slightly less positive attitudes (not reported here).

A Quandary

The financial success of the business suggested that continuing in the same vein would be feasible, but Benjamin questioned whether the income generated justified his time. It seemed pretty clear that he wouldn't make $1 million within the next 7 years unless he made some changes. Increased competition in the clearance business was evidenced by the number of sales being conducted for similar and related merchandise. If Benjamin had any thought of getting out of the business, now would be the opportune time to sell out. At least one of his "lieutenants" was interested in taking over the reins.

Benjamin left for the Lakeshore University sale while mulling over his options. The drive provided time to think, but a decision would have to be made soon. It was already May, and he would graduate on June 4.

Analytical Problem

1. What should Brad Benjamin do? If he stays in business, what measures are required to solve or at least reduce his operating problems?
2. Evaluate Benjamin's current merchandise management practices. Suggest some improvements.
3. Does the type of city affect market potential? Would your recommendations to Benjamin differ if he was considering your university's town?
4. What additional information should be gathered, how, and from whom?

NORTHEASTERN APPLIANCES:
Merchandise Budgets and Plans

Background
Northeastern Appliance was a chain of twenty retail stores located in northeast Florida. Established in 1957, the chain was now a major force in this market. It offered a full line of major brands of home appliances including washers, dryers, dishwashers, trash compactors, television sets, videocassette recorders, stereo systems, and many other products. The firm's executives attributed its steady growth to the company's philosophy of putting the customer first in every corporate decision. Northeastern was a highly ethical organization that constantly strove to serve its customers' needs. Employees were frequently reminded that Northeastern's number-one priority was customer service.

Although price was a very important concern in the home appliance market, Northeastern stressed competitive prices backed up by the firm's commitment to customer service. Northeastern seldom sold at a price lower than competition, but it was seldom "out-of-line" with local market prices.

In September of 1982, Bob Schwartz, Northeastern's Merchandise Manager, read an article about compact disc players, a product that he thought Northeastern should consider for its product line.

New Product Development
The Sony Corporation of Japan and the Dutch firm N. V. Phillips had been co-developing the compact disc (CD) player since June of 1980. The design of the player featured two advanced technologies, the laser optical scanner and computer-based digital audio. The firms' objective was to eliminate the limitations of the conventional 12-inch long-playing (LP) record player/turntable and raise the state of the art in audio reproduction to a standard never before thought possible—near perfection. Toward the end of 1982, Sony realized the fruits of this labor and introduced a version of the compact disc player in the Japanese market. Sony sold over 100,000 units in the first month, and had to double production to meet demand. Given that the price of the new player was $1,000, Sony was pleased with this new entry into the Japanese marketplace.

Sony's competitors did not overlook the CD player's early success. More than two-dozen firms began offering their versions of the player by licensing the technology from Sony/Phillips. John C. Koss, chairman of a firm that manufactured headphones and loudspeakers, announced that this new technology represented "the next generation of improvement."

The high interest in this high-priced, high-tech product for the home stereo system can be explained by examining the product's advantages. The CD player offered several benefits, especially audio performance. The dynamic range (the dif-

This case was prepared by George B. Glisan, Illinois State University, and Jon M. Hawes, University of Akron.

ference between the quietest and loudest passages of music) of the new format approaches 90+ decibels. This compares with a range of approximately 50+ decibels for conventional 12-inch LP records and turntables. The decibel system of measuring sound is a logarithmic function. In other words, for every three-decibel increase in sound level, there is a doubling of sound volume. Thus, the CD player is not merely 50 percent better than conventional records in sound intensity but is many times better. The result is a range that comes close to matching that of an actual concert performance.

The CD player also offers other performance benefits. Because the discs rotate at such high speeds in the player (200 to 500 revolutions per minute versus 33 1/3 for conventional records), speed variations known as "wow and flutter" are simply nonexistent. Another benefit of this new technology is that it generates better transient response than conventional players. That is, the transition from a high to a low musical note, for example, occurs so instantaneously that it duplicates the original musical performance. Additionally, the CD format can reproduce an extended frequency response. Conventional records have great difficulty in reproducing frequencies below 45 Hz (the low bass notes found in music). Although such low bass notes are not encountered often in music, the CD player can reproduce them. Thus, the full impact of a low C on a pipe organ is thunderously reproduced.

A final performance benefit is the absence of extraneous noise when playing CDs. When playing conventional LP records, the listener frequently encounters pops, ticks, and other surface noises. Also heard is a background hiss, which emanates from the master tape (the recording format) used to produce the record. All of these annoyances are missing from CDs. Partly responsible for this performance benefit is the recording method. The music information on a CD is stored on the disc as pits, or spots, etched onto the surface. These pits are then "read" by the optical scanning laser in the player. The result is an uncanny silence between musical passages, and a lack of noise intrusion during the music.

At the heart of this superb music reproduction system is the digital audio technology. When the music is recorded at the studio, recording technicians dispense with the conventional analog method (sequential recording onto a reel-to-reel tape recorder) and use machines that convert music information to binary code (0 or 1) and then store, or record, it. Each sample of music is converted into a 16-bit "word." About 4.3 million (yes, million) bits are scanned each second by the digital processor. This system's precision is a virtual one-for-one recording of the original performance. To take advantage of this recorded performance necessitates a digital playback device. The CD player is this device.

Although performance is the principal strength of this new technology, there are additional latent benefits. The discs themselves represent a series of advantages over conventional records. Their smaller size (4.7 inches in diameter) makes them easier to handle and store. Furthermore, the CDs are not susceptible to the kinds of warpage that conventional vinyl records are, because the discs are made of aluminum and sheathed in hard plastic. Additionally, dust, fingerprints, even scratches to the plastic will not diminish playback quality as they do on conventional records.

Sony and most of the other manufacturers have incorporated additional features into their players. For instance, many of the machines are programmable. If you desired to listen to selections 3, 7, and 1 on a disk, you could program the CD player to play only those selections, even in that out-of-sequence order. Some of the manufacturers have such features as seek and scan, memory, and remote control.

Without question, the state of the art in home music reproduction has been significantly raised by the advent of the CD player. After Sony's successful introduction in Japan during the fall of 1982, it set its sights on the U.S. market. With its past business success in consumer electronics innovation, Sony was optimistic. Past successes include the pocket transistorized radio, high-performance color television (the Trinitron), videocassette recorders (Betamax and Betamax HiFi), and portable stereo (the Walkman). With the introduction of the CD player in Japan, U.S. consumer hi-fi publications heralded the form as the greatest innovation since the transition from high fidelity to stereophonic playback in the 1950s.

New Product Introduction

Since Northeastern was an authorized Sony dealer and the firms had an excellent business relationship, Schwartz was eager to place a large order for Sony CD players as soon as they were available in 1983. Northeastern bought no other brands of CD players. Northeastern introduced the products to its market with great fanfare, advertising extensively in the local media through a co-op arrangement. Salespeople were thoroughly trained to sell the new high-tech product. Preferred locations were used in each store to display the CD players. As was Northeastern's policy, the Sony CDs were priced to be competitive with Sony CD players sold by other local retailers, as well as other brands.

At the end of 1983, however, Schwartz was reassessing Northeastern Appliance's commitment to the line of Sony CD players. Northeastern had sold far fewer CDs than expected during 1983. This chain was not alone, however, in its disappointment with the sales of CD players. In fact, Northeastern had done better than most of its competitors. Unfortunately, in the United States these items did not come close to the early level of sales success achieved in Japan. The problem was not specific to Sony, however, as none of the other manufacturers had yet achieved any hint of sales success. Several reasons were offered for the lack of widespread acceptance of the CD player in the United States. Consumer resistance to the $1,000 price was an important factor. Consumers viewed the player as an alternative to the conventional turntable, which had an average price (with cartridge) of $350. This product generated a very respectable sound. The $650 difference, many buyers pointed out, could be used to buy a lot of albums, or a better amplifier and speakers if a new system were purchased.

Another dilemma was software, that is, the discs themselves. Although all the major record companies offered at least some CDs, conventional records still offered a much better selection. Buyers were reluctant to buy a CD player if there was little to play on it. Sony established a joint venture with CBS to bring out several hundred titles by the end of 1983, as had Toshiba and EMI. Poly Gram, one of the largest record companies in the world, had hoped to have about 600 titles in its catalog by the end of the year. Unfortunately, the record companies' hopes were not met. Even though more titles were being released each month, many record retailers were reluctant to carry many of the discs. They cited two difficulties. First, the discs retailed for about $18 each, double the price of conventional record albums. Second, retailers were reluctant to stock the discs until more of the players had been sold.

Consumer electronics analysts pointed out that even more fundamental difficulties existed for the acceptance of CD players in the United States. First, to fully realize the benefits of the new technology, all components of the stereo system had to be high quality. If, for example, the user's amplifier put out 25 watts per channel, the user would discover rather quickly that the amplifier had difficulty meeting the demands of the digital audio signals. It was not uncommon to reach instantaneous peaks of 200 watts. For retailers, however, this was an opportunity to upgrade the buyer's amplifiers and speakers as "digital ready" to take advantage of this opportunity. Needless to say, these new components were quite expensive, and many consumers were unwilling to pay for this "upgrade."

Another dilemma that the analysts mentioned were American listening habits. The majority of U.S. hi-fi owners listened to rock music. Yet, the full audio potential of CDs is not realized in this type of music. Classical music posesses the greater frequency response and dynamic range. While there are many U.S. consumers who enjoy classical music, far more prefer popular or rock music.

A final point that the analysts emphasized was the range of choices facing electronics consumers in 1983. Videocassette recorders, computers, satellite receiving dishes, and even such new items as cordless telephones, also competed for the consumer's attention. Indeed, some retailers were repositioning themselves as consumer electronics stores so that they could sell buyers something, even if it wasn't CD players.

As Schwartz considered all of these issues, he remembered the four-channel stereo that was introduced in the early 1970s. It never caught on and is now just an unpleasant memory. Four-channel offered sonic improvement and faced some of the same challenges as the CD player, yet it failed terribly in the marketplace. For Schwartz, this whole issue of what to do with this Sony line of CD players had to be resolved quickly. Next year's merchandise plans were due by the end of the month.

Analytical Problem

Assist Bob Schwartz by writing a report that addresses the following issues:

1. Should Northeastern continue its high-level commitment to the Sony line of CD players in 1984?
2. If sales in 1984 do not increase significantly, how long should Northeastern remain fully committed to the Sony line of CD players?
3. What else could Northeastern do to enhance sales opportunities for the new line of Sony CD players?
4. What effect does the chain's commitment to the line of Sony CD players have on Northeastern Appliance's image?

Carol MacDonald owns and operates the Mainline Gift Shop in suburban Houston. Carol purchased the business seven years ago, and its sales have grown gradually from less than $200,000 to more than $900,000. The business has an excellent reputation, is beautifully decorated, and is stocked with gifts from all parts of the world. Carol is pleased with her success and attributes her prosperity to total dedication, close contact with her clients, appropriate merchandise, and a good marketing plan. Carol admits to having serious problems, however, and has talked about them to several of her friends, including her accountant, lawyer, and banker. The problems concern location as well as some internal changes that she feels she might have to make.

When Carol purchased the business seven years ago, the landlord would not give her more than a one-year lease. Because the previous owner of the business had no difficulty renewing the lease each year, Carol did not expect to encounter problems in this area either. Further, when Carol was starting out, she was somewhat reluctant to commit herself to a lease of more than one year because she had doubts about her ability to successfully run the business. But the business did succeed, and for the last seven years the lease was renewed. Three months ago, however, the landlord died, and his widow turned over all property management to her son, Andrew. Naturally, Carol expected the lease arrangement to remain the same as it had been in the past, and indeed, Andrew assured her that when her present lease expired she would receive a new one. But at the end of the year, Carol received a new lease for five years with a rent increase from $1,000 to $3,000 per month, or 5 percent of total annual gross receipts, whichever was higher. Needless to say, Carol was furious and contacted Andrew. He told her there would be no adjustments and that if she did not like the new terms, she could move. Andrew insisted that the rental he was asking was fair based on comparable rental values throughout the community. Andrew did offer "for old times' sake" to give her a six-month extension on her present lease at the new rate. Carol told him she would give him an answer in a few weeks.

Carol does not want to move because she has spent a lot of time building her business at that location and does not want to risk $900,000 in sales and profits. On the other hand, she cannot afford either 5 percent or $45,000 a year in rent. Since her business is growing at the rate of 20 percent per year, she knows moving would set her back. She contacted several real estate brokers and finally located a vacant lot 10 blocks from her present location. The new location would have room for parking and future expansion and still be close enough to keep most of her present clientele. The total cost of the building would be $375,000. She could get a mortgage for $300,000, which would require payments of $3,600 monthly for 15 years. The earliest she should move into the location would be 6 to 8 months from

This case is reprinted from John Edward deYoung, *Cases in Small Business Management: A Strategic Problems Approach* (Columbus, OH: Merrill Publishing, 1988).

the present. The builder told her he could make the location reasonably presentable and functional sooner, but it would not be totally complete for about 8 months.

In the meantime, Carol heard that Andrew was thinking about opening his own gift shop at her present location. When Carol confronted him about this, he did not deny it and said that his wife, Shelly May, was going to open up a shop as soon as Carol left. Carol knew Shelly May because she had worked part time for Carol for several years and was in fact quite capable and knew the suppliers, customers, and price structure necessary to operate the business.

Carol asked Andrew if he would be willing to sell the building; he told her he would be willing to sell for $400,000. He would take $100,000 down and hold the mortgage himself at 11½ percent fixed for 20 years; monthly payments would be $3,200. Carol knew the building was not worth that much and that there was little room for expansion. She did not know whether Andrew was bluffing to sell the building or if he really intended to open a gift shop. Since the old lease clearly indicated that all improvements she had made became part of the property of the landlord, a gift shop run by Shelly May would have the same type of decor that Carol had operated under for years. Carol worried about whether all her customers would shop at her new location as well as whether the existence of the two gift shops would cause her to lose business. If sales dropped, she might not be able to afford the mortgage payment on the new building. Carol told Andrew she would think about the purchase and asked for an eight-month extension on her lease, but Andrew insisted that she would have to sign a five-year lease.

Carol is considering another alternative. For some time she has been contemplating opening a shop in a second location and had finally settled on a new growth area in another section of Houston. A new building is available there, which Carol could either lease or purchase. The property is strategically located among a cluster of stores that would complement her business. There is plenty of parking space and room for future expansion. The owner is willing to lease the facility for $2,000 per month on a three-, five-, or ten-year basis, or sell the property for $250,000. The owner will accept $50,000 down and can arrange financing at 12 pecent over a 20-year period. Monthly payments, including principal and interest, would be $2,202. Carol is tempted to call it quits at the old location and start from the beginning in this new growth area; however, when she thinks about the time and effort she has put into the original location, she is hesitant to start over again.

So, Carol's alternatives are (1) to pay an exorbitant rent under a five-year lease at the present property; (2) to purchase, for $400,000, a property that will probably be too small within a few years and is overvalued; (3) to build a new building 10 blocks down the same street and take on a mortgage of $3,600 per month with the threat of having Andrew's wife open the same type of business and perhaps cut into her sales; and (4) to open at a new location in the growth area and start over again, where she would face uncertainty in sales and income. While Carol is more confident than she had been when she opened the original store, she would still have to face it as a new business.

In the meantime, Carol is having other problems. She is not satisifed with her inventory control system. Differences constantly arise between her book inventory and actual physical inventory. At the end of each buying season (such as Easter,

Christmas, or Mother's Day) there is usually an abundance of inventory that must be stored until the following year. When the physical inventory is unpacked and counted there is either a shortage or overage compared to book inventory. Carol thinks perhaps the discrepancy results from returns, withdrawals, or exchanges. In any case, last year's physical inventory was $17,000 lower than the book inventory. Carol has considered purchasing a computer but does not know much about them. She is afraid that if she puts all business transactions into the computer, anyone who can tap into the computer will know the details of her business, just as Shelly May does.

Another problem is that as the business is growing and has more customers, more shoplifting is occurring. Because those she has caught are always clients who can afford to buy the merchandise, Carol has not enforced her own rules. She merely warns shoplifters that if they are caught again she will report them to the police. At one time Carol had dummy TV cameras and mirrors around the store, but when clients complained that they did not like being followed by a camera when trying to shop, she took down the cameras and left only mirrors.

About nine months ago Carol appointed Joyce Lamont as store manager to assist her and fill in when she wasn't at the store. Joyce has done an excellent job and is totally dedicated to the business; she works late and even refuses to take a vacation. Carol has become very dependent upon her. Recently, Joyce pointed out that daily gross cash receipts are not following typical days; for example, cash receipts on a Saturday when the store is packed with customers may be $300 off what they would be on a normal Saturday. Joyce thinks some of the employees may be stealing and has asked for permission to fire people if she does discover thefts. Carol was shocked and told Joyce she should handle the matter carefully because many of her part-time employees were related to influential people in the community. Since all the clerks work fast to relieve the congestion on busy weekends and all the clerks dip into any cash register that is open, it is impossible to hold any one person responsible for a particular cash register. Joyce did report that she had noticed one girl stealing and quietly informed her that she was being let go because they were cutting back on staff. As Joyce pointed out, it would be difficult to prove she was stealing, and it was better not to create a scene. Carol agreed with this approach and commended Joyce on her tactfulness.

Carol became concerned when the same thing happened several more times over the next few months. She wondered if something else had been overlooked, since the same scenario keeps occurring. She thought about getting fidelity insurance, but learned that it would be extremely expensive for the gift shop business. She also considered hiring an outside organization that investigates employees by coming into a store and buying items with cash, then leaving without a receipt. She even toyed with the idea of putting a live TV camera near the counter where she could privately monitor activity herself. As yet she has not mentioned this to Joyce because she wants to give it more thought.

Finally, Carol is having a problem with vendors. She has dealt with them since she opened the store, and in many ways, the business would not have survived without their help. Lately, however, other suppliers have been offering much better prices and credit terms. Some have been offered consignment arrangements. Carol feels tremendous loyalty to her old suppliers and has talked to some of them, but they always point out how they helped her when she needed them. Some have given her better prices and terms and made other concessions; however, unless she complains, nothing happens to prices and terms. Carol wonders how long she should operate under these conditions. After all, she adjusts her prices for her customers constantly, and she cannot understand why her suppliers cannot do the same. She wonders whether she should give some of the new suppliers a chance or stick with the old vendors who helped her when she started the business.

Analytical Problem

1. What alternative would you advise Carol to take concerning her location and rental arrangement? Be specific and consider all alternatives.
2. How would you handle the problems of inventory control?
3. What should Carol do about the shoplifting problem?
4. Should Carol computerize her operation?
5. Do you think there is any relationship between the shoplifting and the difference between the physical and book inventories? Explain.
6. Do you agree with the manner in which Joyce Lamont has been handling the theft problem? Should she have reported the employees to the police?
7. Should Carol use some other system to determine what is happening to cash receipts? Do you think she should install a private monitoring system? Should she inform Joyce?

VALDOSTA STATE COLLEGE BOOKSTORE:
Managing Merchandise in a Not-for-Profit Environment

Valdosta, Georgia, a city of 50,000 people, is 15 miles north of the Florida border on Interstate 75. Named the Azalea City for its abundance of that flower, Valdosta is surrounded by rich farmlands. Agriculturally, Valdosta is a leader in forestry production as well as cash crops of tobacco, soybeans, cotton, and corn. Valdosta is also a trading, shopping, medical, manufacturing, and business center for a ten-county area in Georgia and Florida. Throughout its history, diverse industry, agribusiness, and tourism have contributed to the economic development of Valdosta and Lowndes County. The city is the home of high-tech electro-chemical companies and is becoming a regional health-care center. In addition to Moody Air Force Base, Valdosta State College also has a significant economic impact on the city.

Valdosta State College (VSC), serving over 6,500 students, primarily offers a liberal arts education with diverse educational programs that include a strong business school. The college serves as a regional educational center for southeast Georgia. It has a school of nursing and programs such as preengineering, premedicine, and prelaw. The college offers master's degrees in several disciplines including business and nursing. It has a cooperative doctoral program in education with Georgia State University and the University of Georgia. Many of VSC's students come from within a 100-mile radius of the college. At least 5 to 10 percent of the students, however, come from Florida, other states, or foreign countries.

The VSC Bookstore is located in the Union Building, in the center of the main campus. The store has been owned and operated by VSC as a part of its Auxiliary Services Division since the college was founded in 1913. The current bookstore was professionally designed in 1976 by Ken White, one of the most prominent college bookstore designers in the country. It is housed in a two-level structure, with raised borders on the top level, giving its exterior a three-level appearance. The bookstore will soon undergo extensive remodeling on both levels. The VSC Bookstore has an annual sales volume of approximately $1.8 million.

Mission and Objectives

The VSC Bookstore falls under the guidelines of the Division of Auxiliary Services within the State of Georgia University System. It exists to meet the service function of supplying textbooks and other campus-life needs for the student population. The bookstore is expected to be self-supporting, and it receives no funding from the State or the University System. The bookstore therefore generates its own revenues to meet all of its expenses. According to its manager, Tommye Miller, the VSC Bookstore is a full-fledged retail business operatng in an academic environment under the strict guidelines of the university system with the objective of serving the needs of the student population in the following:

This case was prepared by Allan C. Reddy, Valdosta State College, Georgia, and C. P. Rao, University of Arkansas.

☐ Sale of new and used textbooks
☐ Sale of school and business supplies
☐ Sale of outside reading materials and student guides
☐ Sale of trade books
☐ Sale of school insignia clothing and supplies
☐ Repurchase of used textbooks

Strategy

The VSC Bookstore's basic strategy was to meet the textbook, school and art supply, campus housekeeping, and other miscellaneous retail needs of its student customers as economically as possible. This had to be done while still generating the revenues needed to pay all its own operating expenses. The bookstore had a marketing plan to increase the student demand for all the product lines carried. Also, it planned to add new products that students wanted.

Promoting and expanding its nontextbook product line was necessary so that the bookstore would not be so dependent on the sales of textbooks, which accounted for 90 percent of the dollar volume of total bookstore sales. The national average for college bookstores is only 75 percent. Expansion of nontextbook sales would allow the bookstore to reduce the markup on textbooks by generating more gross margin from other areas of its product line. Exhibit 21–1 shows the proportion of sales by each department.

The bookstore was also attempting to develop a marketing strategy that would pull the student customers through the store and down to the lower level. This would allow the store to use the downstairs space more effectively. Another marketing strategy consideration was attempting to educate the student customer about the actual cost and profit basis of a bookstore operation.

According to Miller, the bookstore had a poor image among students. They perceived it as an exploiter of a captive market and as selling textbooks and supplies at high prices. Miller explained that the typical VSC student had never purchased textbooks before, since books were provided at no cost to the student in most public high school systems. On entering college, the students were shocked to discover that textbooks are extremely expensive, costing approximately $150 or more per quarter for a normal load of three courses. Because of these high prices, stu-

EXHIBIT 21–1
Valdosta State College Bookstore Annual Sales by Department

Department	Sales ($000s)	Total Sales (%)
New textbooks	1,080	60.05
Used textbooks	545	30.3
Trade books	12	.7
School/art supplies	126	7.0
Clothing	18	1.0
Cards and gifts	18	1.0
Total	1,800	100.0

dents felt that the bookstore used the absence of other convenient private textbook sources to make huge profits. According to Miller, the students must be educated that publishers, not the bookstore, regulate textbook costs and that the store had a gross margin of only 25 percent on textbooks.

Another issue was the improved system that was being developed to give the bookstore management better and faster information on all the financial aspects of the operation. This would allow maintenance of better financial control and would assist in the basic goal of cutting the costs associated with the retail delivery of textbooks to students.

Policies

The VSC Bookstore operated as a retail establishment and treated all students entering the store as valued customers. They were shown courtesy and were entitled to the same rights and privileges that any retail operation extends to its customers. Miller was *very* emphatic about this important store policy.

The bookstore had a return merchandise policy that allowed return of unused or defective merchandise within the first 2 weeks of any quarter for a full refund if accompanied by the sales receipt. The bookstore also had an aggressive used-book buy-back policy and repurchased textbooks that would be used again during the next quarter.

To better serve the student consumers and to learn more about their needs and wants, the VSC Bookstore conducted a survey of the student population. As a result, Miller planned to expand the product line into new areas of interest to students to generate additional revenues and gross margins. The results of the survey are summarized in Exhibit 21–2, and the questionnaire is shown in Exhibit 21–3.

EXHIBIT 21–2
Independent Student Market Survey

> A small, independent market survey of fifty-seven members of the student population of Valdosta State College was conducted during the previous Summer Quarter. These are some of the results:
> 95% Felt the textbooks were overpriced
> 77% Have made nontextbook purchases
> 13% Had bought clothing
> 51% Had bought gifts or greeting cards
> 58% Use the bookstore only once a quarter
> 49% Don't shop there more often because the prices are too high
> 49% Don't shop there because of the lack of parking
> 10% Have never been downstairs
> 60% Had been downstairs more than three times
> Suggestions for new product lines included beer, cassettes and albums, food and snacks, film, and video rentals
> Note: Most of the students do not attend classes during the Summer. This survey therefore can only be considered a pilot study of student opinion. Exhibit 21–3 shows the questionnaire used to gather student views.

EXHIBIT 21–3
Questionnaire: VSC Bookstore

Dear Student: Please take a few minutes to fill out this questionnaire about the VSC Bookstore. Your viewpoints on these topics are important and will be given directly to the bookstore manager. Thank you.

DIRECTIONS: Check "yes" or "no" to these questions.

1. Do you think VSC textbooks are overpriced? YES____ NO____
2. Do you know that the bookstore is a nonprofit, self-supporting auxiliary service of the college? YES____ NO____
3. Have you ever made a nontextbook purchase at the bookstore? YES____ NO____
4. Have you ever bought clothes at the bookstore? YES____ NO____
5. Have you ever bought cards or gifts at the bookstore? YES____ NO____
6. Has a required textbook ever been out-of-stock when you needed to purchase it? YES____ NO____
7. Were you adequately helped by bookstore personnel on your last visit to the bookstore? YES____ NO____
8. Do you know there is a bookstore outlet at Langdale Hall? YES____ NO____
9. Would you use a bookstore outlet at Pound Hall? YES____ NO____
10. Would you use a bookstore outlet at the Education Center? YES____ NO____

DIRECTIONS: Circle the statement that best answers the question. You may circle more than one answer.

11. Which statement best describes your student status?
    a. Live in dormitory
    b. Live off campus
    c. Commute from out of town
    d. Take classes at North Campus only
    e. Between the ages of 18 and 25
    f. Over 25 years old
12. How often do you visit the bookstore?
    a. Once a quarter
    b. Once a month
    c. Once a week
13. What is (are) the biggest reason(s) you don't shop at the bookstore more often?
    a. Prices too high
    b. Lack of parking
    c. Doesn't carry what I need
    d. Poor service
14. How often have you been downstairs at the bookstore?
    a. Never
    b. One to three times
    c. More than three times
15. List three items you would like the convenience of purchasing at the bookstore that are not now being stocked by the bookstore.
    a. _____ b. _____ c. _____

Management

The bookstore's manager, Miller, was previously its associate director from 1976 until early 1984. At that time she'd been specifically responsible for managing the book departments (both textbooks and trade books) and for inventory control for the whole store. From early 1984 until late 1985, Miller worked for a subsidiary of the National Association of College Stores in Oberlin, Ohio, that sells trade books to college and university bookstores. Miller returned to VSC in September of 1985 as bookstore manager. She developed a long- and a short-range plan for remodeling and remerchandising the store. As manager, she was responsible for creating and implementing the annual bookstore budget of approximately $1.8 million under the university system regulations and guidelines for auxiliary services.

The bookstore also employed an assistant bookstore manager, a textbook buyer and assistant, a store secretary, a full-time accounting clerk, and several cashiers.

The VSC Bookstore Target Market

The VSC Bookstore served the entire student population of the school, which totalled approximately 6,500 students. Miller stated that although she would welcome outside competition as proof to her student customers that her pricing structure is fair and competitive, she felt that VSC was simply too small for an independent retail operation to successfully (profitably) compete with the college bookstore.

The general public was allowed to shop at the VSC Bookstore, but the store did not advertise outside of college publications. Both Miller and the administration felt that it was unfair to compete with taxpaying retail operations in the general public market. This was one of the biggest dilemmas Miller faced in the bookstore operation. The bookstore functioned as a retail operation that had to pay its own way as an auxiliary service, but its customer base was restricted to VSC students. The university system provided no profit motive, either for the bookstore as an entity, or for the employees. All profits had to return to the auxiliary reserve account for use on approved Auxiliary Services projects. The Director of Auxiliary Services and the Vice President for Business and Finance determined the usage of auxiliary reserve funds. Incentive pay for bookstore employees, for example, was *not* an approved expenditure.

Marketing Strategies

Products

The main product of the VSC Bookstore was, naturally, textbooks. Ninety percent of the approximately $1.8 million annual sales at the bookstore was generated by textbook sales. The bookstore also sold study guides, trade books, school supplies, insignia clothing and school supplies, greeting cards, small gift and knick-knack items, magazines, and art supplies. The bookstore also ran a small outlet store in Langdale Hall, a student dormitory building on campus, which sold drugs and sundries, health and beauty aids, and some snack items. Miller felt that there was great need for a market survey of the student population (see Exhibits 21-2 and 21-3) to better anticipate the needs and wants of the student population for nontextbook product lines. She felt that if a better mix could be established in these other lines, the increased gross profits would allow her to reduce the price of textbooks.

Pricing

Textbook pricing was determined by a markup of 33 percent from cost, which represented a 25 percent gross margin on the retail selling price of new textbooks. This did not, however, account for text freight costs. Other nontextbook product items varied in markups. For example, the bookstore achieved a 50-percent gross margin on the retail selling price of greeting cards, a 45-percent gross margin on school supplies, and a 40-percent gross margin on clothing and art supplies.

The store purchased used textbooks from students at half the original purchase price on an anticipated-need basis. Used books carried a higher profit margin than new books but also carried a higher risk, according to Miller. She stated that she could easily get "stuck" with a shelf full of used textbooks when one of the department heads did not give sufficient notice of a change in textbooks. When this happened, she could absorb a complete loss, because other outlets for the books might no longer be available.

The bookstore planned to change its buy-back policies the following fall. To date, the bookstore had bought textbooks back at one half the original purchase price and sold them for three fourths of the new book's retail price. For example, a student who had bought a used book would receive only one half the used-book price when selling that book back to the bookstore. The bookstore realized a higher profit margin percentage on these books by reselling the same book at three fourths of the *new*-book price.

To better serve students next fall, Miller instructed her staff to begin paying one half of the *new* price for all textbooks that were bought back, regardless of whether they were purchased new or used. She also changed the refund policy. As mentioned, this policy had been to provide a full refund for the first 2 weeks of the quarter with a sales receipt; after this period, the store paid only the buy-back price at the end of the quarter. Miller developed a sliding-scale refund policy up to the sixth week of classes so that those students who had dropped courses by midterm would realize more value from their textbooks when they returned them to the bookstore. They would no longer have to wait until the designated buy-back period to resell their textbooks.

Miller felt that the bookstore should be run as a retail operation with a profit motive. However, because the store could not use any profits or provide salary or bonus incentives for its employees for increasing sales and gross margins, the profit objective lacked meaning. The University System had never told Miller what the profit margin should be, but she said that historically it fluctuated from 1 to 8 percent, all of which entered the auxiliary reserve fund. She felt frustrated that the bookstore was expected to function as a retail operation but was not allowed to initiate the same goals and rewards as a retail operation. She was also frustrated that she could not reward her employees for outstanding performance through salary increases or bonuses.

The bookstore, which in Miller's opinion was very poorly designed for a retail application because of its upstairs–downstairs floor plan, would soon be remodeled under her direction. Miller stated that one of the major problems facing the store was drawing customers through it, especially to the downstairs selling areas. On completion of the remodeling project, she intended to introduce a different product mix to increase profits in the nontextbook area, enabling a decreased markup in textbooks. The bookstore then would not be so dependent on the gross profits of textbook sales to meet operational expenses.

Promotion

The VSC Bookstore conducted only minimal advertising and promotions. Because of university guidelines, the only media in which the bookstore was allowed to advertise was the college newspaper. The advertising—done about once a month—produced only mediocre results, according to Miller. The bookstore spent less than $500 advertising in the college newspaper last year. (Note: A quarter-page ad in every issue of the paper would cost the bookstore less than $3,000 per year, which represented less than two tenths of 1 percent of the store's sales.)

Miller found that bookstore coupons printed in the newspaper produced the best results. The bookstore was not allowed to advertise in off-campus media because of university regulations against competing with tax-paying retail organizations, and Miller agreed with this policy. But she had to obtain special permission from the administration even to advertise in fraternity and club publications or in special events of these groups. Next fall, the bookstore would again advertise on the back cover of the VSC football program to attract a segment of the general public attending the college athletic events. For the first time, a drawing for $250 worth of VSC insignia clothing would be promoted on the football program.

Purchasing

Textbook purchasing was based on the book requests from the different department heads, who usually based their textbook quantity estimates on information gathered from early registration. But, this was often poor information at best, according to Miller. She said that to determine textbook quantities needed for each course the bookstore kept its own internal records about previous enrollments, and these were more accurate than those of the academic departments. But Miller normally ordered the quantity of textbooks that the professors requested for the fall quarter because even if they overanticipated their needs, she could sell those books in the next quarter. This system often created an unused inventory of textbooks, tying up funds. She satisfied the faculty members for the fall quarter, however, by ordering according to their estimates. During the winter and spring quarters, she found it necessary to begin adjusting the department head orders for textbooks based on her own internal records.

Because the bookstore had only four major buying periods during the year (counting the summer quarter), Miller wanted to develop a just-in-time inventory method to reduce the carrying costs for the bookstore. But she knew that if she made too many changes with text orders, she would face the ire of the faculty when out-of-stocks occurred. She felt that she was literally between a rock and a hard place concerning inventory controls and faculty requests.

Miller said that the goal concerning inventory purchases was to receive most of her merchandise the month before each academic quarter. Then, the invoices would become due during the month in which the quarter began, and funds would be available for timely payment. University bookstores throughout the country, however, all order the same textbooks at about the same time. Those on the semester system are about a month ahead of those functioning on the quarter system. She needed enough lead time in her orders so that if the publisher had a stock-out she could still receive the textbooks before the quarter began. Miller said that, on the average, shipments require 4 to 8 weeks.

Miller had a lot more freedom in inventory control and levels with her non-textbook product lines. These lines, however, made up less than 10 percent of the total sales, so most of the problems of inventory carrying costs were in an area over which she had less control. In addition, the employee in charge of inventory and placing the orders for this other merchandise was inexperienced and had not yet developed good control over inventory levels on these nontextbook product lines.

Finance

Miller felt that it was important to understand the role of Auxiliary Services under the University System of Georgia to fully appreciate the bookstore's financial problems. Every unit in Auxiliary Services (such as the Bookstore, Food Services, Residence Life, Student Health, College Vending, Laundry Facilities) was expected to be self-supporting and received no funding from the state or the University system. As manager of the bookstore, Miller administered the $1.8 million budget.

The bookstore's revenue had to pay for all stock purchases, salaries, employee benefits, direct operating expenses (a percentage of the revenues was paid to the school as rent to cover these direct operating expenses), plant operations such as the phone bill, and other indirect operating expenses such as postage, repair and maintenance of equipment, and so on. In addition, 5 percent of revenue had to enter an Auxiliary Services reserve fund, which was used at the administration's discretion but, by System policy, was spent only for the operation of the Auxiliary Services units.

Miller felt the bookstore had a serious problem with receiving financial information to assist her in decision making. The bookstore obtained most of its financial information and its profit and loss statements from the Office of Business and Finance. Miller stated that this information arrived at least 3 weeks after the end of any monthly reporting period. During the summer months, when the fiscal year ended and the annual report was being produced, as much as 2 months elapsed between the closing of a financial period and Miller receiving a financial statement. She felt that this information lag time and the lack of a departmental breakdown of profits and expenses was harmful to the bookstore operation. She wanted to develop a system of internal accounting procedures so that she could generate her own internal accounting records tailored to the needs of the bookstore operation.

Miller's expertise was not in accounting, and she needed outside help to implement an internal accounting system. As part of the current remodeling project, the bookstore had ordered a new cash register system capable of providing inventory and sales reports by department. Miller needed assistance in devising an accounting system for the bookstore that could use the information generated by the new cash registers. The major objective of the VSC Bookstore operation was to produce a small profit or at the least operate at break-even. As stated previously, the net profit of the bookstore had fluctuated from 1 to 8 percent, and all net profits had to be deposited in the auxiliary reserve account. Even these profits therefore were not at Miller's disposal to spend as she saw fit. The bookstore cost of goods sold was approximately 74 percent (see Exhibit 21–4).

Miller compared the markup statistics she found in reports of national bookstore surveys (conducted by the National Association of College Bookstores) to those at the VSC bookstore. She made some minor adjustments, based on some unique aspects of the VSC customer environment, and as a result, most of her profit margins were a little below the national average for bookstores generating approximately the same level of sales.

According to Miller, the bookstore did not have a cash-flow problem. She managed her inventory and cash flow by holding invoices and credits at the bookstore until she had the available funds, and then she sent the invoices to the cashier's office to be processed and paid. Turnaround time from invoice receipt by the cashier's office to check issue was about 3 days. Thus, Miller could control the cash flow fairly well during peak periods using this procedure. The usual terms with suppliers were "net 30 days." Most of the suppliers, however, did not demand payment for at least 60 days. This gave her a little flexibility if she found it necessary to hold invoices. Miller stated that these suppliers also served other colleges and were quite familiar with the inventory and revenue flows of college bookstores. They knew when and for how long they would have to wait for their money. Miller therefore never had any problem in this area.

Relationship with the College Administration

Miller felt that she had an excellent relationship with the administration and was well supported by both the office of Business and Finance and the Vice President of Academic Affairs. Her frustrations with the accounting systems of the business and finance office stemmed from the fact that the bookstore's accounting needs differed from most other operating units within the college. She also had always been able to talk to the Vice President of Academic Affairs and reach an agreement

EXHIBIT 21–4
Valdosta State College Bookstore Distribution of Revenues

Description	Amount ($000s)	Percentage of Total Budget
Cost of Goods Sold	1,332	74
Personnel	198	11
Direct Expenses	72	4
Plant Operations	36	2
Auxiliary Reserves	90	5
Net Profit	72	4
Total	1,800	100

when she'd had problems with the faculty over textbook orders. Miller felt that the primary problem was not between administration and the bookstore but rather that there was an inherent problem of a retail operation trying to function within an academic environment.

Analytical Problem

Tommye Miller contacted Dr. Smith, a marketing professor at VSC, and arranged for the VSC Bookstore to be a "live case" in his senior-level marketing management class. As one of Dr. Smith's top students, you have been assigned to handle the "case" and to provide consulting services to Miller. Prepare a written consulting report on the VSC Bookstore. Be sure to incorporate responses to the following questions in the report:

1. What do you consider to be the three most important problems/opportunities that Miller faces? What solutions would you recommend? Why?
2. Should the bookstore be able to initiate the same types of goals and rewards as a retail operation in a commercial environment?
3. Miller states that getting customers downstairs is a major problem. What suggestions do you have for her that would alleviate this problem?
4. Should the VSC Bookstore increase its advertising in the college newspaper next year?
5. What would be the overall effect of educating the student customer about the actual cost and profit basis of the bookstore operation?
6. Please evaluate the store's previous and its planned book buy-back policy.
7. How would you interpret the results of the summer quarter survey? How could the research design be improved?

PART SEVEN
Retail Price Management

CASE 22   **TOBY JUG:**
Setting Restaurant Prices

In 1972 four partners pooled their resources to purchase a 100-year-old wood-frame house and the adjoining property on Main Street in Danbury, Connecticut. The site was 1/4 mile from the center of town, close to a major highway that later became interstate Route 84 (see Exhibit 22–1). After extensive renovation, restoring the original yellow with black trim exterior, the house became the newly founded Toby Jug Restaurant.

The impetus to establish Toby Jug came from the success that two of the partners experienced with the King Neptune Seafood Restaurant in nearby Ridge-field. Located about 7 miles from Danbury, King Neptune had been in operation since 1946. Its good reputation and association with the newly opened Toby Jug contributed to the latter's quick acceptance.

From its inception, Toby Jug specialized in seafood, initially limiting its menu to five seafood and five nonseafood items. Over the years, as customers requested seafood entrees that were offered only at King Neptune, the Toby Jug menu was expanded to include these additional items.

In 1983, three of the partners worked at King Neptune while the fourth partner, Tom Smeriglio, managed Toby Jug. Separate books were kept for each establishment, but the restaurants did share some of the same suppliers as a means of achieving purchasing economies.

During the inflationary years preceding 1983, the costs of fish and other purchased foods had increased steadily. As Toby Jug's manager, Smeriglio found it necessary to raise his prices two or three times annually to maintain his margins. It was now time to print new menus and Smeriglio was seriously considering which items he should reprice and by how much.

Toby Jug had an image as a moderately priced casual seafood restaurant, serving a clientele of families and other diverse groups. Dinner customers included families, couples, and some business diners on weeknights. Occasionally, Toby Jug

---

This case was prepared by Professor Fred W. Kniffin and Harriet A. Allen of the University of Connecticut as a basis for class discussion rather than to illustrate either effective or ineffective handling of an administrative situation.

EXHIBIT 22–1
Toby Jug Map

catered parties of up to fifty-five persons in the front room; these parties were often business groups for dinner meetings or smaller groups of ten to thirty persons for lunches.

Smeriglio felt strongly that Toby Jug should remain primarily a seafood restaurant, because in his words, "that's what we're known for." To attract a luncheon trade, however, he realized that he had to offer a variety of sandwiches and non-seafood items.

A goal of Smeriglio's was to have a menu with "reasonable and fair prices," since he felt that the present clientele was "price sensitive." As evidence, he cited the fact that the restaurant often received telephone inquires as to the prices charged for certain items on the menu.

In 1982, annual gross sales of Toby Jug were between $500,000 and $550,000. For the same year, the gross profits were approximately $350,000 and the profit before taxes was 8 percent. Profitability depended, according to Smeriglio, on the proper combination of volume and pricing, and the correct management of waste, portion control, and purchasing. As for the pricing of food items, with which Smeriglio was not concerned, he stated, "We're probably not priced properly on some items. For instance, when we can't get a reasonable or full price for an item, we pick up the profit on other items." As an example, Smeriglio cited the sale of king crab dinners, which were now priced at $21.95 but which entailed a cost of $14.00 for only the meat portion of the dinner (see Exhibit 22–2). He stated that for king crab, if he charged what would cover total costs plus a reasonable profit margin, the price of the meal would be "ridiculous." However, because the most significant cost of the meal—the cost of the crab—showed no signs of going down, he had been gradually raising its price over the last few years, hoping to ease customers into accepting the price they should be paying. The possibility of eliminating king crab from the menu or decreasing the portion size was not considered, because as Smeriglio said, "We have always been known for our king crab dinners, as well as for the portion sizes of all our meals."

The types of food that could be served at Toby Jug were presently constrained by the restaurant's kitchen facilities, which were primarily geared to frying and broiling. Ninety-nine percent of the food was cooked to order, with only desserts, batters, and salad dressings made in advance. Smeriglio stated that numerous sauces or other intermediate preparations were not needed, because the type of food served was "simple food, simply prepared." Furthermore, any change in the kitchen would require considerable expenditures, for which the partners were not willing to commit funds at this time. Basically, Smeriglio wanted to continue to serve the same clientele with much the same type of food, yet improve his volume and profitability.

Currently, menu prices at Toby Jug were determined on a rule of thumb cost plus basis. In restaurants, according to Smeriglio "One should always recover from three to four times the food costs in the price of an item." Thus, the price for the scrod dinner for which the fish costs were $2.25 per pound would be calculated as follows:

$4.50 = 2 lbs. = 3 orders
$1.50 = meat cost for 1 order
  .30 = cost of roll, butter, salad (estimated)
$1.80 = total cost of food for 1 order

$1.80 × 3   = $5.40 = "too cheap"
$1.80 × 4   = $7.50 = "too expensive"
$1.80 × 3.5 = $6.30 = about right; Smeriglio rounded
     price to $6.10, which seemed to him more
     "reasonable."

Scrod dinner = $6.10 (see Exhibit 22–2)

Using this method of calculating prices, the price of some dinners covered close to four times the food costs, while others covered only about three times the food costs. Smeriglio stated, "I usually multiply higher-costing items, such as steak, by about 3, and lower costing items, such as hamburger, by about 4 when figuring my prices, to ensure that meals are neither exorbitantly priced nor underpriced." Also, he could adjust the calculated end price for a meal to create a more "reasonable" or "attractive" price for it, as in the scrod dinner.

Any Time From Our Bar **KING SIZE COCKTAIL**	**ALASKAN KING CRAB**	**TOBY PLATTER**	**SHRIMP SCAMPI**
Any **1.75** Cocktail Double **2.95** Does Not Include Special Brands or Extra Dry	Direct from cold Arctic waters. Giant points of delicious meat broiled in their own paper-thin shells. Served with drawn butter, potato, cole slaw or salad **21.95** Queen Size Portion ———	Worthy of the Captain's Table. A jumbo platter of fried Shrimp, Clams, Scallops, Sole and Onion Rings. Served with tartar sauce, potato, cole slaw or salad — **9.95**	POTATO SALAD OR COLE SLAW — **9.95** Inquire at desk concerning small banquet or dinner parties

APPETIZERS

Scampi	**4.25**
Shrimp Cocktail	**3.75**
Marinated Herring	**2.25**
Fruit Cup	**.95**
Tomato Juice	**.85**
Old Fashioned Clam Chowder	**2.25** bowl — **1.15** cup
New England Clam Chowder	**2.25** bowl — **1.15** cup

SERVED DURING LUNCH ONLY Mon. thru Sat.

Hot Pastrami	**3.25**
Hot Corned Beef	**3.25**
Hamburger	**2.35**
Roast Beef	**3.35**
Steak Sandwich	**4.75**
Boiled Ham	**2.75**
Boiled Ham & Swiss	**2.95**
Shrimp Salad Sandwich	**3.35**
Roast Beef, Swiss Cheese, Lettuce—Russian Dressing	**3.50**
White Meat Turkey	**2.95**
Turkey, Ham, Lettuce & Mayo	**3.35**
Chef Salad	**3.95**

Served With Potato Salad, Cole Slaw or Home Fries When Available

BROILED BEEF

Filet Mignon	**9.95**
N.Y. Strip Steak	**8.95**
Toby Steak	
Chopped Sirloin Steak	**4.25**

FRIED SEAFOOD

Ipswich Clams	**6.95**
Sea Scallops	**8.85**
Shrimp	**9.10**
Fish & Chips	**4.75**
Filet of Fish	**4.40**

BROILED SEAFOOD

Boston Scrod	**6.10**
Blue Fish	**5.85**
Flounder	**6.95**
Sea Scallops	**9.95**

All Dinners Served With Baked or French Fries and Salad or Cole Slaw

Garlic Bread	**1.25**
Gorgonzola Cheese Salad	**2.75**

OPEN FRIED SEAFOOD SANDWICHES

Clam	**3.95**
Shrimp	**4.65**
Sea Scallops	**4.25**
Fish	**2.95**

Served With French Fries and Slaw

Have a Platter of Crisp French Fried Onion Rings 1/2 Order **1.25** — Full Order **2.50**
One Entree For Two **1.50** Service Charge
WATER SERVED ON REQUEST ONLY

BEVERAGE

Coffee—Tea—Sanka—Milk	**.40**
Iced Tea or Coffee	**.60**

EXHIBIT 22–2
Toby Jug Menu, 1983

170

Smeriglio applied the three to four times food costs rule of thumb when calculating original prices for new items on the menu or for spot-checking existing prices when the food costs were fluctuating. Small amounts however (i.e., 15 cents, 20 cents, 35 cents), often were added to existing prices when the menu was reprinted to account for recent variations in the costs of food (see Exhibit 22–3). He arrived at these minor additions to existing prices intuitively. In this case the amount of the change was not the result of any calculation; rather, it was based on an intuition that a certain adjustment in price seemed reasonable in light of changing food costs. In some cases, he'd changed an item's price in this way several times, and several years may have elapsed since he'd applied the three to four times cost rule of thumb. In fact, looking back at his old menus, it was hard for Smeriglio to determine how often or when he'd applied the three to four times cost rule to any particular item (see Exhibits 22–2 to 22–4).

While the method of multiplying food costs by three to four was meant to ensure that total costs and profit were covered in the price of a meal, it was true that the proportion of food to labor costs of a meal varied. In general, lunch items involved proportionally higher labor costs to food costs than did dinner items.

Prices were displayed on the menu and its attachments (see Exhibits 22–3 and 22–4). Those items printed on the menu were always available, while items on the attachments usually were offered because a certain fish was in season.

"Specials" were advertised on a blackboard in the front foyer, and these reflected items available only that day. The blackboard also often included high priced items for which more preparation was required or dinners that included more extras. The typical price for a dinner listed on the blackboard was $9.95 and rarely exceeded $11.00.

Although Smeriglio was satisfied with Toby Jug's sales revenue, he was always interested in improving volume. In terms of potential, the restaurant could serve 300 meals in an afternoon or evening, assuming that slightly less than three times capacity was more realistic for dinners, since such a high turnover probably would not be attainable during weekday lunch hours. Currently, on an average Monday to Thursday weekday, between seventy-five and one hundred lunches and forty and sixty dinners were served. On Fridays and Saturdays, the average number of dinners served was between 175 and 200. Friday lunches averaged ninety to one hundred, while Saturday lunch volume usually dropped to about forty. Toby Jug was closed on Sundays.

Greater volume would neither necessitate hiring extra help nor incur higher overhead costs. Serving more meals, however, would result in the present kitchen staff putting in longer hours, at an average labor cost of $6.00 an hour. These costs, however, would be more than offset by the additional revenues generated. The average sale for a lunch meal was $7.50 including $1.50 for drinks, and the average dinner meal revenue was $13.50 including $2.50 for liquor.

Smeriglio rarely thought about the competition or even considered other restaurants to be his rivals because, "in this business, if you do things right it will pay off, but if you don't satisfy the customer, you'll lose money, regardless of the competition." Comparing Toby Jug prices with other restaurant prices was futile, since

NOT RESPONSIBLE FOR LOSS OR EXCHANGE OF PERSONAL PROPERTY

Any Time From Our Bar **KING SIZE COCKTAIL**	**ALASKAN KING CRAB**	**TOBY PLATTER**	**SHRIMP SCAMPI**
Any **1.55** Cocktail Double **2.60** Does Not Include Special Brands or Extra Dry	Direct from cold Arctic waters. Giant points of delicious meat broiled in their own paper-thin shells. Served with drawn butter, potato, cole slaw or salad **17.50** Queen Size Portion **11.75**	Worthy of the Captain's Table. A jumbo platter of fried Shrimp, Clams, Scallops, Sole and Onion Rings. Served with tartar sauce, potato, cole slaw or salad **9.75**	POTATO SALAD OR COLE SLAW **9.75** Inquire at desk concerning small banquet or dinner parties

APPETIZERS

Scampi	4.10
Shrimp Cocktail	3.50
Marinated Herring	2.25
Fruit Cup	.85
Tomato Juice	.85
Old Fashioned Clam Chowder	2.25 bowl — 1.15 cup
New England Clam Chowder	2.25 bowl — 1.15 cup

SERVED DURING LUNCH ONLY Mon. thru Sat.

Hot Pastrami	3.25
Hot Corned Beef	3.25
Hamburger	2.35
Roast Beef	3.35
Steak Sandwich	4.75
Boiled Ham	2.75
Boiled Ham & Swiss	2.95
Shrimp Salad Sandwich	3.35
Roast Beef, Swiss Cheese, Lettuce—Russian Dressing	3.50
White Meat Turkey	2.95
Turkey, Ham, Lettuce & Mayo	3.35
Chef Salad	3.95

Served With Potato Salad, Cole Slaw or Home Fries When Available

FRIED SEAFOOD SANDWICHES

Clam	3.85
Shrimp	4.25
Sea Scallops	4.00
Fish	2.95

Served With French Fries and Slaw

Have a Platter of Crisp French Fried Onion Rings 1/2 Order **1.25** — Full Order **2.50**
One Entree For Two **1.50** Service Charge
WATER SERVED ON REQUEST ONLY

BROILED BEEF

Filet Mignon	9.75
N.Y. Strip Steak	8.95
Toby Steak	4.25
Chopped Sirloin Steak	

FRIED SEAFOOD

Ipswich Clams	6.95
Sea Scallops	8.50
Shrimp	8.95
Fish & Chips	4.35
Filet of Fish	4.25

BROILED SEAFOOD

Boston Scrod	5.95
Blue Fish	5.65
Flounder	6.75
Sea Scallops	9.80

All Dinners Served With Baked or French Fries and Salad or Cole Slaw

Garlic Bread	1.25
Gorgonzola Cheese Salad	2.75

Bay Scallops	
FRIED	9.25
BROILED	10.25
BAKED or FRENCH FRIES SALAD or SLAW	
OPEN SANDWICH	
FRENCH FRIES & SLAW	

BEVERAGE

Coffee—Tea—Sanka—Milk	.40
Iced Tea or Coffee	.60

When Available — Broiled	
RED SNAPPER	11.50
STRIPED BASS	
SEA TROUT	6.25
SERVED WITH POTATO	

EXHIBIT 22–3
Toby Jug Menu, 1982

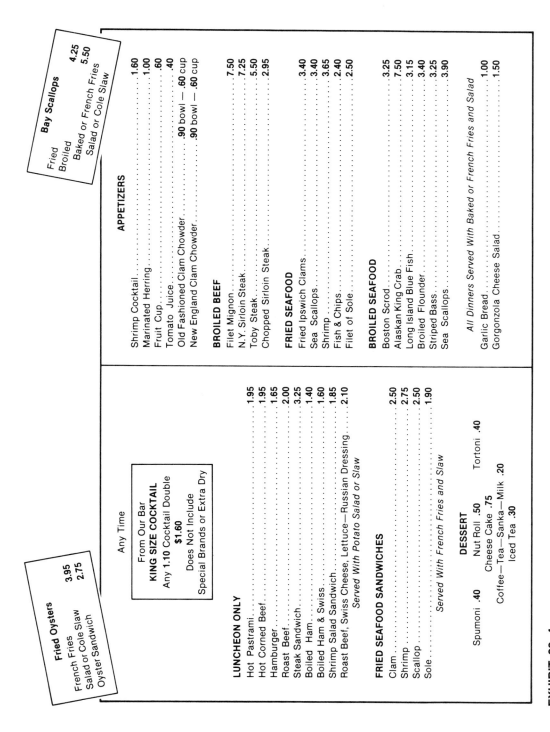

Bay Scallops
Fried 4.25
Broiled 5.50
Baked or French Fries
Salad or Cole Slaw

Fried Oysters
French Fries 3.95
Salad or Cole Slaw 2.75
Oyster Sandwich

APPETIZERS

Shrimp Cocktail 1.60
Marinated Herring 1.00
Fruit Cup .... .60
Tomato Juice .... .40
Old Fashioned Clam Chowder ... .90 bowl — .60 cup
New England Clam Chowder ..... .90 bowl — .60 cup

BROILED BEEF

Filet Mignon 7.50
N.Y. Sirloin Steak 7.25
Toby Steak 5.50
Chopped Sirloin Steak 2.95

FRIED SEAFOOD

Fried Ipswich Clams 3.40
Sea Scallops 3.40
Shrimp 3.65
Fish & Chips 2.40
Filet of Sole 2.50

BROILED SEAFOOD

Boston Scrod 3.25
Alaskan King Crab 7.50
Long Island Blue Fish 3.15
Broiled Flounder 3.40
Striped Bass 3.25
Sea Scallops 3.90

All Dinners Served With Baked or French Fries and Salad

Garlic Bread 1.00
Gorgonzola Cheese Salad 1.50

Any Time

From Our Bar
KING SIZE COCKTAIL
Any 1.10 Cocktail Double
$1.60
Does Not Include
Special Brands or Extra Dry

LUNCHEON ONLY

Hot Pastrami 1.95
Hot Corned Beef 1.95
Hamburger 1.65
Roast Beef 2.00
Steak Sandwich 3.25
Boiled Ham 1.40
Boiled Ham & Swiss 1.60
Shrimp Salad Sandwich 1.85
Roast Beef, Swiss Cheese, Lettuce—Russian Dressing ... 2.10
Served With Potato Salad or Slaw

FRIED SEAFOOD SANDWICHES

Clam 2.50
Shrimp 2.75
Scallop 2.50
Sole 1.90
Served With French Fries and Slaw

DESSERT

Spumoni .40   Nut Roll .50   Tortoni .40
Cheese Cake .75
Coffee—Tea—Sanka—Milk .20
Iced Tea .30

EXHIBIT 22-4
Toby Jug Menu, 1976

	(12-month) average cost of meat	Weight or size of one serving	Cost of meat/one serving	12-month average cost FF or potato and salad or cole slaw[a]	Total cost of food for meal	Preparation time	Total cost of meal
Shrimp	$6.95/lb.	9 shrimp	1 lb. = 26-30 shrimp 1 serving = $\frac{9}{28}$ × $6.95 = $2.233	$.30	$2.53	1½ hr to clean 25 lbs. 3.6 min. to clean 1 lb. 3.6 × $\frac{9}{28}$ = 1.16 min. to clean 1 serving Min prep. 8.0 T = 9.16 min.	
N.Y. Strip	$3.55/lb. before waste	approx. 12 oz.	1 strip = 12-13 steaks 1 strip = 14-16 lbs. 15 lbs. = 14 steaks 1.071428 × $3.55 = $3.80	$.30	$4.10	10 min.	
Blue Fish	$.90 whole 50% waste $1.80/lb.	10 oz.	$1.125	$.30	$1.425	10 min.	
Sea Scallops	$6.00/lb.	10 oz.	$3.75	$.30	$4.05	10 min.	
Chopped Steak	$1.70/lb	8 oz.	$.85	$.30	$1.15	10 min.	
Flounder							
Scrod							
etc.							

[a]12-month average costs: baked potato or FF, $.12 + salad or cole slaw, $.18 = $.30 total average cost.

EXHIBIT 22–5
Tom's Cost Worksheet

according to Smeriglio, it was like "comparing apples to oranges. You don't really know if they're serving the same amount or the same quality that you are."

New menus were printed at a cost of $100 when they were needed or whenever the menus got dirty and Smeriglio wanted to change some prices. Now he was preparing to change some prices and send the new menu to the printer. This time he thought he would give a more careful look at his costs, and he began with the worksheet shown in Exhibit 22–5.

Analytical Problem

Assume the role of a business consultant and advise Smeriglio on price strategy, menu preparation, and retail management.

ELEGANT INTERIORS:
Evaluating Price-Setting Methods and Policies

Elegant interiors, Inc., was a small interior design retailer located in Springdale, a small town in New England. The firm had six full-time employees (including the two owners/managers) and predicted a sales volume of almost $650,000 during fiscal 1984. Elegant Interiors was committed to a retail strategy of sales growth while maintaining its reputation as a status-oriented provider of upscale products such as furniture, floor and wall coverings, and accessories, as well as interior design services and advice of the highest caliber.

The operational mission of Elegant Interiors was to generate a reasonable rate of return and profit for its owners and to provide a revenue base capable of generating an income for its employees. The firm was particularly concerned about its image and made every effort to enhance the prestige of shopping at Elegant Interiors. It consciously practiced a "soft-sell" orientation to support other image-enhancement tactics.

Elegant Interiors had been in the same location since it was founded by the Robertson family in 1876. Although much of the historical information was no longer available, the store was believed to have begun as a general retail furniture store that primarily served Springdale (the county seat) and the rest of the county. Over the years, as population, demographics, transportation, and the structure of the regional economy changed, the retail store gradually expanded its geographic coverage and targeted its offerings more toward the "upper-end" of the market. In 1974, the firm changed ownership, and the store's name was changed from Robertson's Furniture to Elegant Interiors. This reflected the store's continuing interest in providing an even more complete range of professional services to customers through its increasing attention to interior design.

Structure and Personnel

When the company's ownership changed in 1974, Alan and Linda Swift acquired Robertson Furniture from Lois George in March of that year. In the five or so prior years, the store's sales and profitability had slumped badly. This was primarily due to some problems associated with absentee-ownership. The Swifts gradually made managerial and strategic changes and the company subsequently made considerable progress. Although 1982 was a disappointing year, much of this was explained by the economic environment.

Alan Swift was president of Elegant Interiors. He relied heavily on the expertise of his wife, Linda, and all of the other employees for conducting the company's operations. Everyone worked together, and Alan practiced a democratic decision-making and leadership style. This participative management approach was illustrated by the way Elegant Interiors formulated its promotional messages and made

This case was prepared by Joseph W. Leonard, Miami University, and Jon M. Hawes, University of Akron. Although the case is based on an actual retailer, names and certain facts have been disguised or altered.

buying decisions. Swift sought employee input through informal staff meetings and brainstorming sessions before making promotional, buying, and other important decisions. Although Swift retained ultimate authority and made the final decisions, the opinions of all employees were sought and considered.

Other information about company personnel is summarized in Exhibit 23–1.

Physical Facilities

Elegant Interiors, Inc., operated from a three-story building located on the square in Springdale. The building (owned by Linda and Alan Swift) was leased to the corporation. The 109-year-old building contained about 8,000 square feet of display area and another 2,000 square feet for storage and office use. Over the years, the building had been remodeled several times, most recently in 1981. The building was designed to display the staff's professional expertise through its various room setting displays (e.g., outdoor furniture, contemporary furniture, leather furniture, etc.). The building construction was typical of older buildings. The building was brick, with adequate utilities and an old (1891) elevator that barely continued to pass state inspection for use by the staff (not customers) only.

The company owned a large delivery truck, a van, a station wagon, a four-door sedan, and other general business necessities such as a typewriter, photocopy machine, and other office furnishings.

EXHIBIT 23–1
Personnel Fact Sheet

Years with Elegant Interiors	Name	Primary Duties	Education
11	Alan Swift (President)	General manager	B.A., 1966 Oklahoma City University (psychology); M.A., 1969 Boston University (sociology)
11	Linda Swift (Vice President)	Head designer and sales clerk	B.S., 1968 Boston University (interior design)
11	Jane Jones	Designer and sales clerk	B.S., 1971 University of Hartford (interior design)
5	Marilyn Carson	Designer and sales clerk	B.S., 1976 University of Vermont (interior design)
8	Jim Johnson	Delivery, drapery installation, general maintenance	High school graduate
6	Karen Grant	Secretarial, administrative, bookkeeping	High school graduate
4	Jeannine Wynnt (1/2 time)	Cleaning	High school graduate

Retail Strategy

Elegant Interiors sold high-quality furniture, floor and wall coverings, draperies, and accessory products to complement its residential interior design services. The firm also did some commercial business with banks, churches, and various professional offices, but over 85 percent of all sales were made in the retail market. Elegant's products were intended to appeal to the "high-end" and "near high-end" of the market. Special orders made up approximately 90 percent of sales. The average delivery time was about 30 days from receipt of the order but ranged from 3 to 8 weeks or more. The special-order orientation enabled Elegant Interiors to offer an extremely wide range and a very deep assortment of products to its customers.

Elegant Interiors advertised through several newspapers, the yellow pages, and direct mail. It also depended heavily on favorable word-of-mouth recommendations from satisfied customers. These previous customers also represented the retailer's best source of potential future sales. In the past, the company also advertised on local radio stations and employed the services of an advertising agency. The Swifts did not consider these to be cost effective, however, and dropped them.

In addition to the hometown newspaper, Elegant Interiors regularly advertised in nearby communities: *The Decatur Press* (a small town weekly newspaper), *The River City Palladium Item* (a daily publication), and the Newton News Examiner (daily except Sunday). The retailer usually advertised once a week in these three newspapers. Elegant Interiors promoted its direct (toll-free) telephone lines from Decatur and River City. It also had a small yellow pages ad under various listings in each of these community's telephone directories.

In addition, the retail firm maintained files on past clients and had developed a mailing list of about 3,350 names. Direct mailings were sent (bulk rate) about five times per year to each of these homes to promote the store's services and merchandise.

Like most other furniture retailers, Elegant Interiors had two peaks in sales each year. Before the mid-1970s, most retail furniture stores had sales volume peaks in February and in August. Since then, the two seasonal peak volume periods had spread out to January to February and to July to August. More recently, the seasonality of the industry had been even less well defined.

Unlike most retail furniture stores, where virtually every item appears to be "on sale" at all times, Elegant Interiors usually set prices based on the manufacturer's suggested retail price. For special-order merchandise, the following schedule normally was used:

Twenty-percent discount off the manufacturer's suggested retail price for orders above $650

Fifteen-percent discount on orders ranging from $500 to $650

No discount for orders under $500

In those rare cases when floor samples were sold, a flat 20-percent discount usually was provided to customers, regardless of the order's total price.

Elegant Interiors provided free delivery to customers living within 50 miles of the store. The state sales tax was collected on all in-state sales but waived for out-of-state deliveries. About 85 percent of the deliveries were made in the company's van with the large delivery truck used for the balance. Part-time delivery helpers were hired and paid on an hourly basis.

Elegant Interiors subcontracted the installation of its customer's carpeting to a reliable provider. Most customers assumed the installers were employed by Elegant Interiors. The fee was on a square-yard basis. Elegant Interiors did not, however, install wall coverings. Instead, it recommended individuals whom customers could contact directly.

About half of the store's sales included a complete set of some furniture grouping, such as an entire living room arrangement. A typical sale ranged from $1,000 to $5,000, but orders totaling $10,000 or more were not uncommon.

Typical payment terms required the customer to make a deposit of one third of the purchase price at the time the order was placed. The balance was billed shortly after delivery of the product. A "late payment" charge of 1½ percent per month was applied after 30 days. The retailer also accepted bank credit cards, but they seldom were used. Elegant Interiors had also recently worked out an agreement with the Farmer's Bank in Springdale for customer financing at competitive interest rates. Over the past several years, Elegant Interiors had virtually no losses from bad checks or nonpayment on its customer accounts.

Selling Style

Although the business used a variety of selling techniques to accommodate the diversity of customer needs served, perhaps the most frequent selling scenario can be described as follows.

A prospective client entered the store and was greeted by a designer/sales clerk. The client explained a need (perhaps to redecorate a room), and they discussed requirements and preferences for floor and wall coverings as well as furniture and accessories. The designer/sales clerk showed several available general alternatives and when necessary made an appointment for a home visit to further study the design problem and to make specific recommendations. After evaluating the home visit and/or the needs, the designer/sales clerk closed the sale. Sometimes this was done in the home; however, most often a follow-up appointment in the store was needed to present the design solution and close the sale.

Financial

Elegant Interiors maintained an inventory of about $220,000 (at cost). The company purchased most of its merchandise directly from the manufacturers, most of whom were located in the eastern half of the United States. It bought a small quantity of special-order merchandise from nondomestic sources. It bought nearly all its merchandise on a net 30-day basis. Although Elegant Interiors usually paid its bills when due, it did have a line of credit arranged through a local bank. Elegant Interiors paid all freight charges on its purchases, and these charges generally ranged from 7 to 11 percent of the cost for the merchandise. Other financial information is contained in Exhibit 23–2.

EXHIBIT 23–2
Income statement and balance sheet

	March 31, 1984, 9 months ($)	June 30, 1983 ($)	June 30, 1982 ($)	June 30, 1981 ($)	June 30, 1980 ($)	June 30, 1979 ($)
Income statement (short form)*						
Total sales	448,906	531,330	373,432	486,713	402,883	323,452
Cost of goods sold	244,887	281,837	185,028	279,528	205,070	170,925
Gross profits	204,019	249,494	188,405	207,185	197,814	152,527
Total operating expenses	180,535	203,772	196,564	189,659	174,352	122,074
Net income	23,483	45,721	(8,160)	17,526	23,462	30,453
Balance sheet (short form)						
Assets						
Cash and savings account(s)		6,038	4,012	28,376	(852)	2,747
Accounts receivable		25,338	14,663	28,297	44,300	35,150
Inventory		158,653	160,281	107,738	102,297	67,441
Other		1,500	1,200	1,364	5,320	2,300
Total current assets		191,528	180,126	165,811	151,065	107,637
Fixed assets		12,845	10,484	12,008	16,924	21,660
Total assets		204,373	190,609	177,819	167,988	129,297
Liabilities						
Accounts payable		18,462	19,203	11,970	9,833	13,606
Customer deposits		22,372	21,012	(3,161)	8,324	12,035
Notes payable		33,000	65,000	58,838	49,175	13,000
Other		6,250	6,629	8,646	3,693	809
Total current liabilities		80,085	111,843	76,292	71,025	39,451
Total liabilities		80,085	111,843	76,292	71,025	39,451
Capital						
Common stock		8,000	8,000	8,000	8,000	8,000
Retained earnings		70,567	78,926	75,999	65,502	68,295
Net profit/loss		45,721	(8,160)	17,526	23,462	13,552
Total capital		124,288	78,766	101,526	96,964	89,846
Total liabilities and capital		204,372	190,609	177,819	167,989	129,297

*Note: All income statements are for 12 months, except for 1984.

The Problem

Alan Swift was reconsidering Elegant Interiors's price strategy. Swift felt that the firm needed to continue to increase its sales volume to remain a viable organization. While considerable progress had been made, Swift wanted Elegant Interiors to increase its sales by 20 percent annually over each of the next 5 years. He thought that price strategy was a critical factor influencing sales volume.

The initial markup percentage in this industry was quite high. But while most other furniture retailers engage heavily in markdowns, Elegant Interiors seldom practiced this policy. Other than the previously mentioned discounts on special orders of more than $500 and floor samples, this firm based its prices on the manufacturer's suggested retail price with no plans for markdowns. In some cases, though, the store made modest price concessions to customers who argued that they could purchase the same item at another store for a lower price.

Swift evaluated a number of pricing alternatives that might help the store reach its sales volume objectives. First, Swift considered the greater use of price negotiation with clients. Since the firm was small and his two designer/sales clerks were paid a 20 percent commission based on the gross margin of their orders, he wondered if he should encourage his employees to vary prices when necessary to make the sale (subject to his approval).

Furthermore, Swift questioned whether Elegant Interiors should develop an enhanced markdown policy. This might involve setting an even higher initial retail selling price, but marking the somewhat inflated price down after a short period of time. Then, customers would think their purchases were made at special, "on-sale" prices. He was hesitant to do this, however.

Also, almost none of the previous advertising for Elegant Interiors had stressed prices. Instead, the ads stressed the full range of professional design services that Elegant Interiors provided to its customers. The ads were designed to enhance the prestige and status of shopping at the store. Swift questioned the wisdom of placing ads promoting reduced, "sale" prices on the store's products.

Swift was in doubt as to what strategies should be employed to achieve the firm's sales goals.

Analytical Problem

Assume that Alan Swift has hired you as a consultant. What would you suggest in terms of a pricing strategy? Provide him with at least three different price-setting and price-adjusting alternatives. Outline the pros and cons of those alternatives, and recommend one to Swift. Be sure to justify your recommendation. Keep in mind that your alternatives and recommendations should be appropriate to Swift's operation and the home decorating and furnishing industry.

ZIPCO DISCOUNT SALES:
Pricing Under Markup Constraints

Zipco was a national chain of discount stores with over 250 units in operation. Like most discount chains, Zipco was very promotional in character. It ran weekly advertisements, featuring savings on its already low prices, in the local newspapers of the cities it served.

In addition to these weekly traffic builders, Zipco had many special promotions. Almost every holiday was covered: Christmas and Easter, Washington's Birthday and Labor Day, Thanksgiving, and New Year's Day. Furthermore, special spring promotions were run by the garden shop, and the whole store participated in the back-to-school promotion. Preseason outerwear sales were run in July, and the linen and bedding departments ran January, May, and August "white" sales.

One of the very special and effective promotions by Zipco was its semi-annual Dollar Days sale, which was run for a week in February and again in August. Regular departments marked closeout and special items to even-dollar figures wherever possible. The closeouts represented the prior season's final clearance. The specials were not different from those run weekly except that the sale prices were usually set at even-dollar figures. Zipco, like most discount chains, had a central buying office. The company had over 100 buyers who purchased the merchandise, priced it, determined when specials would be featured, and worked with the company's advertising department in developing effective advertisements to be placed in local newspapers.

Dollar Days presented a unique problem for some of Zipco's buyers. Over the years, Zipco had often promoted some specially purchased items during Dollar Days. These items, not regularly carried in the Zipco units, were bought and shipped in just for the sale. They were featured in a full-color, eight- to ten-page supplement to local Sunday newspapers. While other items appeared in the supplement, the specially purchased items were the leaders and were offered at $1.00, $2.00, and $3.00 price points.

Value was stressed for these items, and fairly low markups on the retail base were used in pricing. However, the store did want to make some profit from selling the items. Therefore, it strived to buy items that, when sold at a particular price point, would yield a 21-percent markup on retail base.

Beginning in January, even before the February Dollar Days sale had begun, Zipco buyers were in the market searching for items to be sold during the August Dollar Days. The problem faced by the buyers was that the prices on the items that could be obtained in the market did not always yield a 21-percent markup when placed into the $1.00, $2.00, or $3.00 price lines.

Since the items usually sold out completely during the 7-day sale, the problem involved buying the right quantities (excessive quantities might not sell out during the sale period) of the various items offered by suppliers, so as to yield a 21-percent

This case is reprinted with permission from John S. Berens, *Contemporary Retailing: Cases from Today's Market Place*, 2d ed. (Danville, IL: Interstate Printers & Publishers, Inc., 1985), 153–156.

initial markup on the total *assortment* of the special purchase items offered for sale at *each* of the three price points ($1.00, $2.00, and $3.00). Ms. Wilma Chalmers was the housewares buyer for Zipco. Since most of the items that were placed in the sale at the various price points were housewares items, a major part of her job was to select the housewares items that would be featured by Zipco during Dollar Days.

Many different items were carried by a typical housewares department at Zipco. Examples included cooking pots and pans, flatware, cooking utensils, drinking glasses and pitchers, decorative canisters, plastic wares, ironing boards, small metal tables and cabinets, and closet accessories, such as garment bags and clothes hangers.

In buying for Dollar Days, Ms. Chalmers normally estimated just how much of an item she felt could be sold during the 7-day period by the "typical" or average Zipco store. Then, she multiplied that amount by the number of stores in the chain, projected by August to be 276 retail outlets.

Ms. Chalmers had to estimate how many items of a given manufacturer's line of plastic housewares to purchase for the Dollar Days sale. Although the items had differing costs, all of these had to be placed at the $1.00 price point. She now had to decide which specific items she should buy to come as close as possible to the 21-percent initial markup that management wanted to achieve on the sale of Dollar Day items. She did not want to greatly exceed 21 percent since this would degrade the quality of the assortment and reduce its promotional impact.

She was looking at the following items:

Item	Price per Gross	Unit Pack
Large pail	$125.00	2 gross
Small pail	$100.00	1 gross
Cutlery tray	$ 96.00	2 gross
Waste basket	$120.00	1 gross
Dish pan	$118.00	1 gross
Vegetable bin	$114.00	1 gross
Sink drainer set	$120.00	1 gross
Tool carry-all	$120.00	1 gross
Small pail and sponge set	$120.00	1 gross
Plastic broom	$128.00	1 gross
Dust pan and crumb tray set	$ 95.00	3 gross
Laundry basket	$120.00	1 gross

Ms. Chalmers wanted to carry at least five of the different items she was reviewing. She also felt that she should have a total of 14 gross of the plastic items for each store. (One gross represents 12 dozen or 144 products.)

She also wanted to be sure that there was one plastic pail item and a laundry basket in the assortment. Although she definitely would include the laundry basket, she was undecided about which pail to purchase. The large pail was the size usually used for household chores, but it had one of the highest prices in the assortment. The small pail would yield the greatest markup, but it was less desirable to house-holders. On the other hand, the pail and sponge set had added appeal. Its pail was small, but the large household sponge enclosed in the pail pack would give the customer added incentive to purchase the item. In her opinion the assortment would be strong if the plastic broom was included; however, because of its high cost, she had mixed feelings about buying it.

Ms. Chalmers had given the problem some thought and was now ready to write up her total order for August Dollar Days.

Analytical Problem

Assume that you are Ms. Chalmers, and write up the order. Explain your reasoning in a written report.

RICH'S DEPARTMENT STORE:
Developing an Effective Retail Advertising Strategy

The Executive Committee meeting had been a lengthy session, lasting through most of the morning, but Mr. Dick Mills, vice president and sales promotion director of Rich's Department Store, had returned to his office knowing that a major advertising decision was still not ready to be made. And Mr. Mills realized that it would be his responsibility to submit a final recommendation on media strategy at the next meeting.

Mr. Mills stared at the two neatly bound research reports that he had placed side by side on his desk. The pair of documents represented summaries of the two presentations that had been made to the Rich's Executive Committee that morning. These studies had been based on exactly the same data, drawn from the same in-store survey of Rich's customers. Each report had been prepared by an experienced and professional marketing researcher. Mr. Mills had expected the strong self-interests of the researchers to be reflected in their presentations and interpretations of the survey results, but he was confident that neither man would misrepresent the actual facts.

Mr. Mills had to admit to himself that he had been very surprised at the apparent major contradictions between the two presentations that he had heard earlier that morning. Mr. Mills and the research director of Rich's, who had also attended the morning presentations by the two outside researchers, had discussed the situation briefly after the meeting. The two men had decided to separately review the written reports and, then, to meet later in the afternoon to decide what additional steps to take.

Before rereading the reports, Mr. Mills thought back over the events of the past 3 months that had eventually led to this situation.

Rich's Department Store was both the largest merchant and the largest single advertiser in Atlanta, Georgia. The store had been founded in 1867 and had grown to an annual sales volume of approximately $200 million through its downtown store and six branch stores located in major suburban shopping centers. The Rich's market share was 40 percent of department store sales in Atlanta and 25 percent of all general merchandise sales.

The Rich's advertising strategy in the past had been to emphasize newspaper advertising for specific sales items and to utilize broadcast media primarily for image purposes. Newspaper was also used for some image-oriented advertising, with occasional direct mailings used to promote specific sales items of merchandise. Rich's is the largest local advertiser in both print and broadcast media.

The two principal daily newspapers in Atlanta are *The Atlanta Journal* (evenings) and the *Atlanta Constitution* (mornings). These are two of the largest circulation newspapers in the South, and both have distinguished journalism traditions, including Pulitzer Prizes. Although both newspapers are owned by the same company, Atlanta Newspapers, Inc., there is little overlap of readership except for the combined Sunday morning edition.

This case was prepared by Kenneth L. Bernhardt. Copyright © 1987, Kenneth L. Bernhardt.

There are six TV stations and forty radio stations in the Atlanta market. However, broadcast media are dominated by WSB-TV and WSB Radio, both of which are owned by Cox Broadcasting Corporation.

Mr. Mills recalled that several months earlier, executives of Cox Broadcasting and of their two local stations had met with key executives of Rich's. One topic discussed at that meeting had been possible use of broadcast media to promote individual sales items. WSB had offered to participate with Rich's in a market test to determine the abilities of different media to sell specific items of merchandise.

As a result of these discussions, Mr. Mills had held a series of meetings with Mr. Jim Landon, research director of WSB-TV and Radio, and Mr. Ferguson Rood, research director of the Atlanta Newspapers, Inc., to design the market test. It was eventually decided to conduct the test during Rich's annual Harvest Sale, which has been the merchandising highlight of the year since 1925. This sale runs for 2 weeks each fall. The test was to center on ten specific items of merchandise, which would be advertised in both print and broadcast media during the first 3 days of the sale. During this same period, in-store interviews would be conducted by professional interviewers, with all purchasers of these ten items in three representative stores (see [Appendixes 25–1 and 25–2 and Exhibits 25–1 to 25–19] for detailed survey design, sample questionnaire, and media plan).

At the conclusion of the survey period, the Research Departments of both Atlanta Newspapers, Inc., and WSB were furnished duplicate computer card decks [data files] by Rich's containing survey data. [These data] served as the basis for the presentations that Jim Landon and Ferguson Rood had made to the Rich's Executive Committee. Excerpts from *The Atlanta Journal* and *Constitution* report are in Appendix 25–1, and excerpts from the WSB report are presented in Appendix 25–2.

These were the two presentations that Mr. Mills would have to reconcile to arrive at a decision about future media strategy for Rich's. Mr. Mills knew that a decision would have to be made quickly, in view of TV production lead times, if any change in media mix were to be considered for the upcoming Christmas sales season.

Appendix 25–1
An Analysis of a Rich's In-Store Study of Advertising Effectiveness on Specific Purchase Decisions*

Foreword
This report is the result of an innovative research study conducted by Rich's Department Store in partnership with Atlanta Newspapers, Inc., and Cox Broadcasting Corporation.

The study was designed to measure:

1. The relative performance of newspapers, television, and radio as a source of influence on shoppers' decisions to purchase specific items.
2. Shoppers' exposure to specific item advertising messages.

---

*Presented by *The Atlanta Journal* and *Constitution* Research & Marketing Department.

The advertising period covered in this study consisted of three days (beginning Sunday, September 20) prior to Rich's annual Harvest Sale.

A total of 2,176 interviews were made on Monday and Tuesday, September 21 and 22. The interviews were made in three of Rich's seven stores—Downtown, Lenox Square, and Greenbriar, and focused on the ten departments in each store where the advertised items were sold.

An Atlanta interviewing firm was employed by Rich's to interview shoppers in each department immediately after they made their purchase. To qualify for the survey, shoppers had to purchase the specific advertised item or a directly related item.

Summary and Interpretation

More than nine out of ten shoppers covered in this survey had the specific purchase in mind before going to Rich's, or knew it was *on special.*

Three fourths of all shoppers recalled being recently exposed to advertising messages for specific items.

More than half of all shoppers' decisions to purchase specific items were attributed to advertising.

Attributions to newspapers were more than twice those of television and radio combined in influencing specific item purchase decisions (71 percent versus 33 percent).

Dollar for dollar . . . newspapers delivered more than three times the influence on specific item purchase decisions than television and radio combined.

The advertising schedule placed in newspapers . . . was conspicuously more effective and more efficient . . . in influencing specific purchase decisions . . . than the saturation schedule placed on television and radio.

Appendix 25–2

Analysis of Rich's In-Store Survey*

Introduction

First, we would like to state that WSB television and radio were pleased to have the opportunity to participate in this research effort with Rich's. We have one basic characteristic in common with Rich's—both WSB-TV and WSB Radio, like Rich's, are dominant in the Atlanta market. Like Rich's, we are an Atlanta institution and have enjoyed dominance since our origination.

In this presentation, we will not attempt to interpret the results of your research from a marketing standpoint. You have your own market research department, and we are sure that they have done a capable job of analyzing and interpreting the results of the study from that aspect. Instead, we will concentrate on interpreting the results from a media standpoint, which is our particular area of experience.

The following pages contain our detailed analysis of this research for Rich's management.

---

*Presented by WSB-TV, WSB Radio, and Cox Broadcasting Research.

(Appendix 25–2, continued)

EXHIBIT 25–1
Newspaper advertising
schedule*

	Sunday Journal and Constitution (Inches)	A.M. Constitution (Inches)	P.M. Journal (Inches)
Sunday	1,064		
Monday		172	247
Tuesday		0	505
Total	1,064	172	752

*1,989 column inches, the equivalent of 11.6 pages, made up the newspaper
schedule covered in this survey.

Pre-Harvest Sale Advertising Weight

Rich's Pre-Harvest Sale was heavily promoted with a "mix" of three media: radio,
TV, and newspaper.

On the broadcast side, Rich's ran 261 radio spots on five stations and 177 TV
spots on five stations promoting 10 different items during a three-day period. It
can be estimated that the total radio campaign reached about 90 percent of the
Atlanta adult metro population, with the average listener exposed to seven commercial announcements (all products combined). The total television campaign also
reached an estimated 90 percent of the Atlanta adult population, with the average
viewer exposed to 10 commercial announcements.

The newspaper campaign consisted of 13 ads for the specific items and 11
ads for related* items, or a total of 24 ads representing 1,987 inches of space in
the *Journal* and *Constitution.* Rich's also ran 6,140 inches of other newspaper advertising during the three-day period. We have no way of estimating the reach and
frequency of the newspaper ads.

Pre-Harvest Sale a Success

Rich's total advertising effort helped make the store's pre-Harvest Sale a tremendous success.

Monday, September 21, and Tuesday, September 22, were two of Rich's biggest days of the year according to traffic and sales volume. As far as we know,
the departments participating in the test were all up considerably in sales volume
compared to a year ago.

Unfortunately, sales results for the *specific items* tested were not available.
However, it is our understanding that the departmentwide sales results reflected the
success of the individual items in those departments that were tested.

The advertising effort for the pre-Harvest Sale represented one of the few
times that Rich's has used a media-mix for *item selling.* Radio and TV have been
used extensively by Rich's for institutional advertising and to announce sale events,

*Same item but different price than in the radio and TV commercial.

(Appendix 25–2, continued)

but item selling has been limited in the past primarily to newspaper and direct mail. *The media-mix for item selling worked from a sales results standpoint.*

Summary of Media Recall Findings

After analyzing the results of the survey, we found the following to be the most significant findings:

1. Because of the confusion and particularly the conditioning factor regarding newspaper, the three media cannot be completely compared in recall.
2. Recall for both radio and TV was significantly higher on Tuesday versus Monday, indicating that the broadcast media were building in impact on customers. Sales results were also generally better on Tuesday versus Monday.
3. Both radio and TV did *best* in recall (compared to newspaper) for items having the *least* amount of newspaper advertising. Radio and TV did *poorest* for items having the *greatest* amount of newspaper advertising.

EXHIBIT 25–2
Broadcast schedule*

	Television			Radio		
	Sunday	Monday	Tuesday	Sunday	Monday	Tuesday
6 A.M.		X			X	X
7		X			X	X
8		X	X		X	X
9		X	X		X	X
10		X		X	X	X
11		X			X	X
12		X	X	X	X	X
1 P.M.	X	X	X	X	X	X
2	X	X	X	X	X	X
3	X	X	X	X	X	X
4	X	X	X	X	X	X
5	X	X	X	X	X	X
6	X	X		X	X	
7	X	X		X	X	
8	X	X				
9	X	X				
10	X	X				
11	X	X				
Total spots	42	86	49	53	121	87
Average number per schedule hour	3.8	4.8	6.1	5.3	8.6	7.2

*438 30-second spots were scheduled to run on five television and five radio stations, for an average of 8 spots per hour, between 6 A.M. and 11 P.M., over the 3 day period.

(Appendix 25–2, continued)

4. In general, items where radio and TV did *best* in recall (compared to newspaper) had better sales results than items where radio and TV did poorest.
5. All three media performed better among high-priced items and for items where customers decided to buy before coming into the store.
6. Radio and TV balanced newspaper quite well by reaching younger adults than the print medium.

[See Exhibits 25–17 through 25–19.]

Three Types of Media Recall in the Study

The questionnaire used in Rich's in-store survey obtained information about customers' recall of advertising media in three areas:

1. Ideas to Buy

For customers purchasing the item being tested, those that indicated having in mind buying that specific merchandise before coming to the store were asked *what gave*

EXHIBIT 25–3
Comparison of advertising schedule and budget

	Broadcast spots			Newspaper Space (Inches)
	TV	Radio	Total	
Hard goods				
Mattress	12	19	31	35
Carpeting	12	23	35	150
Draperies	16	26	42	407
Vacuum sweeper	15	22	37	172
Color television*	0	0	0	150
Soft goods				
Handbags	15	27	42	189
Girdles†	15	27	42	0
Shoes	15	27	42	398
Shirts*	56	64	120	86
Pant suits	21	26	47	400
Total ten departments				
Sunday	42	53	95	1,064
Monday	86	121	207	420
Tuesday	49	87	136	505
Total	177	261	438	1,989
Budget			$27,158	$16,910

*The original broadcast schedule included twenty TV and twenty-four radio spots for the color television sets to run Tuesday. Since all the sets were sold on Monday, this commercial time was switched to shirts.

†While no Playtex girdle ads were scheduled to run in newspapers, other foundation advertising during the test period supported the influence.

(Appendix 25–2, continued)

them the idea to buy the item. In this question, answers involving media came from top-of-mind recall (not aided). Nonmedia answers to this question, such as "needed" item, "wanted" item or "had past experience" with item were accepted.

2. Learned of Special

Those customers who were aware of the store having a special on the specific item purchased were asked *where they learned about it.* In this question, answers involving media also came from top-of-mind recall and nonmedia responses such as "saw on display" or "friend told me" were accepted.

3. Direct Recall

Customers were also asked if they recalled seeing or hearing any advertising that may have reminded them or helped them decide to buy the specific item. If they answered in the affirmative, they were then asked *where they saw or heard it.* If radio, newspaper, TV, or mail circular were not mentioned by the respondent, they were also asked if they happened to hear a radio commercial, see a newspaper ad, and so on (aided recall). For purposes of analyzing the results, the unaided and aided answers to direct recall have been combined in this question.

EXHIBIT 25–4
Interviews

	Number	Percent
Total	2,175	100%
Women	1,764	81
Men	380	18
Couples	31	1
Under thirty-five	963	44
Thirty-five to forty-nine	817	38
Fifty and older	394	18
White	1,966	90
Nonwhite	209	10
Hard goods	527	24
Mattress	71	3
Carpeting	45	2
Draperies	123	6
Vacuum sweeper	134	6
Color television	154	7
Soft goods	1,649	75
Handbags	284	13
Girdles	249	11
Shoes	393	18
Shirts	483	22
Pant suits	240	11
Distribution of interviews by store		
Downtown	683	31
Lenox Square	848	39
Greenbriar	645	30

(Appendix 25–2, continued)

Effect of Confusion and "Conditioning"
First, we would like to emphasize three points that should be taken into consideration when evaluating each advertising medium's performance based on the recall results of the study:

1. Because of the heavy amount of Rich's advertising activity in all media during the three-day period of interviewing, there was a certain amount of confusion that occurred among the customer-respondents regarding where they saw or heard advertising. This fact will be documented in the pages to follow.
2. Because Rich's traditionally has done the vast majority of its *item* advertising in newspaper, customers are "conditioned" to this particular medium;

EXHIBIT 25–5

"Before coming to Rich's today, did you have in mind buying this specific brand/item, or did you decide after you came into the store?"
Sixty-three percent of all shoppers had the specific purchase in mind before going to Rich's.
These shoppers described the following as sources of influence on their buying decision when asked: "What was it that gave you the idea to buy this brand/item?"

Advertising	52%
Needed or wanted it	23
Past experience with it	16
Outside source suggestion	6
Other	7

EXHIBIT 25–6

"Was the store having a special on this specific brand/item today, or were they selling at the regular price?"
Eighty-four percent of all shoppers said the brand/item was on special.
These shoppers gave the following sources when asked: "Where did you learn about that?"

Advertising	63%
Store display/crowds	27
Outside source	6
Other	4

(Appendix 25–2, continued)
> i.e., more inclined to think of Rich's merchandise being advertised in a newspaper.
> 3. During the three-day period of the study, *other department stores* were also running *newspaper* ads for items similar to Rich's items being tested. Some newspaper ad recall in this study could have been due to confusion with other stores' ads.

These points can all be substantiated by the following results.

Only Slight Confusion for Radio Commercials
There were *no* radio commercials for color TV sets, since the spots were canceled before they were scheduled to run on Tuesday afternoon.
- 0%   Claimed they got the idea to buy a color TV set from radio commercials.
- 1%   Thought they learned of color TV sets being on sale from radio commercials.
- 2%   Said they recalled hearing radio commercials for color TV sets.

Only Slight Confusion for TV Commercials
There were *no* TV commercials for color TV sets, since the spots were canceled before they were scheduled to run on Tuesday afternoon.
- 0%   Claimed that they got the idea to buy a color TV set from TV commercials.
- 0%   Thought they learned of color TV sets on sale from TV commercials.
- 5%   Said they recalled seeing TV commercials for color TV sets.

EXHIBIT 25–7
Advertising influence

> Fifty-five percent of all shoppers attributed their specific purchase decision to advertising. Of these, 71% attributed their purchase to newspapers, 33% to broadcasts (28% to television and 9% to radio), and 9% to mail circulars.
>
> Newspapers and broadcast accounted for 94% of all advertising influence. Sixty-one percent of these influences were attributed to newspapers exclusive of broadcast. Twenty-three percent were attributed to broadcast exclusive of newspapers, and 10 percent were attributed to both.

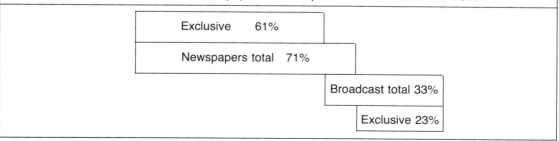

(Appendix 25–2, continued)
Some Confusion and "Conditioning" for Mail Circular
In the mail circular that Rich's distributed to its customers the week prior to the survey, there were *no* ads for any specific items, yet among the total sample of customer-respondents purchasing any of the eleven items tested:

- 3%   Claimed they got the idea to buy the specific item from a mail circular.
- 5%   Thought they learned of the specific item being on sale from a mail circular.
- 18%   Said they recalled seeing a mail circular for the specific item.

Greater Confusion and "Conditioning" for Newspaper Ads
There were *no* Rich's newspaper ads for Playtex girdles, yet:

- 12%   Claimed they got the idea to buy girdles from newspaper ads.
- 15%   Thought they learned of girdles being on sale from newspaper ads.
- 16%   Said they recalled seeing newspaper ads for girdles.

EXHIBIT 25–8
Advertising influence

Newspapers and television accounted for 90% of all advertising influence. Sixty-two percent of these influences were attributed to newspapers exclusive of television. Nineteen percent were attributed to television exclusive of newspapers, and 9% were attributed to both.

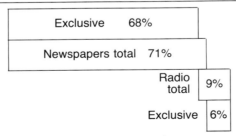

Newspapers and radio accounted for 77% of all advertising influence. Sixty-eight percent of these influences were attributed to newspapers exclusive of radio. Six percent were attributed to radio exclusive of newspapers, and 3% were attributed to both.

(Appendix 25–2, continued)

EXHIBIT 25–9
Advertising influence—by
shopper demographics
(among the 55 percent of all
shoppers who were influ-
enced by advertising)

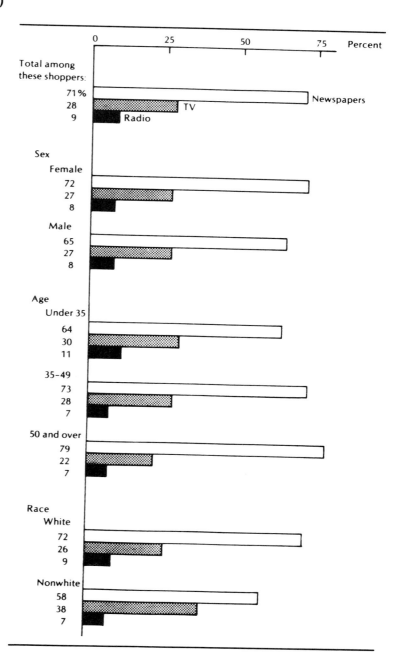

(Appendix 25–2, continued)

EXHIBIT 25–10
Advertising influence—by shopping patterns (among the 55 percent of all shoppers who were influenced by advertising)

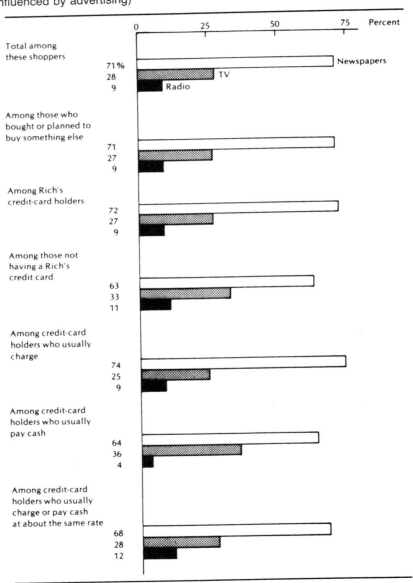

(Appendix 25–2, continued)

There were *no* Rich's newspaper ads for mattresses on either Sunday or Monday of the survey, yet among customers interviewed on Monday:

27%   Claimed they got the idea to buy a mattress from newspaper ads.
30%   Thought they learned of the mattress being on sale from newspaper ads.
49%   Said they recalled seeing newspaper ads for mattress.

Caution in Comparing Media by Recall!

As you can see, the extent of erroneous recall of newspaper advertising ranged from a low of 12 percent to a high of 49 percent. For this important reason, it is impossible to derive any accurate yardstick for measuring the separate value of each medium, dollar for dollar. In addition, these results cannot be converted to any type of advertising-to-sales ratio.

Radio May Have Been Higher with More WSB Spots

Due to the problem created by trying to find enough availabilities on WSB only in morning and evening drive time (because of the agency's buying criteria) to handle commercials for eleven different items in 3 days, Atlanta's dominant radio station was not able to contribute as much weight as it should have to most of the media schedules. As a result, a higher proportion of spots ran on WQXI (primarily teens), WAOK (primarily ethnic) and WRNG (primarily 50 + listeners), and WPLO (lower socioeconomic level). A brief analysis of the number of radio commercials that ran for each item, showing the light proportion of WSB spots, is shown in the accompanying table.

	Total Spots	WSB Spots	WSB morning Drive Spots*
Career shirts	48	10	0
Carpeting	23	6	3
Color TV	—	—	—
Draperies	26	7	2
Dress shirts	15	6	2
Girdles	27	5	1
Handbags	27	5	1
Mattresses	19	6	2
Pant suits	26	8	2
Shoes	27	6	2
Vacuum cleaner	22	5	2
Total	260	64	17

*Monday or Tuesday.

Television versus Newspaper

While TV budgets were fairly even, newspaper budgets ranged from $260 for mattresses up to $4,412 for draperies. TV versus newspaper performance in all RTH types of recall showed a good relationship to the amount of money spent in news-

(Appendix 25–2, continued)
paper. The smaller the newspaper budget versus TV, the better TV performed versus newspaper in recall, and vice versa:

1. TV did *best* in all types of recall *compared to newspaper* for mattresses, career shirts, and vacuum cleaners. These items had the *smallest amount* of advertising space in the newspaper compared to the others.
2. TV did *poorest* in all types of recall *compared to newspaper* for draperies, pant suits, shoes, and carpeting. These items had the *greater amount* of advertising space in the newspaper.

Radio versus Newspaper
Again, radio budgets were fairly even compared to the wide range in newspaper budgets. Radio versus newspaper performance in all types of recall also showed a fairly strong relationship to the amount of money spent in newspaper. The smaller the newspaper budget versus radio, the better radio performed versus newspaper in recall, and vice versa:

1. Radio did *best* in all types of recall *compared to newspaper* for mattresses, vacuum cleaners, and career shirts. These items generally had the least newspaper space.
2. Radio did *poorest* in all types of recall *compared to newspaper* for draperies, pant suits, and handbags. These items generally had the greatest newspaper space.

EXHIBIT 25–11
Share of budget versus share of influence

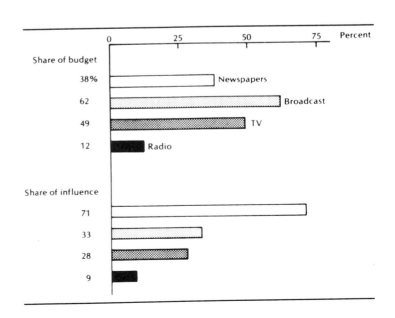

(Appendix 25–2, continued)

Less Newspaper Space—No Harm to Sales Volume
We have just indicated that, as newspaper space was reduced, both radio and TV
did better in recall.
How about Rich's Sales volume?
There appeared to be little, if any, correlation between the amount of newspaper
space and sales volume as measured by department sales increases. If anything,
the reverse occurred:

	Monday	Tuesday
TV and radio did best (least newspaper space)		
Girdles	+7%	+92%
Career shirts	+151	+349
Mattresses	+43	+76
Vacuum cleaners	+98	+222
TV and radio did poorest (most newspaper space)		
Draperies	−0	+9
Pant suits	+17	+46
Shoes	−19	+14
Carpeting	−9	+526

EXHIBIT 25–12
Newspaper/broadcast—share of influence versus share of budget by departments

	Newspapers		Broadcast	
	Share of Influence	Share of Budget	Share of Influence	Share of Budget
Total	71%	38%	33%	62%
Hard goods	77	45	30	55
Mattress	43	11	69	89
Carpeting	83	39	23	61
Draperies	83	56	22	44
Vacuum sweeper	70	25	45	75
Color TV	99	100	1	—
Soft goods	68	34	34	66
Handbags	68	41	27	59
Girdles	28	—	74	100
Shoes	87	54	25	46
Shirts	63	12	36	88
Pant suits	82	53	16	47

(Appendix 25–2, continued)

Idea to Buy versus Direct Recall
One probable indication of the "conditioning" of Rich's customers to newspaper advertising comes from comparing initial "idea to buy" recall, where media responses came purely from top of mind, to the direct recall that came later in the interview, concentrating on each medium. All three media gained in regard to the proportion of customers recalling (from idea to buy to direct recall), but newspaper, having been recalled more from top of mind, gained the least, while TV and especially radio, in the background during top of mind "idea to buy," came to the surface more in the direct recall.

	Average Recall, All Items*		
	Idea to Buy	Direct Recall	Percent increase
Newspaper	42%	64%	+52%
TV	16	36	+125
Radio	5	16	+220

*Girdles were eliminated for newspaper, and color TV sets were eliminated for radio and TV because of no advertising.

First-Day versus Second-Day Recall
Analysis of the direct recall results by day of interview produced an interesting fact. The impact of newspaper was initial, while both radio and TV performed significantly better on the second day. This is probably due to the nature of the broadcast

EXHIBIT 25–13
Comparison of advertising schedule/budget/shopper influence*

	Total Ten Departments				
	Broadcast Spots		Newspaper Space		
	TV	Radio	Journal— Constitution	Constitution	Journal
Schedule					
Sunday	42	53	1,064		
Monday	86	121		172	248
Tuesday	49	87		0	505
	177	261	1,064	172	753

*Four hundred thirty-eight broadcast spots versus 1,989 inches; budget—$27,158 for broadcast spots versus $16,910 for newspaper space; and shopper influence—33% for broadcast spots versus 71% for newspaper space.

(Appendix 25–2, continued)

media, which gain impact and effectiveness with *increased frequency* (as listeners and viewers are exposed to more commercials). In addition, sales results for all items were generally better on Tuesday than on Monday, compared to a year ago. This also indicates that, if spots had been spread more evenly over Sunday, Monday, and Tuesday (rather than concentrated on Sunday and Monday in most cases), and if interviewing had been extended through Wednesday, both radio and TV would have performed better in recall, at no increase in budget for either medium.

	Average Recall, All Items*		Tuesday Percent Difference
Newspaper	66%	62%	−6%
TV	33	38	+15
Radio	13	18	+38

*Mattresses were eliminated for newspaper as an invalid comparison, since there were no ads on Sunday or Monday. However, even though there were no radio or TV commercials for career shirts on Sunday or Monday, and no newspaper ads at all, this item was included in this comparison because there was advertising for dress shirts, a related item. Also, girdles were eliminated for newspaper and color TV for radio and TV because of no advertising.

EXHIBIT 25–14
Advertising exposure

Seventy-four percent of all shoppers recalled being exposed to specific advertising messages within the past day or two. Of these, 79% recalled newspapers, 53% recalled broadcasts (46% television, 18% radio), and 24% recalled mail circulars.

Newspapers and broadcast accounted for 96% of all advertising messages. Forty-three percent recalled newspapers exclusive of broadcast. Seventeen percent recalled broadcast exclusive of newspapers, and 36% recalled both.

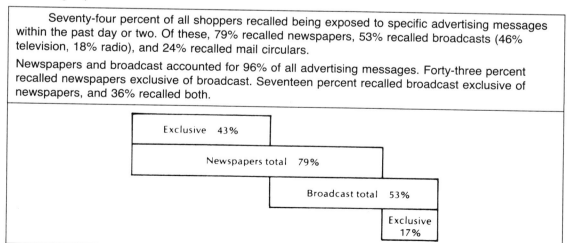

(Appendix 25–2, continued)

High-Priced versus Low-Priced Items
In order to analyze media performance by item *price range,* the items were divided into either a high-price (carpeting, color TV, draperies, mattresses, and vacuum cleaners) or a low-price (career shirts, dress shirts, girdles, handbags, pant suits, and shoes) group. All three media performed better among high-priced items compared to low-priced merchandise, especially radio and TV. However, the differences were greater regarding "idea to buy" recall and "learned of special" recall than with the direct recall. Customers who had made up their minds to buy a large-ticket item were apparently more persuaded by advertising than those coming to Rich's for lower-priced merchandise. However, whether in the market for high- or low-priced items, both type customers were exposed to advertising, as indicated in the direct recall.

	High-Priced Items	Low-Priced Items	High-Priced Percent Difference
Idea to buy			
Newspaper	47%	37%	+27%
TV	20	14	+43
Radio	7	3	+133
Learned of special			
Newspaper	60	42	+43
TV	28	16	+75
Radio	10	5	+100
Direct recall			
Newspaper	69	59	+17
TV	39	34	+15
Radio	18	14	+29

"Had in Mind" versus "Decided in Store"
In order to analyze media performance by the extent to which customers had in mind to buy the item before coming to the store, the items were divided into two groups: "had in mind" and "decided in store," based on results to the question covering this aspect of purchasing. The four items where roughly half of the customers indicated deciding in the store (pant suits, dress shirts, career shirts, and handbags) were placed in the "decided in store" group. The other seven items, where significantly less customers indicated deciding in store, were placed in the "had in mind" group. All three media performed significantly better among items in the "had in mind" group, that is, for items where a greater proportion of customers made their decision in advance. The differences were greater regarding "idea to buy" and "learned of special" recall than with the direct recall.

(Appendix 25–2, continued)

	"Had in Mind" Items	"Decided in Store" Items	"Had in Mind" Percent Difference
Idea to buy			
Newspaper	48%	35%	+37%
TV	19	12	+58
Radio	6	2	+200
Learned of special			
Newspaper	59	38	+55
TV	26	13	+100
Radio	9	4	+125
Direct recall			
Newspaper	70	56	+25
TV	38	32	+19
Radio	16	15	+7

Broadcast Media Recall Reflected Younger Adults
By analyzing media recall by age of customer, it was determined that radio and TV balanced newspaper quite well by reaching younger adults. In all three types of recall, the under-35 age group was proportionately higher for broadcast, especially radio, than for newspaper. These figures are based on all items combined.

Age	Radio	TV	Newspaper
Got idea			
Under 35	56%	44%	36%
35–49	31	38	44
50 and over	13	18	20
Learned of special			
Under 35	50	43	36
35–49	34	41	41
50 and over	16	16	23
Direct recall			
Under 35	49	44	41
35–49	33	38	41
50 and over	18	18	18

Note: Read table. Of those customers indicating that they "got the idea" to buy an item from radio commercials, 56% were in the under-35 age group.

(Appendix 25–2, continued)

Rich's Dominant Position in Atlanta
In concluding this presentation, we would like to announce the results of separate research that we have just completed that indicates the extent to which Rich's dominates the department store market in Atlanta, a domination that we feel is due to:

- ☐ Outstanding management.
- ☐ Quality of merchandise.
- ☐ Attention to customer service and satisfaction.
- ☐ Efficient use of advertising and promotion, *especially the use of a media mix.*

EXHIBIT 25–15
Advertising exposure

Newspapers and television accounted for 93% of all advertising messages. Forty-seven percent recalled newspapers exclusive of television. Fourteen percent recalled television exclusive of newspapers, and 32% recalled both.

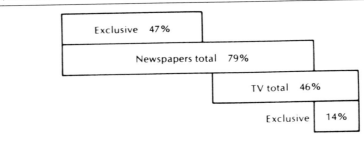

Newspapers and radio accounted for 85% of all advertising messages. Sixty-seven percent recalled newspapers exclusive of radio. Six percent recalled radio exclusive of newspapers, and 12% recalled both.

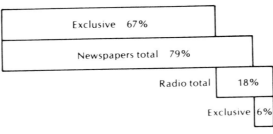

EXHIBIT 25–16
Customer Survey

Questionnaire   HARVEST SALE IN-STORE CUSTOMER SURVEY

Interviewer Name: _____ (1-2)   STORE:. . . . . . Downtown. . . . . Lenox. . . . Greenbriar   (3)
                                                       1   2   3

DATE: M   T   W   TIME OF INTERVIEW: _____   DEPARTMENT: _____   (6)
         1   2   3 (4)   (5)

Hello. We're conducting a short survey among RICH'S customers:

1.   What did you happen to buy in this department today? _____
                                        (PROBE, BRAND, STYLE)
                                                                    (7-8)

2.   Before coming to RICH'S today, did you have in mind buying this specific brand/item, or did you decide after you came into the store?

         HAD IN MIND. . . . ( ) 1   DECIDED IN STORE. . . . . ( ) 2   SKIP TO Q. #3   (9)

         What was it that gave you the
         idea to buy this brand/item? _____

         (IF APPROPRIATE, ASK: Where did you learn about that?) _____

                                                                     (10-11)

3.   Was the store having a special on this specific brand/item today, or were they selling at the regular price?

         SPECIAL. . . . . . ( ) 1   REGULAR PRICE. . . . . . ( ) 2   SKIP TO Q. #4   (12)

         Where did you learn about that? _____

                                                                     (13-14)

4.   Do you recall seeing or hearing any advertising within the past day or two on radio or television or in the newspapers or in a mail circular that may have reminded you or helped you decide to buy this _____ today?

         YES. . . . . ( ) 1   NO. . . . . ( ) 2   SKIP TO Q. #5   (15)

         a. Where did you see or hear it? _____   (16)

	4a. UNAIDED RECALL	5. AIDED RECALL		
		YES	NO, DK	
RADIO.	1	1	2	(17)
NEWSPAPERS	2	1	2	(18)
TELEVISION.	3	1.	2	(19)
MAIL CIRCULAR	4	1	2	(20)
OTHER, DON'T KNOW	5			

ASK FOR EACH MEDIUM NOT CHECKED IN Q. #4a.

5.   Did you happen to see or hear any of the following within the past day or two:
A radio commercial for this specific _____? A newspaper ad for this specific _____? A television commercial for this specific _____? A mail circular for this specific _____? _____

6.   Have you bought anything else at RICH'S today, or do you plan to buy anything else at RICH'S today?

         YES. . . . . ( ) 1   NO. . . . . ( ) 2

7.   Do you (or your wife/husband) have a RICH'S credit card?

         YES. . . . . ( ) 1   NO. . . . . ( ) 2   (21)
                                                                    (22)

         a. Do you usually charge or pay cash for most of your purchases at RICH'S?

         CHARGE . . . . ( ) 1   CASH. . . . . ( ) 2   SAME. . . . . ( ) 3   (23)

8.   What is the name of the county where you live? _____   OUT-OF-STATE . . ( )   (24-25-26)

ESTIMATE AGE: UNDER 35 YEARS. . ( ) 1   SEX: FEMALE . . . ( ) 1   RACE: WHITE . . . . ( ) 1   (27)
                 35 - 49 . . . . ( ) 2   MALE . . . . ( ) 2   NON WHITE. ( ) 2   (28)
                 50+ . . . . ( ) 3   (29)

(Appendix 25–2, continued)

Presentation Summary

1. With use of media mix for item selling, the pre-Harvest Sale was a success. All departments participating in the test were up in sales volume.
2. Because of confusion and conditioning factors, recall results are not completely comparable between media.
3. In general, as the amount of newspaper space was reduced, the proportion of recall for both TV and radio was increased, and sales results were generally more favorable.
4. Sales volume was up significantly on Tuesday versus Monday in all departments, indicating a relationship with broadcast media recall, also up significantly on Tuesday as frequency increases.
5. All media had higher recall for higher-priced items and items where customer generally decided in advance.
6. Separate research confirms Rich's dominance of the Atlanta market, especially versus Davisons. Rich's uses radio and TV effectively, Davison's uses very little broadcast media.

EXHIBIT 25–17
Summary of newspaper recall

Item	Budget	Day/Ads	Got Idea	Learned of Special	Direct Recall
Draperies	$4,412	Sun.-2, Tues.-2	48%	68%	81%
Pant suits	3,359	Sun.-2, Mon.-1, Tues.-3	50	56	63
Shoes	2,834	Sun.-1, Mon.-2, Tues.-1	48	55	72
Handbags	1,670	Sun.-1, Tues.-1	30	30	60
Carpeting	1,503	Sun.-1	61	63	80
Color TV	1,503	Sun.-1	62	68	66
Dress shirts	859	Sun.-1	40	40	54
Vacuum cleaner	780	Mon.-4	36	62	64
Mattresses	260	Tues.-1	30	37	54
Career shirts	—	—	19	27	45
Girdles	—	—	12	15	16
Averages, all items*			42	51	64

*Excludes girdles (no ads), but includes career shirts because of ads for dress shirts, a related item.

(Appendix 25–2, continued)

EXHIBIT 25–18
Summary of television recall

Item	Budget	Adult Audience (000)	Got Idea	Learned of Special	Direct Recall
Career shirts	$2,998	1,373.4	15%	16%	27%
Draperies	2,714	776.5	11	15	37
Pant suits	2,494	885.4	8	9	39
Playtex girdles	2,364	752.1	25	34	32
Dress shirts	2,028	824.8	16	16	29
Handbags	1,922	649.2	10	10	34
Shoes	1,909	724.7	11	14	41
Vacuum cleaner	1,867	627.4	19	36	42
Carpeting	1,790	624.5	8	12	29
Mattresses	1,627	691.9	40	48	49
Color TV	—	—	0	0	5
Averages, all items*			16	21	36

*Excludes color TV (no commercials).

EXHIBIT 25–19
Summary of radio recall

Item	Budget	Adult Audience (000)	Got Idea	Learned of Special	Direct recall
Career shirts	$903	489.1	2%	6%	17%
Draperies	560	654.3	1	2	8
Shoes	544	566.8	5	6	14
Pant suits	539	633.9	1	2	12
Carpeting	513	590.9	8	7	24
Dress shirts	498	496.4	4	5	12
Girdles	482	553.0	6	9	11
Mattresses	477	527.6	11	23	29
Handbags	476	475.1	2	3	20
Vacuum cleaner	453	482.1	7	8	10
Color TV	—	374.2	—	1	2
Averages, all items*			5	7	16

*Excludes color TV (no commercials).

CASE 26 COLUMBIA FURNITURE COMPANY:
Analysis of Retail Salesmanship

The Columbia Furniture Company is located in a large southwestern city. It is a retail chain consisting of ten units located both in the downtown area and in surrounding suburbs. Sales growth has continued to be satisfactory, although market share has begun to slump. Alarmed about this situation, management retained a consulting firm to analyze company operations and to determine where changes might be required.

Problem

Detailed analysis showed most aspects of company operations to be excellent. There was cause for concern, however, over the performance of the sales force. Sales volume per employee was relatively high, and turnover was low; yet, there were definite signs of customer alienation caused by a lack of sales force efforts to build future patronage through an attitude of genuine helpfulness. In other words, making the sale is only one aspect of the total job a salesman is expected to perform.

It became apparent that data were needed on salesmen's performance, using criteria other than sales volume and observation by management. Therefore, a two-phase study was undertaken. Phase One concentrated on the entire sales force and generated a rating of total performance for each member. Phase Two consisted of a further analysis of sales performance in the Country Fair store, the largest unit in the chain. This unit, in turn, was the center of most customer complaints and thus warranted further study in order to identify the problems. Each of these phases is discussed below.

Phase One

Salesmanship was defined for purposes of this study as "showing people how they can satisfy their needs, wants, or desires through the purchase of goods or services." It must clearly be distinguished from *order taking*, in which the salesman often makes no effort to convert a prospect into a customer.

Salesmanship can be detected only imperfectly from sales records, and a specific methodology was needed to analyze salesmanship with a sufficient degree of accuracy. Indeed, a proper evaluation can only be made in terms of whether or not the salesman has convinced the shopper that his needs can be satisfied through purchase. Thus, in this study, the evaluation of salesmanship was made by people who acted the part of prospective customers.

This case is reprinted with permission from James F. Engel and W. Wayne Talarzyk, *Cases in Promotional Strategy*, rev. ed. © RICHARD D. IRWIN, INC., 1971 and 1984. (Homewood, IL: Richard D. Irwin, Inc., 1984), 215–222.

Methodology

A number of young adults were trained to perform the role of active shoppers, and six different selling situations were utilized.

1. A young couple tells the salesman they are going to be married in a few months and that they will want to purchase furniture at that time. At the present, they are only looking for ideas.
2. A person tells the salesman that he wished to furnish a specific room in his house.
3. A person explains to the salesman that he is confused concerning different styles of furniture.
4. A customer does not realize that he is having difficulty in choosing attractive color combinations.
5. A couple states that they are just looking around to get ideas, and they become upset when a salesman tries to inject comments.
6. A customer keeps dickering on the price.
7. A husband and wife have differing tastes in furniture. What appeals to one is not pleasing to the other.

No individual salesman received more than six of the seven situations on the above list.

Each salesman was approached at least several times for purposes of evaluation. The person doing the evaluation carried a hidden tape recorder and filled out a detailed questionnaire covering the following items:

1. Appearance
   a. Clothing
   b. Hair
   c. Personal hygiene
   d. Posture
   e. Other factors
2. Personality
   a. Courtesy and so forth
   b. Ability to make customer feel at ease
   c. Other noticeable traits
3. Enthusiasm
   a. Speed of approach
   b. Interest shown in being of help
      i. Questions to explore needs
      ii. Attempts to get into the home
      iii. Suggestions
      iv. Use of imagination
   c. Control of enthusiasm
   d. "Romanticizing" furniture

4. Product knowledge
   a. Explanation of construction and so forth
   b. Visualization of needs and good suggestions
   c. Explanation of styles
   d. Justification of price differentials
   e. Explanation of warranty
   f. Other related points
5. Human relations
   a. Use of tact
   b. Ability to make customer feel he made the decisions
   c. Creation of impression that "customer is king"
6. Selling ability
   a. Ability to "get in" with prospect
   b. Development of shopper into prospect
7. Contribution to the store
   a. Conveying good store image
   b. Attempts to encourage return visits and future sales
   c. Thorough explanation of management policies.

The shoppers rated the salesman on each point using a scale ranging from 1 (excellent) to 9 (poor). The sales volume record of each salesman was later evaluated by company management using the same scale so that comparisons could be made between volume and customer ratings of salesmanship.

The accuracy of the shoppers' ratings was evaluated through use of a hidden tape recorder. This recorder was built into a handbag carried by the shopper, and an objective record was thereby provided. With few exceptions, the accuracy of shoppers' evaluations was verified.

Data were analyzed by computing an average evaluation score along each criterion for each salesman. These data are graphically presented later in this report.

The majority of the salesmen also were later interviewed by one of the investigators. Fourteen selling situations were listed, and the salesman was asked how he would handle each situation. Company management previously had determined the proper response, and the answers given were rated from 1 to 9 in terms of the degree to which the answer correctly reflected company policy and procedures. This rating is referred to as "expected performance."

In summary, the following information was collected: (1) a rating of salesmanship performance, (2) a rating of "expected" performance on fourteen selling situations (collected only for a smaller sample of salesmen), and (3) a rating of sales volume.

Data Analysis
Only certain highlights of the findings are given in this section. Two summary figures have been prepared, and they provide a graphic indication of the results. [In Exhibit 26–1,] salesmen are listed in terms of sales rank. Sales performance is graphed by the dotted line. Also, an average salesmanship rating was computed for each sales-

man using the arithmetic mean of ratings given by prospects on appearance, personality, enthusiasm, product knowledge, human relations, selling ability, and contribution to the store. Thus, sales volume and salesmanship, as measured in this study, may be compared at a glance.

It will be noticed that the salesmanship performance, on the average, is quite good. In fact, the average score for all salesmen is 3—an unusually high rating. This provides a definite indication that salesmanship is sufficiently high to verify that

EXHIBIT 26–1

A Graphic Comparison of Salesmanship and Sales Volume

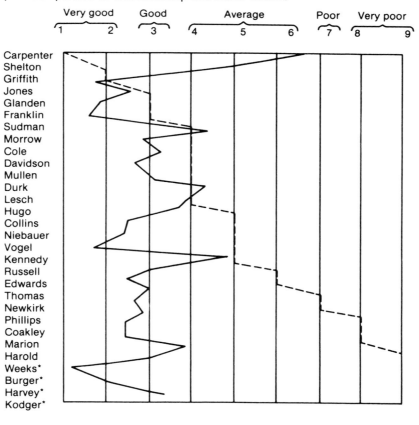

*No sales rating

―――――― Salesmanship

- - - - - -Sales volume

training is being reflected, for the most part, in performance. There are some low ratings, however, and comments on individuals appear in the next section.

[Exhibit 26–2] provides a sharper measure of sales performance. A review of the data disclosed that enthusiasm, product knowledge, and selling ability proved to be the most meaningful ratings provided by shoppers. Thus, the average score for each salesman on these dimensions was plotted graphically. Once again, salesmen are listed in the order of their sales rank.

Notice that, with the exception of Carpenter and Shelton, high-volume salesmen tend to receive the highest ratings on these three criteria. In turn, the low-volume salesmen also have excellent ratings. The lowest ratings, on the average,

EXHIBIT 26–2
A Graphic Comparison of Enthusiasm, Product Knowledge, and Rated Selling Ability

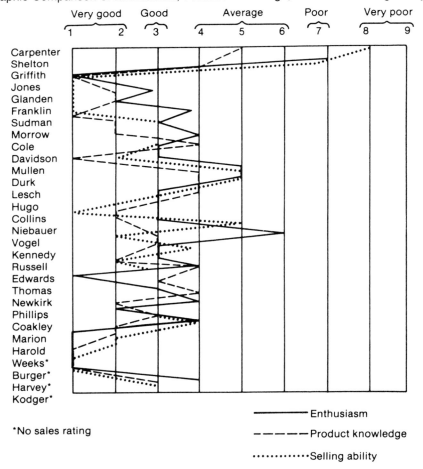

*No sales rating

———————Enthusiasm

— — — — —Product knowledge

············Selling ability

are earned by the middle-ranking salesmen, although in few cases are ratings sufficiently low to be of any real concern. The interesting conclusion from this analysis is that the low-volume salesmen may be spending so much time in helping prospects that they are failing to convert them into buyers. In analysis of certain individuals, this tendency seems to be quite apparent.

It is very clear to the investigators that appearance is not a factor that weighs strongly in the prospect's mind. In many instances, the appearance of those rating highest in salesmenship was not felt to be especially good.

It also should be pointed out that salesmen's responses to the fourteen-item questionnaire were, for the most part, excellent. The action they say they would take in each situation closely parallels that specified by management.

There are several implications for sales training that should be noted briefly here. First, enthusiasm and interest in the shopper are the most valued behavior as stated by prospects. If this enthusiasm and level of interest is high, then the prospect, in all probability, will have a high opinion of Columbia as a place to shop and buy. Product knowledge also weighs heavily, and it cannot be emphasized too strongly that the shopper is looking for reasons to buy. If this information is not volunteered by the salesman, the salesmanship rating tends to suffer.

Phase Two

The first phase of this project focused on the manner in which individual salesmen handle complex selling situations. The data, however, did not fully illuminate the problem of treatment of browsers, especially in the Country Fair store. As a result, a further study was undertaken to evaluate whether or not browsers are being approached properly at Country Fair and are being turned into prospects.

Methodology

A total of twenty-two couples served as shoppers for this purpose. They were instructed to visit the store at different times of the day and week and simply to indicate that they wished to browse. At a later point in the visit, however, instructions called for them to begin to show interest in an item in such a manner that it would be observed by an alert salesman. Various data were collected during the visit including the time of first contact by a salesman and the time of any subsequent recontacts. Also of interest were the names of the salesmen, the nature of sales activity during contacts, a record of the number of people in the store, and a general overall evaluation of the extent to which they were satisfied as customers.

Data Analysis

The shopper usually was contacted within the first 5 to 10 minutes after entering the store (over 50 percent reported contact within 4 minutes). Several went a considerable period before first contact, however, and one left after 28 minutes without seeing a salesman. In 82 percent of the instances, the initial contact was made by a member of the sales force. The hostess at the door performed this function only once.

It is disturbing to note that no recontact was made in 41 percent of the visits. Moreover, many shoppers were neglected for as long as a half hour. Finally, the same salesman who made the initial contact returned in only 23 percent of reported instances.

Of the recontacts made, only a few could be evaluated as being real selling where definite help was given based on an awareness of what browsers had been doing and the merchandise they had been examining. In remaining situations the recontact was usually made by a different salesman and consisted merely of a casual offer to help. No salesman, however, followed through on such an offer.

One might expect a problem of neglected browsers in a crowded store. This was seldom the case, however, as it was the opinion of the great majority of the participants that the store was not busy. In addition, idle salesmen were observed in nearly 60 percent of the visits. There were frequent comments about the idle sales force:

> Four sales personnel, a red-haired woman and three gentlemen, were standing immediately in front of the door conversing with each other.
>
> There were twenty people in the store. We noticed two salesmen sitting down and talking to each other while two groups of shoppers looked at furniture nearby. Another salesman was sitting talking to the woman at the desk. None of the salesmen made any offer of assistance as we browsed near them.
>
> Mr. Harvey said, "Believe it or not, there are eight salesmen hidden around here somewhere—sometimes it's difficult to give customers the service they deserve."

Implications

There is no doubt that browsers are being neglected at Country Fair. This neglect, in turn, has led to a predominantly negative attitude by participants. Each person was asked to rate the store and its procedures using a seven-point scale. It ranged from 1 (excellent) to 7 (poor), with 4 signifying neutrality. The average rating was 5.1—a strong indication that many shoppers are being alienated. More light is shed on the ratings by consideration of some of the individual comments:

> I received the impression that the salesman would be happy to wait on a person if he expressed an interest in something but that little would be done to create an interest among browsers.
>
> I probably never would go back again.
>
> I counted at least six sales people, and my general impression is that they were not interested in making a sale. The attitude on the part of the persons was boredom and impatience. No attempt was made to make a sale, to explain the product, or to get me to come back. I was furious.

It should be pointed out that the numerical ratings may be unduly harsh. The participants differed from the typical shopper in that they were alert to certain types of behavior that normally might not have provoked such negative responses. Nevertheless, a good indication is provided of the magnitude of the problem.

The data support these conclusions:

1. The initial contact, as a rule, is made fairly promptly.
2. When a recontact is made, it usually is by someone other than the first

salesman. There is a strong indication that salesmen do not stay with shoppers and do not attempt to develop them into prospects.

3. The lack of follow-through is dangerous because the presumption is that salesmen on commission can separate hot prospects from browsers. Yet, what criteria are used for this purpose? A person who appears to be a browser can, in reality, be a real prospect, and it is probable that a significant number of sales are being lost by lethargy.

4. The high number of participants who left with a negative reaction indicate the probability that word-of-mouth communication about Columbia is not favorable.

Conclusions

Management is concerned about these findings, and some felt that perhaps compensation should not be based on commission. Others saw a need to change sales training procedures.

Analytical Problem

1. Evaluate the methodology used in this study.
2. What action should management take, if any?

DANCING WITH THE CALIFORNIA RAISINS:
In-Store Promotion of a Hot Item

California Raisin Advisory Board

The California Raisin Advisory Board was formed in the 1940s to promote raisins. The board began promoting sales and use of raisins by supporting the annual Raisin Queen beauty contest and by publishing various recipes using raisins. In 1972, the board decided to use advertising in its promotional efforts. Foote, Cone & Belding, a San Francisco-based ad agency, began promoting raisins as "the natural snack food." This seemed to work for a while, but other producers and distributors began claiming that their product was also "the natural snack." Over time, other strategies were used. By the mid-1980s, however, it became clear that raisins were once again lost in the promotional clutter.

The board was again faced with the decision of how to improve raisin promotion. In 1987, the board sponsored ads that featured singing raisins with music from the 1960s Motown sound. The California Dancing Raisins became stars almost overnight. A "Grapevine" album was released, and it went gold (500,000 units sold) within the first month. The video from the "Grapevine" album was shown during popular TV programs on MTV and VH-1. The board considered making a second album.

Licensing agreements currently have resulted in sweatshirts, T-shirts, key chains, drinking mugs, posters, and a television show, in addition to raisin figurines. "Claymation Christmas Celebration"—an animated television Christmas special by the animators of California Dancing Raisins and using the same type of animation—was aired December 21, 1987, and received a fifth-place Nielsen rating for the evening viewing. A new board game focusing on the California Dancing Raisins theme was released in February of 1988. Additional agreements resulted in other products, such as Halloween costumes, lunch pails, sneakers, backpacks, and pajamas featuring the California Dancing Raisins, and these new products were introduced during 1988. The anticipated product mix (variety and assortment) is shown in Exhibit 27–1.

Johnson's Department Store

The Johnson's Department Store chain was part of a large department store ownership group. The Johnson's stores were full-service department stores based in a major Midwestern city generally occupying the anchor position in major malls and shopping centers. They catered to middle- and upper-level consumers in an effort to remain current with trends and fashion. Johnson's had just completed major structural and departmental updates of all stores within the past 2 years. Using a standardized layout for all stores, each unit's merchandise departments included those shown in Exhibit 27–2. General management activities, including display design and merchandising, were performed from a central operation at the main store in cooperation with each store manager.

This case was prepared by David O. Bisbee and Kenneth E. Mast, University of Akron.

EXHIBIT 27–1
Breadth and Depth of Line
Planned

Item	Size	Quantity
T-Shirts	XXL	5 cases
	XL	5 cases
	Large	10 cases
	Medium	15 cases
	Small	7 cases
Sweatshirts	XL	3 cases
	Large	5 cases
	Medium	3 cases
	Small	2 cases
Stuffed raisins with suction-cup feet		36
Keychains	Large	144
	Small	144
Plastic coffee mugs	12 oz.	144
Plastic miniatures	Set of four	36
Puppets		36
Boardgames		48

The display department at Johnson's Department Stores made recommendations as to the size, content, and arrangement of in-store displays. If the general merchandise manager and individual store managers agreed with the recommendation, the plans were operationalized. After the primary determinations were made, the display department consulted with store managers to select a precise location for the display. Together they chose the desirable fixtures that would be needed for the entire display. The display department supplied these fixtures as well as other equipment, such as additional lighting or electronic equipment. In addition, artists from the display department provided all necessary creative visuals and fixturing for the display.

Current Situation

In early 1988, Roberta Swanson, display manager for Johnson's Department Stores, was contemplating how to capitalize on the current excitement over the Dancing California Raisin craze. She wondered whether this was really just a passing fad or a trend that would last several selling seasons. Just yesterday, *Billboard* announced that the first album released, called "The California Raisins," had gone gold and hit #71 on the charts for the week of January 9, 1988. The album was released in late 1987. The recent holiday season had seen sales of "raisin paraphernalia" skyrocket.

Should a "mini-boutique" be set up for these products? If so, how much floor space should be set aside for it? What type of display should be used and what in-store location selected for the display? What other items (complementary) should be displayed adjacent to the Dancing Raisins? Who will buy these products? Which of the Dancing Raisin products should be carried? What other possibilities exist that

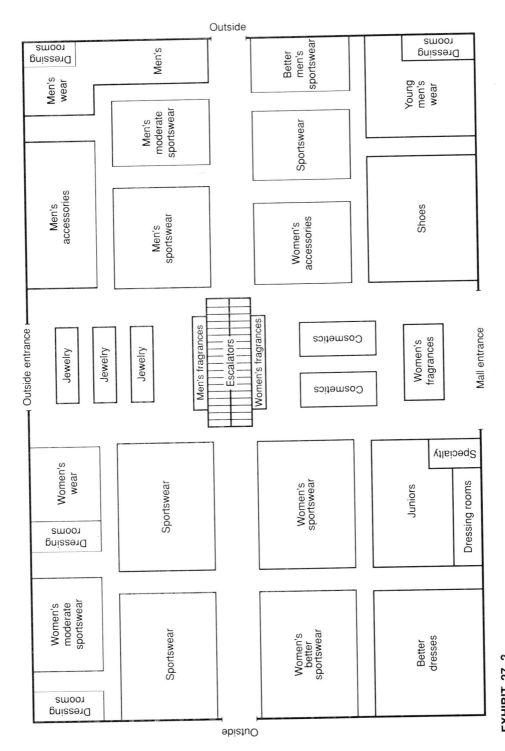

EXHIBIT 27-2
Floor plan

218

would increase the effectiveness by which these hit items could be merchandised? What are the display requirements necessary for successfully merchandising this rather unusual and mixed line of products? These are but a few of the more important questions Swanson had to answer before the end of the month when her season display plan was due. Turning to the store master floor plan (Exhibit 27–2), Swanson started to formulate a plan of attack.

Analytical Problem

Assume the role of Roberta Swanson. Prepare a written report responding to the questions presented at the end of the case. Recommend a course of action for Swanson to pursue. Your plan (course of action) should include recommendations that address the issues of the type, size, location, content, and arrangement of the display. The plan should be supported by visuals (graphics, illustrations, layouts, and/or sketches) that will allow the merchandise manager to fully grasp the impact of the display/boutique concept. Each of the alternatives and decisions associated with the issues enumerated should be fully supported and justified.

PART NINE
Strategic Retail Management

CASE 28   **THE MAGICAL DEER:**
Strategic Retail Management for a Small Business

The Magical Deer was a needle-art design studio that carried high-fashion knitting materials and custom-designed knitwear. Because of the first location's success in Cincinnati, The Magical Deer's partners were encouraged by clientele from Dayton to open a second location. In addition, The Magical Deer's suppliers were eager to lend their support for a second location and offered generous billing terms, including interest-free financing on inventory for 3 months. The partners, Jamie and Cathryn Smith and Debbie Connors, felt they had a wonderful opportunity for growth.

In May of 1985, The Magical Deer opened its second location in Williamsburg Manor Mall, a specialty mall in Dayton located about ¼ mile from a major shopping mall. At this time, Williamsburg Manor had been open for 1 year. It was built with spaces for eighteen main stores and a special center section with smaller spaces for food stands and small shops (see Exhibit 28–1). When The Magical Deer signed a 5-year lease with the Williamsburg Manor owners, fourteen major shops were filled: three women's clothing stores, two men's clothing stores, a children's clothing store, a fine restaurant, a florist, a fine candy store, a toy store, a fine card and gift shop, an oriental rug store, a fine shoe store, and a petrified wood store (ornamental gifts made from petrified wood). The center section of the mall held four food stands. Three more food stands and ten small shops were yet to be rented. The center food area and small shop area were still under construction at the time the lease was signed. Consequently, not many of the spaces were filled. The mall owners intended to fill these stands with fresh produce and meats, as well as fine accessory shops selling handbags, jewelry, perfume, and other items.

Because The Magical Deer had made a large portion of its past profits on made-to-order hand-knit garments that sold for between $150 and $400, the partners hoped to eventually expand their custom designs into other lines such as ultrasuede skirts, high-fashion jewelry, and belts. With this customized concept in mind,

---

This case was prepared by Joseph W. Leonard, Miami University. It was developed to provide a basis for class discussion rather than to illustrate either effective or ineffective handling of organizational issues and practices. All names, places, and dates have been disguised. Copyright © 1986 by Joseph W. Leonard.

EXHIBIT 28–1
MALL LAYOUT

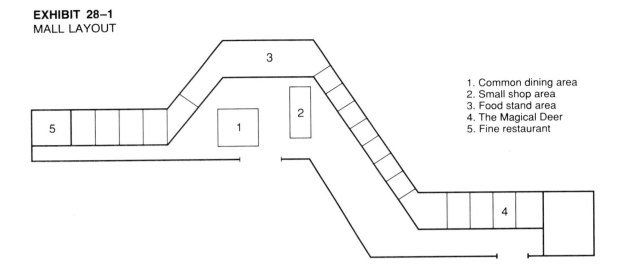

1. Common dining area
2. Small shop area
3. Food stand area
4. The Magical Deer
5. Fine restaurant

the partners leased 2,100 square feet of space (see Exhibit 28–2). This space was approximately two and a half times the size of their Cincinnati shop.

The first 3 months at Williamsburg Manor proved encouraging for The Magical Deer partners. They came increasingly closer each month to reaching their sales goals. In fact, the Dayton location was already outperforming the Cincinnati location.

By October of 1985, however, the tide began to turn for The Magical Deer and many of the other main shops within the mall. Traffic had slowed down considerably, and there was great dissension between the shop owners and mall management on two issues. The first issue concerned evening hours. Most shops were staffed in the evenings by hired help, not the owners. Many owners claimed that the sales brought in during the evening hours did not cover their employees' wages. The Magical Deer partners agreed. In both day and evening hours, their traffic and sales had dropped drastically in what was supposed to be the busiest time of the year for their industry.

The second issue of concern for the owners was the type of shops leasing space in the small center locations. Most of these shops were not in keeping with the specialty theme; for example a video game room and T-shirt shop were two of the new tenants.

In November of the same year, many of the main shops started to leave. Because most shops were held by private individuals, they could not afford to withstand many consecutive months of losses. Some shops went bankrupt; some owners left with their merchandise in the middle of the night.

The tragedy was just as great for The Magical Deer and its partners (see Exhibit 28–3). The bills from suppliers were coming due, but The Magical Deer had no way to pay them. The partners received numerous calls each day demanding that The Magical Deer set up a payment schedule.

The partners were unclear as to what to do. Because they had signed a lease, they feared a lawsuit if they left the mall. The profits from the Cincinnati location

EXHIBIT 28–2
STORE LAYOUT

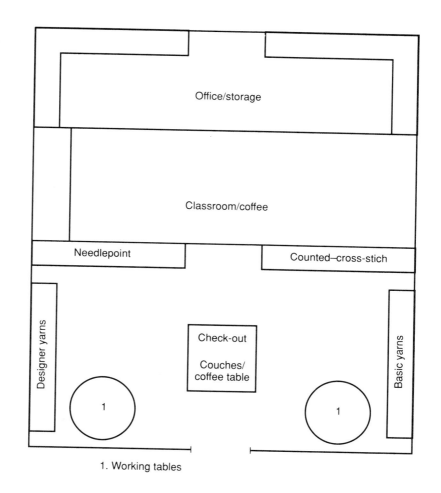

1. Working tables

had dwindled because the credit problems with suppliers had made it difficult to obtain merchandise. Therefore, the Cincinnati shop could not afford to supplement the Dayton shop. Declaring bankruptcy was an alternative. Because the form of business was a partnership, however, the partners feared the loss of their homes and other personal assets. Bankruptcy therefore was a last resort. The next day the partners were to have a critical meeting to determine what alternatives were available and which should be selected.

History

Cathryn Smith began The Magical Deer in May 1984. In October of 1984, Cathryn hired Debbie Connors as a crochet instructor and finisher (sewing together and blocking garments that customers made). Later, in January of 1985, Cathryn's

EXHIBIT 28–3
THE MAGICAL DEER, Dayton Store, Financial Data

Balance Sheet, November 30, 1985	($)
Assets	
Shop fixtures	50,000
Inventory	77,800
	127,800
Liabilities	
Accounts payable—suppliers	63,250
Accounts payable—others*	3,100
	66,350
Owner's equity	61,450
Total liability and owner's equity	127,800

Income Statement, for May 1 to November 30, 1985	($)
Sales	78,610
Cost of goods sold	42,180
Gross profit	36,430
Operating expenses	
Rent ($1,140/month)	7,980
Utilities	723
Payroll†	7,800
Office supplies	1,030
Taxes, licenses	540
Total operating expenses	18,073
Net income before tax	18,357

*Note: There were no long-term debts.
†Owners' Draw is *not* included in this figure.

daughter, Jamie, came to work full-time for The Magical Deer as a bookkeeper and sales clerk.

As the opportunity for a second location became apparent, Cathryn offered partnerships to both Jamie and Debbie if they would invest in the business. The funds from the new partners were used to establish the second location.

The business responsibilities were divided up as follows: design, Cathryn; technical assistance, Debbie; operations, Jamie.

Cathryn Smith

Although Cathryn had no "technical" training in fashion design, she seemed to have a strong flair for it. She had the ability to combine colors and textures both in sweaters and in the shop decor. Cathryn was a shrewd businesswoman who could read people well. She did not, however, like to be bothered with the day-to-day operations of managing the shop. In addition, she much preferred her "intuition" over facts in merchandising her shop as well as in handling the accounting records.

Jamie Smith

Jamie, 20 years old, was Cathryn's daughter. Jamie had past business experience along with 3 years of college as a business major. Jamie was interested in having her own business, but she was not fully aware of the commitment that owning a business required. Jamie felt that her position in the shop should be "behind the scenes." She did not want to work with the public. Jamie was a good salesperson, but often became impatient with customers who were indecisive or who could not quickly master the art of knitting.

Debbie Connors

Debbie, 32 years old, was technically the best knitter of the three partners. Debbie could take Cathryn's or any customer's ideas and translate them into a knitting pattern. Debbie did not care for the business aspect of the firm, but she was excellent at working with people. Because of her family commitments (four children under the age of 6), Debbie often found herself making promises to her customers and to her partners that she was not able to keep.

Decision Making

In the partnership agreement, each partner was supposed to have an equal say in decision making. Because of Cathryn's intuitive nature and Jamie's quantitative nature, they quite often took opposing views on business issues. Discussions often became heated. Jamie, as a result of her monetary obligations to her mother for the purchase of the partnership, usually gave in. Consequently, regardless of what Debbie thought about an issue, Cathryn's decision was usually final.

Store Strategy, Objectives, and Image

All three partners had been in complete agreement on the purpose of The Magical Deer. The broad objective for The Magical Deer was to provide its customers with the area's most complete selection of unique high-fashion materials and customized designs, along with full service. The Dayton location therefore strongly emphasized a contemporary and luxurious setting. Customers were to be greeted personally and offered coffee as they discussed their outfit ideas with one of the three partners (clerks were primarily used at the counter for checkout assistance). One of the partners would then help the customer pick out the appropriate pattern and material for an outfit. Quite often the customer required a pattern that could not be found in a published knitting book. Therefore, one of the partners had to calculate the pattern manually. This was normally done for a minimal charge of $5.00, the standard price of most knit shops in the area. In addition, The Magical Deer provided any necessary assistance to the customer to help her complete the knitting project. As was standard in the industry, this service was provided free of charge. It was not unusual for a customer to require 2 hours or more of assistance to complete the garment.

Although the partners perceived The Magical Deer as more of a fashion-oriented shop than as a "needlework" shop, it still carried about one third of its merchandise in two other types of needlework: counted–cross-stitch and needlepoint. The partners felt that these two other types of needlework were complementary to the knitting yarns and helped to smooth out the slow knitting seasons (spring and summer).

The Knit Industry

The knitting industry had made a strong comeback in the 1980s. It was generally well-known in the needlecraft business that different types of needlework come into popularity in a cyclical nature. Because many of the famous fashion designers' lines (e.g., Ralph Lauren, Calvin Klein, and Perry Ellis) included hand-knit sweaters and knitted suits at this time, knitted garments had become popular.

Because of the high price of hand-knit sweaters in conventional retail stores (usually $260 and up), many women opted to knit their own sweaters from materials that ranged in price from $50 up to $275. This new demand for yarns set off a sales explosion in what had been a stagnant industry. Not only did numerous new foreign and domestic yarn suppliers come into existence, but many new retail yarn shops were established all over the country.

There were hundreds of yarn wholesalers in the industry. Although there were about ten major yarn wholesalers, most were smaller firms that made their own yarns or imported them. Wholesalers sold two types of materials: bread-and-butter yarns and fashion yarns. The bread-and-butter yarns were standard wool and man-made blends. They came in four weights: baby weight, sport weight, worsted weight, and bulky weight. Many discount houses as well as regular knit shops carried these basic yarns. The designer materials were made from wool, acrylic, angora, metallics, paper, wood pulp, and a host of other fibers.

With each wholesaler's line having twenty types of material along with fourteen colors in each type on the average, a knit shop could have a very unique inventory. With all the competition, suppliers were eager to have a shop carry their yarns. The average markup within the industry was 50 percent. The standard terms were 2/10 net 30. Extended billing was typical, however, during the slow spring and summer seasons.

Supplier standards were minimal. As long as funding for a shop existed, most would ship orders small enough for even an "in-home yarn shop." Quite often, retail shops that had to pay overhead found it difficult to compete against in-home shops. In addition to not having to pay overhead, in-home shops often could provide more flexible hours. They also could provide inventory-wide discounts, a practice widely frowned on by the retail segment of the yarn industry.

In-home shops were not the only major competitor of knit shops. Discount retailers such as K Mart offered low-grade materials at greatly reduced prices. Often the inexperienced knitter considered all basic yarns to be the same. The high acrylic content of many discount yarns, however, caused formation of hard fuzz balls on the completed garment's friction points. The small knit shop industry depended on its ability to teach knitters to see the differences in quality and to get them to pay for it.

In addition to competing with the in-home shops, most yarn shops had difficulties overcoming two other problems: dye lot and customer service. When yarn is dyed, it is assigned a unique lot number. It is important when knitting a garment to use skeins that are of the same lot number or the garment may appear to be striped. Most often yarn is sold in bags of eight, ten, or twelve skeins. The amount of material needed for a garment depends on the garment style, size, and the properties of the yarn. If a customer should purchase eight skeins from a 10-skein bag, two skeins of a particular dye lot would be left. These skeins normally had to be sold at a discount.

The second common problem facing knit shops was the extent of customer service required. In most other retail specialty shops, the customer is assisted in selecting a product. The store's customer service responsibility usually ends there. In a knit shop, in addition to helping the customer select the appropriate yarn and pattern for a garment, the shop is responsible for helping the customer knit that garment. Quite often this means helping a customer master a new stitch, fix dropped stitches, and sew the garment together.

In addition to these services, which average approximately 2 hours per garment, the store must assist the customer in finding more yarn of the same dye lot if it did not sell the customer enough during the initial purchase. Also, when the customer finishes knitting a garment, most yarn shops have a policy whereby unused skeins can be returned for credit up to 3 months after the initial purchase. The store's service makes or breaks the business. Without excellent customer service, few customers return to make additional purchases or refer friends to this retailer.

Target Market

The Magical Deer sought to serve the middle- to upper-income segments because the level of service it provided was generally independent of the price level of the yarns sold. Therefore, service to the purchaser of $70 worth of materials would reap more profits than the same amount of service to the purchaser of $30 worth of materials. In addition, the more expensive materials were bulkier and therefore could be knitted more quickly. This would result in the customers returning sooner to make repeat purchases.

Advertising

The Magical Deer had little success advertising in newspapers or on radio. The partners believed they were targeting much too specific a market to use the mass media. Instead, they found much better response to newsletters, postcards, and most of all, word-of-mouth. The advertising budget for the shop was approximately 3 percent of the projected sales for the upcoming year. The bulk of advertising was geared toward announcing upcoming materials and fashion trends in a company newsletter that was sent to previous customers and to prospects once every 3 months.

The Magical Deer's business was somewhat countercyclical to the economy. The lower the funds were for a family to spend on extracurricular activities, the more women were likely to buy yarn projects to work on.

Classes and Special Events

The Magical Deer partners had given much thought to holding classes at the Dayton location to decrease the amount of service given to individuals and to gain new customers. The partners had developed facilities in the rear of the store for these classes. After one group of classes, however, The Magical Deer found that the people attending were not regular customers. Although some repeat business did develop from the classes, the incremental increases in business did not seem to justify the additional expense. The Magical Deer held a variety of other special events including trunk shows, special seminars, and fashion shows, but none of the events seemed to increase sales in the long run.

The partners found that sales were highest when a large inventory of materials was available and new sweater designs were developed and displayed in the shop on a weekly basis. These garments gave customers ideas for upcoming projects and encouraged them to complete present ones. Therefore, most of The Magical Deer's display efforts were in promoting unique designs.

Analyical Problem

As a small business consultant, you are asked to advise The Magical Deer partnership on the following concerns:

1. Identify and cite the relative merits of various courses of action regarding the problems surrounding the Dayton location and its 5-year lease.
2. Make recommendations for improving both the decision-making and management capabilities of the firm's three partners.
3. Make recommendations for improving the current merchandising strategies and tactics as well as suggestions for new marketing actions that would enhance the firm's overall marketing strategy.

CASE 29   SOUTHLAND CORPORATION:
7-ELEVEN STORES—Developing Long-Run Retail Strategies for a
Multinational Corporation

"What you want when you want it"
"Slurp your way to happiness"
"Get more milk for your moo-lah"
"Oh, thank heaven for 7-Eleven"

Even though such messages might seem corny to some, they have served their purpose: to create a good feeling in the millions of hurried Americans who find the neighborhood 7-Eleven store to be their answer to convenient shopping. The 7-Eleven store concept is one of the great retailing stories in history. From an icehouse in 1927, this Dallas-based company has blossomed into the world's largest convenience store chain. In 1987, it had over 11,000 7-Eleven stores throughout the United States, Canada, and eleven other countries. What makes Southland's success even more amazing is that the yearly sales of nearly $8 billion come from customers who spend only about $2.25 per trip.

History

The Southland corporation began in 1927, when Claude S. Dawley bought eight ice manufacturing plants and twenty-one retail ice stores and incorporated them into The Southland Ice Company. One of the original board members and investors in the new company was 26-year-old Joe C. Thompson, Jr., a recent business administration graduate from the University of Texas. "Jodie" had grown up working in some of the Dallas ice plants that were purchased by Mr. Dawley and had acquired a thorough knowledge of the ice business. The hardworking and innovative Thompson was soon named Secretary-Treasurer, and, in 1931, at only 30 years of age, was promoted to president of the company.

Selling products other than ice was the idea of Uncle Johnny Green, one of Southland's dock managers. Mr. Green kept his ice store open in the summer 16 hours every day, 7 days a week, to dispense the block ice that was essential for home refrigeration. Many of his customers hinted or asked that he provide other items besides ice, particularly at night and on Sundays. In the summer of 1927, after a brief but successful trial in his own store, Green persuaded Jodie Thompson to finance an inventory of milk, bread, eggs, cigarettes, and some canned goods to be stocked on the ice dock. The groceries sold, and the next spring, the 55-year-old dock manager strolled into Thompson's office and plopped down $1,000 in cash, Southland's share of the grocery proceeds. At that moment, the convenience store was born.

This case is adapted from Stephen W. McDaniel, "Southland Corporation's 7-Eleven Stores," in *Cases in Marketing Strategy*, eds. Richard T. Hise and Stephen W. McDaniel (Columbus, OH: Merrill Publishing Company, 1984), 269–287. This case was developed to provide a basis for class discussion rather than to illustrate either effective or ineffective retail management.

After Thompson became president of the company, he stocked all of his ice docks with groceries and renamed the stores "Tote'm Ice Stores," to denote that people toted away their purchases. Thompson acquired genuine Indian totem poles to place in front of each store. Soon totem poles began to spring up at ice docks other than Southland's, giving more impetus to this new concept in retailing but taking away from Southland's uniqueness. As a result, the company decided to make a change in its name and promotional appeal. In 1946 a Dallas advertising agency suggested that the company keep all of its stores open from 7 A.M. to 11 P.M., 7 days a week, and then rename them "7-11" stores.

After Mr. Thompson headed a group of investors and bought out the company, he began grooming his two sons, John and Jere, to take over the business. When they were teenagers, he put them to work in the stores and hired them again after they graduated from the University of Texas. As they rose in the company, John and Jere were instrumental in directing the expansion of 7-Eleven stores in Texas, Florida, and other Sun Belt states in the 1950s and 1960s. During this time, a revolution of sorts was taking place in America. Urban dwellers were fleeing to the suburbs and becoming commuters; soon America was in a hurry, and retailing opportunities arose to meet this growing market demand for convenience. This convenience store concept has an advantage over supermarkets in that the supermarket might be several miles from the customer's home and would require him or her to wait in line to buy only a couple of items. It also has an advantage over mom-and-pop grocery stores that do not offer long hours and diverse merchandise.

In the late 1950s, the company decided to try opening stores outside of the Sun Belt. There was some reservation about this move, since the popular 7-Eleven lines like cold beer and ice might not sell as well in colder northern climates. Jodie Thompson decided to open a string of experimental stores in the Washington, D.C. area in 1957. That winter, a blizzard paralyzed the city, and those who could not drive to supermarkets trudged in droves to the nearby 7-Elevens. In the words of a member of the board:

> After that snowstorm hit the Washington area, we sold the stores out to the walls.
> The managers were so busy most of them slept in the stores for several days. People in Washington discovered 7-Eleven because we were there when they needed us.
> This really proved our little convenience store could make it in a cold climate and, in my opinion, it was the making of the company.[1]

Jodie Thompson died in 1961. John and Jere, Chairman and President, respectively, took over and led an aggressive expansion program. In what may have been the most rapid buildup of individual retail stores in American history, the number of 7-Elevens soared from 1,519 at the beginning of 1965 to 3,537 at the end of 1969. During the 1970s, the company achieved a net increase of 200 to 400

---

[1]Allen Liles, *Oh Thank Heaven! The Story of the Southland Corporation* (The Southland Corporation, 1977), 114.

stores each year. By 1981, Southland had over 7,000 7-Eleven stores in six countries, including 6,680 in forty-two states of the United States. The firm continued to grow and operated 11,000 7-Elevens during 1987.

Company Operations

Southland Corporation's business activities are divided into two strategic business segments: convenience retailing and food processing and manufacturing. It also has a 50-percent equity interest in Citgo Petroleum Corporation, the country's largest independent refiner/marketer.

All 7-Eleven stores are controlled by the convenience retailing segment and are under the direction of S. R. Dole. As Executive Vice President of 7-Eleven Stores, Dole oversees stores in forty-nine states (including Alaska and Hawaii), the District of Columbia, and five provinces of Canada. Franchisees operated 38 percent of the 7,672 company units, while ten domestic area licensees operated another 494 stores in twenty states.

By the end of 1986, Southland International was coordinating the activities of 4,102 7-Eleven stores operated primarily by licensees in the United States and eleven other countries. At that time, the company had 2,924 stores in Japan, 183 in Hong Kong, 122 in Taiwan, 44 in Singapore, 31 in Malaysia, 119 in Australia, 3 in the Phillipines, 52 in England, and 1 in Norway. The company's Swedish subsidiary operated sixty-eight 7-Eleven stores, and Southland owned an equity interest in a firm that operated sixty-one convenience stores in Mexico.

Sales from stores in the International Division are not reported as revenues in Southland's annual report. Royalties from licensees, however, are included in the convenience retailing segment's operating profit.

The convenience retailing segment's other operations include Chief Auto Parts. This is a chain of 465 retail automobile supply stores in California, Texas, Nevada, and Arizona. The segment also includes High's Dairy Stores, Quick Mart stores, and Super-7 outlets.

The food-processing and manufacturing segment includes the Dairies Group, headed by Vice President C. O. Beshears. This operation consists of ten regional dairies and is one of the largest dairy processors and distributors in the United States. Its products are distributed in forty-six states, the District of Columbia, Canada, Guam, and the Caribbean from twenty-eight plants and sixty-two distribution points. The Dairy Group's customers include 5,600 7-Eleven stores and thousands of other retail, institutional, and food service accounts.

Other important components of the food processing and manufacturing segment include Reddy Ice, the world's largest ice company and, of course, Southland's original business. It operates nine plants in Texas, Florida, Oklahoma, and Nevada. Another important component is Tidel Systems, a manufacturer of cash-dispensing units and underground gasoline tank monitoring systems. Its "Timed Access Cash Controller" is a microcomputer-based security and dispensing unit used in 7-Eleven stores.

In addition, the Southland Food Labs manufactures a broad line of food ingredients and specialty chemicals for other Southland operations and many other customers. Food flavorings, preservatives, and emulsifiers are sold to domestic and international customers, while dairy product flavorings, cleansers, "slurpee" flavor concentrates, and many others are sold to 7-Eleven stores. This business segment also includes a snack foods division, consisting of the Pate Foods and El-Ge Potato Chip operations.

EXHIBIT 29-1
The Southland Corporation Financial Summary by Operating Group

	($ Thousands)		
	1986	1985	1984
Revenues			
Convenience retailing	8,038,591	8,097,375	7,592,492
Food processing and manufacturing	870,755	840,956	727,639
Corporate	6,805	6,666	2,704
	8,916,151	8,908,997	8,322,835
Intersegment			
Food processing and manufacturing	(296,470)	(286,600)	(282,162)
Consolidated revenues	8,619,681	8,622,397	8,040,673
Operating profits			
Convenience retailing	263,953	259,931	268,240
Food processing and manufacturing	38,203	32,330	29,249
Consolidated operating profits	302,156	292,261	297,489
Interest expense	(59,285)	(57,875)	(57,214)
Corporate expense, net	(56,491)	(55,454)	(42,550)
Equity in earnings (loss) of Citgo	(55,167)	103,319	(25,411)
Gain from sale of half-interest in Citgo	114,732	—	—
Consolidated earnings before income tax	245,945	282,251	172,314
Identifiable assets at December 31			
Convenience retailing	2,311,851	1,831,712	1,597,184
Food processing and manufacturing	288,309	195,978	165,776
Investment in and advances to Citgo	286,584	800,904	44,164
Corporate	534,344	404,924	341,923
Total identifiable assets	3,421,088	3,233,518	2,549,047
Capital expenditures			
Convenience retailing	561,695	327,649	268,528
Food processing and manufacturing	55,369	32,449	25,914
Corporate	169,834	104,756	97,035
Total capital expenditures	786,898	464,854	391,477
Depreciation and amortization expense			
Convenience retailing	152,103	134,621	121, 892
Food processing and manufacturing	18,521	16,040	14,324
Corporate	14,898	12,990	11,662
Total depreciation and amortization expense	185,522	163,651	147,878

Source: Southland Corporation, Annual Report, 1984, 1985, 1986.

Exhibit 29–1 presents the financial summaries of each operating group, while Exhibit 29–2 presents the corporate financial highlights. Exhibits 29–3 and 29–4 contain Southland Corporation's statement of earnings and balance sheet.

The 7-Eleven Store

Generally, all 7-Eleven stores are open every day of the year and are in neighborhood areas, on main thoroughfares, in shopping centers, or in other accessible sites with plenty of parking. Approximately 95 percent of the 7-Elevens now stay open longer than the traditional 7 A.M. to 11 P.M, with 87 percent now operating 24 hours a day. Over half of the U.S. population lives within 2 miles of a 7-Eleven store.

In Southland's early days, the 7-Eleven store contained 1,200 to 1,800 square feet. Today there are three different-sized 7-Elevens—the smallest has 2,000 square feet (50 × 40 feet) and the largest has 2,450 square feet (70 × 35 feet). The most comon size is 2,400 square feet (60 × 40 feet). Southland has developed a standardized layout for all stores. The layout for the 60- × 40-feet store is shown in Exhibit 29–5; the other stores have similar layouts.

The company believes in maintaining a modern, neat appearance for each store, and this involves continual remodeling of each store. While building a new store costs over $300,000, remodels cost anywhere from less than $10,000 to

EXHIBIT 29–2

Financial Highlights: The Southland Corporation

(Year ended December 31)	($ Thousands)		Change (%)
	1986	1985	
Total revenues	8,619,681	8,622,397	—
Net earnings	200,445	212,535	(5.7)
Primary earnings per share*	3.96	4.41	(10.2)
Fully diluted earnings per share*	3.91	4.37	(10.5)
Cash dividends—common stock	53,877	47,405	13.7
Cash dividends per share—common stock	1.12	1.00	12.0
Capital expenditures	786,898	764,854	69.3
Average shares outstanding—common stock ($000s)	48,094	47,400	1.5
Return on average shareholders' equity	13.02%	16.06%	
Financial condition at year-end			
Total assets	3,421,088	3,233,518	5.8
Shareholders' equity	1,667,831	1,496,823	11.4
Long-term debt	639,496	575,586	11.1
Working capital	(205,730)	(391,581)	47.5
Shareholders' equity per share of common stock*	31.91	28.84	10.6
Debt/equity ratio	0.40	0.40	—
Number of shareholders of record—common stock	8,317	8,186	1.6

*Actual dollar value given.

Source: Southland Corporation, Annual Report, 1984, 1985, 1986.

EXHIBIT 29–3
Consolidated Statement of Earnings The Southland Corporation and Subsidiaries

Year Ended December 31	1986	1985	1984
Revenues			
Net sales	8,577,749	8,578,454	7,998,145
Other income	41,932	43,943	42,528
Total	8,619,681	8,622,397	8,040,673
Cost of sales and expenses			
Cost of goods sold (including $983,609, $1,566,691 and $1,191,862 from related parties)	6,603,164	6,733,464	6,279,459
Selling, general and administrative expenses	1,747,856	1,630,269	1,486,742
Interest expense	38,256	38,050	37,227
Imputed interest expense on capital lease obligations (including $3,683, $4,080, and $4,403 to be related parties)	21,029	19,825	19,987
Contributions to Employees' Savings and Profit Sharing Plan	26,170	31,213	19,130
Total	8,436,475	8,452,821	7,842,545
Balance	183,206	169,576	198,128
Equity in earnings (loss) of Citgo	(51,993)	112,576	(25,814)
Gain from sale of half-interest in Citgo	114,732	—	—
Earnings before income taxes	245,945	282,251	172,314
Income taxes	45,500	69,716	12,062
Net earnings	200,445	212,535	160,252
Earnings per common share*			
Primary	3.96	4.41	3.41
Fully diluted	3.91	4.37	3.38

*Actual dollar value given.
Source: Southland Corporation, Annual Report, 1984, 1985, 1986.

$50,000. The company has three different kinds of remodels: (1) the *mini*, a cosmetic remodel done on 2- to 5-year-old units for less than $10,000; (2) the *midi*, a more comprehensive job done on stores built in the early to mid-seventies for $10,000 to $25,000; and (3) the *maxi*, consisting of major work on the oldest stores, such as some in Texas and Florida, which can cost as much as $60,000. The number of necessary remodels has been increasing each year, and the annual rate recently exceeded 1,000.

Top management also wants to make sure the stores are profitable. New stores are expected to show a profit after 6 months; a laggard store is given up to a year to straighten things out, or it is closed. As Chairman John Thompson puts it, "We would rather close them and take our licks." All 7-Eleven stores are continually monitored by computer. Southland executives punch the store number into the computer terminal on their desks, and the store's current sales and earnings and how close it is to budget are flashed on a screen.

EXHIBIT 29–4

Consolidated Balance Sheets The Southland Corporation and Subsidiaries

Year Ending December 31	($ Thousands)	
	1986	1985
Assets		
Current assets		
Cash and short-term investments	71,600	74,688
Accounts and notes receivable	165,738	106,806
Inventories	435,129	353,916
Deposits and prepaid expenses	47,044	49,918
Investment in properties	27,300	61,500
Total current assets	746,811	646,828
Property, plant and equipment	2,272,624	1,722,496
Investment in and advances to Citgo	286,584	800,904
Other assets	115,069	63,290
Total assets	3,421,088	3,233,518
Liabilities and shareholders' equity		
Current liabilities		
Commercial paper and notes payable to banks	215,291	296,620
Accounts payable and accrued expenses	633,899	570,520
Accounts payable to Citgo	53,528	98,866
Income taxes	23,975	50,513
Long-term debt due within one year (including $3,128 and $3,000 due to related parties)	25,848	21,890
Total current liabilities	952,541	1,038,409
Deferred credits and other liabilities	161,220	122,700
Long-term debt (including $34,798 and $38,315 due to related parties)	639,496	575,586
Commitments and contingencies	—	—
Shareholders' equity		
Preferred stock, 5,000,000 shares authorized: Series A Cumulative Convertible Exchangeable Preferred Stock; $50 per share stated and liquidation value; 2,500,000 shares, being all of Series A, issued and outstanding	125,000	125,000
Common stock, $.01 par value; 150,000,000 shares authorized, 48,353,999 and 47,566,413 shares issued and outstanding	484	476
Additional capital	676,224	639,871
Retained earnings	866,123	731,476
Total shareholders' equity	1,667,831	1,496,823
Total liabilities and shareholders' equity	3,421,088	3,233,518

Source: Southland Corporation, Annual Report, 1984, 1985, 1986.

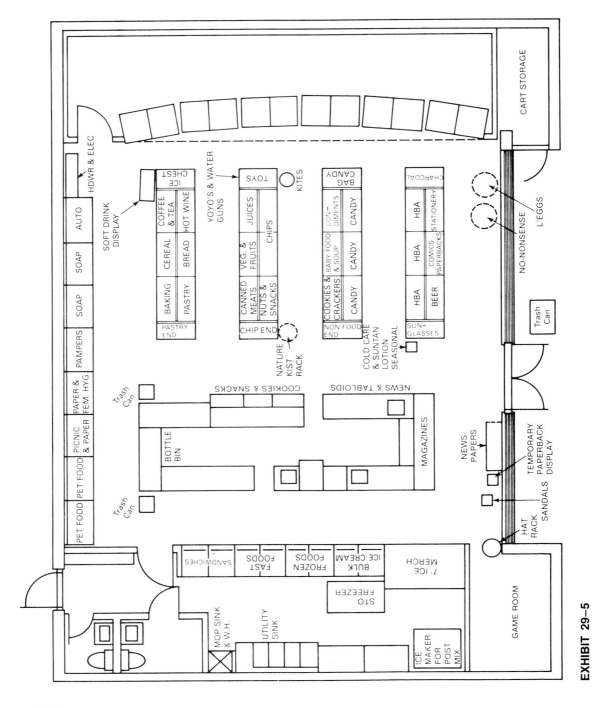

EXHIBIT 29–5

Sixty- by Forty-Feet National Store Layout—Existing Stores.

EXHIBIT 29–6
7-Eleven Store Sales (by
Principal Product Category)

Product Categories	Years Ending December 31 (%)		
	1976	1980	1984
Gasoline	6.8	23.0	24.5
Groceries	14.6	12.4	10.5
Tobacco products	14.7	12.3	14.4
Beer wine	14.4	11.7	11.4
Soft drinks	10.7	10.1	10.5
Nonfoods	10.2	8.0	7.0
Dairy products	9.6	6.7	5.7
Other food items	4.7	5.6	5.3
Candy	5.4	4.0	4.0
Baked goods	5.3	3.4	3.6
Health/beauty aids	3.6	2.8	2.8
Total	100.0	100.0	100.0

Product Mix

7-Eleven Stores have come a long way from the bread, milk, and eggs product mix of the early days. Now, the average 7-Eleven store carries approximately 3,200 items; over 25 percent of those are 7-Eleven's private brands. The percentage of store sales based on the total dollar volume of store purchases is shown in Exhibit 29–6.

Generally speaking, Southland goes for the high-margin, fast-turnover product, preferring to carry only one brand of a product, or at least as few brands as possible. As one Southland executive states, "There is no room to store a lot of different brands of the same product. Our customers don't have time to make choices anyway."[2]

7-Eleven tries to maintain at least a 25-percent profit margin on each item it sells, with many items yielding a much greater margin. Supermarkets generally achieve an average gross margin of 20 to 22 percent. Exhibit 29–7 provides a summary of product category sales and gross margins for the entire convenience store industry.

An exception to Southland's high-margin rule has been gasoline, which yields the lowest profit margin. It has become, however, the number-one selling item for 7-Eleven as well as for the entire convenience store industry. As a result of the increase in the number of customers wanting self-service gasoline and a decrease in gasoline brand loyalty, 7-Eleven began emphasizing gasoline in the mid-1970s. By 1986, 7-Eleven offered self-serve gasoline at 3,594 of its stores. Even though

---

[2]Michael Kierman, "Conveniently, 7-Eleven Sprawls Along with Suburbs," *The Washington Star*, 26 Nov. 1978, F-12.

Category	Sales ($000s)	Sales Rank	Sales Percentage of Total	Average Percentage	Gross Margin ($000s)	Gross Margin Rank	Gross Margin Percentage of Total
Bread and pastry	600,000	7	4.8	27.4	164,400	7	4.3
Cookies and crackers	195,000		1.6	30.4	59,280		1.6
Chips and snack foods	395,000	10	3.2	31.9	126,005		3.3
Dairy (incl. cheese and eggs)	1,450,000	2	11.7	23.4	339,300	5	9.0
Ice cream	310,000		2.5	33.6	104,160		2.8
Beer	1,425,000	3	11.5	28.9	411,825	3	10.9
Wine	110,000		0.9	35.1	38,610		1.0
Liquor	15,000		0.1	20.0	3,000		0.1
Soft drinks	1,250,000	5	10.1	32.0	400,000	4	10.6
Chilled juices	60,000		0.5	38.5	23,100		0.6
Frozen, fountain beverages	95,000		0.8	39.9	37,905		1.0
Hot beverages	55,000		0.4	47.4	26,070		0.7
Fresh and frozen meat	60,000		0.5	33.4	20,040		0.5
Deli	395,000	10	3.2	33.3	131,535	9	3.5
Hot sandwiches	300,000		2.4	31.9	95,700		2.5
Other fast foods	175,000		1.4	41.6	72,800		1.9
Produce	80,000		0.6	41.7	33,360		0.9
Grocery	1,375,000	4	11.1	32.1	441,375	2	11.7
Frozen foods (excl. meat)	210,000		1.7	41.7	87,570		2.3
Tobacco	1,790,000	1	14.4	27.2	486,880	1	12.9
Candy and gum	640,000	6	5.2	34.4	220,160	6	5.8
Books, magazines, papers	520,000	8	4.2	22.3	115,960		3.0
Health and beauty aids	455,000	9	3.7	32.3	146,965	8	3.9
Ice	100,000		0.8	54.6	54,600		1.4
General merchandise	300,000		2.4	42.4	127,200	10	3.4
Miscellaneous	40,000		0.3	40.4	16,160		0.4
Total in-store sales	12,400,000		100.0	30.5	3,783,960		100.0
+ Gasoline	5,900,000			5.0	295,000		
Total sales	18,300,000			22.3	4,078,960		

Source: Reprinted with permission from *Progressive Grocer* 60 (April 1981): 113.

EXHIBIT 29-7
Anatomy of Industry Sales and Profits

the 5-percent gross margin is well below that of in-store products, sheer volume has made gasoline a profitable product. There are other plusses, too. Once the pumps are installed, the customer pumps his or her own gasoline and enters the store to pay the cash register attendant. Little extra effort for the retailer is involved. Also, a 7-Eleven study has shown that 30 percent of the people who buy gasoline also buy something else during that store visit.

7-Eleven is also aggressively expanding its specialized customer services, including automatic teller machines (ATMs), money order sales, and videocassette rentals. The ATM program provides convenient 24-hour cash dispensers using a wide variety of bank cards at 1,500 stores. More than one third of 7-Eleven ATM customers visit the stores primarily because of the machine, and many purchase gasoline or other merchandise. Today, 7-Eleven is second only to the U.S. Postal Service in money order sales. Over 5,500 stores now have new, timesaving electronic money order machines.

The desire to provide what customers want and, at the same time, to maintain as high a profit margin per item as possible, has led to continuous changes in the 7-Eleven product mix. A 7-Eleven store may sell many nonfood items such as shotgun shells, school supplies, beach and picnic supplies, Christmas trees, television tubes, cancer insurance, and even services like TV rentals, and floor waxing and polishing machine rentals. "Movie-Quicks," a videocassette rental program, was recently introduced. It provides videos to consumers in easily accessible locations that never close, at competitive prices, and a regularly rotated 200-tape selection including the most frequently requested movies. About 40 percent of all U.S. households own VCRs, and 80 percent are projected to have them by 1990. In addition, each rental involves two customer trips to the store.

Today, the biggest nonfood sellers are products such as cigarettes, disposable diapers, and Playboy magazines (of which 7-Elevens sell far more than any other retailer). Recently, the big push has been for the "Hot-to-go" fast foods such as pies, hamburgers, hot dogs, sandwiches, burritos, and pizzas, all of which can be heated in the store's microwave oven. In 1980, 7-Elevens added "Hot-to-go breakfast" as well, featuring such items as the "Egg Hamlet" and the "Sausage and Egg with Cheese." New post-mix soda fountains have been installed in all 7-Eleven stores, giving each store the ability to serve a complete fast-food meal. The success of these fast-food items has made 7-Eleven the third-leading fast-food retailer in the United States.

Pricing

7-Eleven stores sell convenience. As a result, prices tend to be higher than prices at the supermarket because people are willing to pay a little more for convenience. Exhibit 29–8 shows the results of a price comparison study done in a Southwestern city over a 2-day period. A random sample of products in nine product categories was selected, and price comparisons were made between a 7-Eleven store, a Skaggs Alpha Beta store, and a Kroger store; 7-Eleven was higher for virtually every product. In this one study, the only exception was milk, which the company tries to price competitively with supermarkets.

EXHIBIT 29–8
Price Comparisons of a Sample of Products

	7-Eleven ($)	Skaggs ($)	Kroger ($)
Groceries			
Ragu Spaghetti Sauce w/meat 15.5 oz.	1.29	.99	.91
Starkist Tuna (solid white) 7 oz.	2.19	1.49	1.59
Ranch Style Pinto Beans 15 oz.	.59	.45	.43
Del Monte Sweet Peas 17 oz.	.75	.49	.49
Ocean Spray Jellied Cranberry Sauce 16 oz.	.89	.57	.57
Maxwell House Instant Coffee 6 oz.	4.25	2.95	2.93
Nabisco Oreo cookies 15 oz.	1.99	1.79	1.47
Log Cabin Syrup 12 oz.	1.55	1.19	1.13
Kellogg's Corn Flakes 12 oz.	1.35	.91	.83
Oscar Meyer Bologna 8 oz.	1.39	1.23	1.19
Beer/wine			
Cella Bianco 750 ml	3.59 (cold)	3.09	2.99
Mateus Rose 750 ml	4.29 (cold)	3.39	3.69
Lite 12 oz., 6 pack	2.75	2.39	2.49
Schlitz 12 oz., 6 pack	2.65	2.39	2.45
Budweiser 12 oz., 6 pack	2.65	2.29	1.89
Candy			
M&M's 7.5 oz.	1.59	1.29	1.25
Tootsie Roll 38 g	.30	.23	.23
Certs	.35	.23	.25
Health and beauty aids			
Contac 10 capsules	2.19	1.79	1.79
Pepto Bismol 8 oz.	3.05	2.29	1.89
Flex shampoo 16 oz.	3.39	1.79	1.69
Dry Idea Anti-Persp. 1.5 oz.	2.85	1.89	1.79
Bayer Aspirin 50 tablets	1.89	1.19	1.19
Kleenex 125	.89	.79	.62
Nonfoods			
Tide 49 oz.	2.39	2.05	1.84
Clorox 64 oz.	1.05	.73	.73
SOS 10 pads	.99	.69	.59
Pampers 12 toddler	2.49	2.09	2.19
Hefty Trash Bags 10	2.25	1.79	1.59
Purina Dog Chow 5 lbs.	2.69	2.09	2.13
Kodak Film 35-mm-Color Print-36	4.69	2.89	3.29
Baked goods			
Mrs. Baird's Honey Bun	.49	.41 (Hostess)	.41
Dolly Madison Variety Donuts 12	1.59	1.39 (Hostess)	1.39
Mrs. Baird's Xtra Thin White 24 oz.	.99	.89	.89

EXHIBIT 29–8 *(continued)*

	7-Eleven ($)	Skaggs ($)	Kroger ($)
Beverage soft drinks			
6 pack, 12 oz. cans	2.39	2.29	2.25
6 pack, 16 oz. non-returnable	2.49	2.39	2.45
2 liter bottle	1.69	1.53	1.55
Hawaiian Punch-Red 46 oz.	1.35	.85	.85
Dairy products			
Oak Farms Milk 1/2 gallon	1.33	1.23 (Pure)	1.45 (Borden's)
Oak Farm Half & Half Cream pint	.79	.69 (Quality Check)	.83 (Borden's)
Minute Maid OJ (carton) 32 oz.	1.19	.99	.89
Farm Field Lowfat Yogurt	.45	.39 (Swiss Style)	.39 (Yubi)
Tobacco products			
Copenhagen Snuff 1.2 oz.	1.05	.59	.75
Levi Garrett Chewing Tobacco large	.99	.75	.88
Single Pack Cigarettes	.95	.80	.75

Regarding 7-Eleven's relatively high prices, one Wall Street analyst observed:

> It is perplexing to us why Southland's revenue growth has accelerated when rising prices have stretched the consumer's budget to a considerable extent. Perhaps it is time rather than money which is the precious commodity to most Americans.[3]

A New York analyst offers the following:

> The appeal of convenience stores has nothing to do with price. It has to do with people's lifestyles and their constant need for fill-ins. The more tightly the pocketbook is pinched, the less frequently the housewife shops at her supermarket, and the more need she has for last minute fill-ins.[4]

The 7-Eleven Customer

Southland Corporation does extensive research on the type of people who shop at a 7-Eleven. A list of some of the findings follows.

---

[3]Michael Kierman, "7-Eleven Creates a Mood of Convenience at a Price," *The Washington Star*, 27 Nov. 1978, A-10.

[4]Michael Kierman, "7-Eleven Creates a Mood of Convenience at a Price," *The Washington Star*, 27 Nov. 1978, A-10.

- Over 70 percent of customers are male.
- Over 50 percent are in the 25- to 54-year age group.
- Over 80 percent are in the 18- to 49-year age group.
- Twenty-two percent shop between 11 P.M. and 7 A.M.
- Over 80 percent live or work less than 1 mile from the store.
- Customers average 4.4 trips per week.
- Thirty-five percent of customer visits are on weekends.
- The average purchase is two or three items (including one nonplanned).
- The average purchase amount is about $2.25.
- Over half the goods are consumed within 30 minutes of purchase.
- The average customer spends less than 4 minutes in the store (as compared to 26 minutes in a supermarket).

Distribution

As a result of the close relationship between the operating groups, 7-Eleven stores have a definite advantage over most other convenience store chains. Presently, Southland's dairies serve 5,600 of the 7-Eleven stores, supplying 60 percent of the dairy products sold by all the stores.

Another source of competitive advantage over other convenience stores is the network of the five regional distribution centers located in Florida, Illinois, California, Texas, and Virginia. These five Food Centers presently supply 7,672 stores in forty states and the District of Columbia with approximately half of their merchandise (other than gasoline). Because of their size, convenience stores depend on frequent deliveries of small amounts of merchandise to maintain high in-stock positions. For each of the past 7 years, the distribution centers have achieved a 98-percent order fill rate. Southland has done this by developing a highly sophisticated merchandise distribution system that enables each store to order prepriced merchandise in less than case losts. This enables the store to improve inventory turnover, stock fresh merchandise, and realize high levels of sales and profits from the available selling space. In addition, this provides flexibility for the stores to change the product mix in response to customer preferences and seasonal demands.

The order process, which is almost completely controlled by computer, begins at each store. First, the store personnel complete a computer-generated order list. The lists, customized for each store's special merchandise needs, are then gathered at the 7-Eleven district offices and transmitted through terminals to the computer center in Dallas. The information is then relayed to the appropriate distribution center, where orders are filled and loaded by delivery sequence into custom-built trucks that have separate compartments for dry, chilled, and frozen merchandise. In addition, the computer schedules and routes each vehicle to achieve maximum time and energy savings.

Southland provides fast foods and ice products for the stores whenever practical. Products not available from or not supplied by the company are purchased from various independent wholesalers, distributors, and rack jobbers. Each store orders inventory from vendor and merchandise lists that Southland periodically prepares, based on the buying habits of the specific areas.

Advertising

Southland Corporation is the only convenience food store chain that uses national advertising. The firm uses television, radio, and newspaper advertising extensively to promote fast foods and other products, particularly its most profitable products. In 1981, the company spent almost $20 million on advertising, the third-largest amount of any food retailer in the United States. The company first tried prime-time television advertising in 1978 and found it very successful. In 1980 the company ran five major campaigns, each of which coordinated national television advertising, radio spots, and newspaper advertising. In 1980 the company also began advertising on weekend cartoon shows, promoting the semifrozen carbonated drink, Slurpee.

In the past, all 7-Eleven advertising has been handled by the company's in-house Stanford Agency. In late 1981, however, the company decided it needed additional creative input, particularly with its increasing use of television advertising. It turned over all national advertising responsibilities to Young & Rubicam Advertising. Along with this shift, the company increased the advertising budget considerably over the next few years.

The Convenience Store Industry

The number of convenience stores in the United States has increased considerably over the past few years, as shown in Exhibit 29–9. Although some industry analysts feel that the market for convenience stores might become saturated, Southland is not worried. Southland's executives feel that industry growth will not slow soon. They believe there are several reasons for this; the major one is the trend for supermarkets to become fewer in number but larger in size. Supermarkets have gone from 7,500 square feet to 30,000 and now 50,000 square feet and have moved from the neighborhoods closer to the shopping centers.

This shift has created the market served by 7-Elevens. Another reason for optimism is the fact that 80 percent of 7-Eleven customers live or work within 1 mile of the store. Top executives interpret this as indication that, potentially, there could be a 7-Eleven store every square mile. Although this view is an extreme, they do believe it points out the tremendous room for continuous growth.

EXHIBIT 29–9

Number of Food Stores and Food Store Sales

	Number of Stores				Sales ($Billions)			
Year	Inde-pendent	Chain	Convenience Stores	Total	Inde-pendent	Chain	Convenience Stores	Total
1986	87,545	17,455	47,000	152,000	132.670	150.730	21.600	305.000
1983	99,965	17,635	40,400	158,000	117.055	130.245	16.500	263.800
1980	112,600	18,700	35,800	167,100	105.285	103.115	12.400	220.800
1977	124,890	20,930	30,000	175,820	79.160	76.260	7.380	162.800
1974	151,240	24,190	22,700	198,130	64.275	61.240	5.320	130.835

The Future

The Southland Corporation has come a long way in a relatively short period of time. The neighborhood 7-Eleven store is fast becoming an American tradition. However, management realizes that the company did not get where it is today by doing things the way they did them yesterday. The company is always evaluating itself, looking at its operations, and deciding what it needs to do differently. Presently, S. R. Dole, Executive Vice President, 7-Eleven Stores, is involved with several strategic decisions, all of which relate to trying to maintain growth performance of the 7-Eleven stores. The following are a few of the questions Dole is pondering:

- ☐ Is our store size most effective? One of our competitors, National Convenience Stores, is building some "super stores" with 3,600 square feet. Should we go in that direction?
- ☐ Should we adjust our product mix? Should we expand or reduce? Should we cut out some product lines and add others? Some consumer activists are calling our "hot-to-go" items nothing but junk food and saying that most of our products are of non-nutritional value. Should we start selling items like fresh meat, fruits and vegetables, or other nutritious items?
- ☐ Should we change our pricing strategy? Consumer activists and others of the general public complain about our relatively high prices on our products. Should we try to be more price competitive with the supermarkets?
- ☐ Where should we try to locate our stores in the future? Should we build more neighborhood stores or more downtown stores?
- ☐ What about our target market? Should we broaden our scope and try to appeal to more women or other segments?
- ☐ Should we make any adjustments to our store layout? Should we change placement of products, traffic flow, or any other elements?

Analytical Problem

Assume the role of a marketing consultant and provide a detailed report of your analysis of the Southland Corporation's 7-Eleven stores. Be sure to address the questions facing Dole shown at the end of the case.

**K MART CORPORATION:
Corporate Strategy at the Crossroads**

K Mart, Inc., in 1987, included discount department stores, variety stores, restaurants, financial services, home improvements centers, and specialty shops in the United States and Puerto Rico as well as several foreign countries, including Canada, Australia, and China. Measured in sales volume, it was the second-largest retailer and the largest discount department store chain in the United States.

By the mid-1980s, the discount department store industry had reached maturity. It was characterized by a reduced number of store openings and a diminishing sales growth, which was due to changes in basic economic factors. In 1985, K Mart had a retail management strategy that was developed in the late 1950s. The firm was at the crossroads, in terms of corporate strategy. The problem was what to do over the next 20 years.

The Early Years

K Mart was the outgrowth of an organization founded in 1899 in Detroit by Sebastian S. Kresge. The first S. S. Kresge store represented a new type of retailing that featured low-priced merchandise for cash in low-budget, relatively small (4,000- to 6,000-square-foot) buildings with sparse furnishings. The embracing of the "5¢ and 10¢" or "variety store" concept, pioneered by F. W. Woolworth Company in 1879, led to rapid and profitable development of the S. S. Kresge Company.

Kresge believed he could substantially increase his retail business through centralized buying, control, developing standardized store-operating procedures, and expanding with new stores in heavy traffic areas. In 1917, the firm was incorporated. It had 150 stores and, next to Woolworth's, was the largest variety chain in the world. Over the next 40 years, the firm experimented with mail-order catalogs, full-line department stores, self-service, a variety of price lines, and the opening of stores in planned shopping centers.

By 1957, corporate management became aware that the development of supermarkets and the expansion of drugstore chains into general merchandise lines had made inroads into market categories previously dominated by variety stores. It also became clear that a new form of store with discount merchandising was also emerging.

The Cunningham Connection

In an effort to regain its competitiveness and possibly save the company, Frank Williams, the President of S. S. Kresge Company, nominated H. B. Cunningham as General Vice President in 1957. This maneuver was undertaken to free Cunningham, who had worked his way up the ranks in the organization, from operating responsibility. He was being groomed for the presidency and was assigned to study existing retailing business and recommend marketing changes.

This case was prepared by James W. Camerius, Northern Michigan University. Copyright © 1988 by James W. Camerius.

In his visits to Kresge stores, and those of the competition, Cunningham became interested in discounting—particularly a new operation in Garden City, Long Island. There, Eugene Ferkauf had recently opened large discount department stores called E. J. Korvette. They had a discount mass-merchandising emphasis that featured low prices and margins; high turnover; large, freestanding departmentalized stores; ample parking space; and a location typically in the suburbs.

Cunningham was impressed with the discount concept, but he knew he had to first convince the Board of Directors, whose support would be necessary for any new strategy to succeed. He studied the company for 2 years and presented it with the following recommendation:

> We can't beat the discounters operating under the physical constraints and the self-imposed merchandise limitations of variety stores. We can join them—and not only join them, but with our people, procedures, and organization, we can become a leader in the discount industry.[1]

In a speech delivered at the University of Michigan, Cunningham made his management approach clear by concluding with an admonition from the British author, Sir Hugh Walpole: "Don't play for safety, it's the most dangerous game in the world."[2]

The Board of Directors had a difficult job. Change is never easy, especially when the company has a proud heritage. Before the first presentation to the Board could be made, rumors attributed the following statement to one shocked senior executive:

> We have been in the variety business for 60 years—we know everything there is to know about it, and we're not doing very well in that, and you want to get us into a business we don't know anything about.[3]

The Board of Directors accepted Cunningham's recommendations. When President Frank Williams retired, Cunningham became the new President and Chief Executive Officer and was directed to proceed with his recommendations.

The Birth of K Mart

Management conceived the original K Mart as a conveniently located, one-stop shopping unit where customers could buy a wide variety of quality merchandise at discount prices. The typical K Mart had 75,000 square feet, all on one floor. It generally stood by itself in a high-traffic, suburban area, with plenty of parking space, and with a floor plan common to other units in the organization.

The firm made an $80 million commitment in leases and merchandise for thirty-three stores before the first K Mart opened in 1962 in Garden City, Michigan.

---

[1]Robert E. Dewar, "The Kresge Company and the Retail Revolution," *University of Michigan Business Review* (27 July 1975): 2.

[2]Dewar, "Kresge Company," 2.

[3]Dewar, "Kresge Company," 2.

As part of this strategy, management decided to rely on the strengths and abilities of its own people to make decisions rather than employing outside experts for advice.

The original variety store operation was characterized by low gross margins, high turnover, and concentration on return on investment. The main difference in the K Mart strategy would be the offering of a much wider merchandise mix.

The company had the knowledge and ability to merchandise 50 percent of the departments in the planned K Mart merchandise mix and contracted for operation of the remaining departments. In the following years, K Mart took over most of those contracted departments. Eventually, K Mart operated all departments, except shoes.

The Maturation of K Mart

By the late 1970s, K Mart's corporate management considered the discount department store industry to be at a level of maturity. K Mart itself was the largest discount department store organization, with 2,100 stores serving 80 percent of the population. The industry was characterized by a reduced number of store openings, reduced expansion of square feet of floor space, and similar product offerings by competitors. Although maturity was sometimes looked on with disfavor, K Mart executives felt that this did not mean a lack of profitability or lack of opportunity to increase sales. The industry was perceived as being "reborn." It was in this context that the program, later referred to as "K Mart for the 80s," was developed.

Many retailers such as Target, who adopted the discount concept, generally attempted to reach an upscale customer. The upscale customer tended to have a household income of $25,000 to $44,000 annually. Other "pockets" of population were being served by firms like Zayre, which served consumers in the inner city, and Wal-Mart, which served the needs of the more rural consumer in secondary markets. Senior management at K Mart felt that all firms in the industry were facing the same situation. First, they were very successful 5 or 10 years ago but were not changing and, therefore, were becoming somewhat dated. Management that had a historically successful formula, particularly in retailing, was perceived as having difficulty adapting to change, especially at the peak of success. Typically, management waited too long and then had to scramble to regain competitiveness.

K Mart executives found that discount department stores were being challenged by several new retail formats. Some retailers were assortment-oriented, with a much greater depth of assortment within a given product category. To illustrate, Toys-R-Us was an example of a firm that operated 20,000-square-feet toy supermarkets. Toys-R-Us prices were very competitive within an industry that was very competitive. When the consumers entered a Toys-R-Us facility, they usually had no doubt that if the product wasn't there, no one else had it.

Other retailers were experimenting with the "off-price" apparel concept, selling name-brands and designer goods at 20- to 70-percent discounts; with home improvement centers that were warehouse-style stores with a wide range of hard-line merchandise for both do-it-yourselfers and professionals; and with drug supermarkets that offered a wide variety of high-turnover merchandise in a convenient location.

In these cases, competition was becoming more risk oriented by putting $3 or $4 million in merchandise at retail value in an 80,000-square-foot facility and offering genuinely low prices. The F&M stores in the Detroit market, Drug Emporium in the Midwest, and a series of independents were examples of organizations employing the entirely new concept of the drug supermarket.

Competition was offering something that was new and different in terms of depth of assortment, competitive price image, and format. K Mart management perceived this as a threat because these competitors were viable businesses and hindered the firm in its ability to improve and maintain its market share in specific merchandise categories.

Corporate research revealed that on the basis of convenience, K Mart served 80 percent of the population. One study concluded that one out of every two adults in the United States shopped at K Mart at least once a month. Despite this popular appeal, strategies that had allowed the firm to have something for everybody were no longer felt to be appropriate for the 1980s. K Mart found that it had a broad customer base because it operated nationally. Its strategies assumed the firm was serving everyone in a market.

K Mart was often perceived as aiming at the low-income consumer. The financial community believed the K Mart customer was blue collar, low income, and upper-lower class. The market served, however, was more professional and middle class because K Mart stores were initially in suburban communities where the growth was occurring.

Although K Mart had made a major commitment in more recent years to secondary or rural markets, these were areas that had previously not been cultivated. The firm, in its initial strategies, perceived the rural consumer as different from the urban or suburban customer. In re-addressing the situation, it discovered that its assortments in rural areas were too limited and that management held too many preconceived notions regarding what the Nebraska farmer really wanted. The firm discovered that the rural consumer didn't always shop for bib overalls and shovels but shopped for microwave ovens and all the things everyone else did.

The goal was not to attract more customers but to get the customer coming in the door to spend more. Once in the store, the customer was thought to demonstrate more divergent tastes. The upper-income customer would buy more health and beauty aids, cameras, and sporting goods. The lower-income consumer would buy health and beauty aids, toys, and clothing.

In the process of trying to capture a large share of the market and get people to spend more, the firm began to recognize a market that was more upscale. When consumer research was conducted, and management examined the profile of the trade area and the profile of the person who shopped at K Mart in the past month, they were found to be identical. K Mart was predominately serving the suburban consumer in suburban locations.

In "life-style" research in markets served, K Mart found that two-income families had increased, families were having fewer children, more married women were working, and customers tended to be homeowners. Customers were very careful about their purchases and were perceived as wanting quality, in distinct contrast to the "throw-away" orientation of the 1960s and early 1970s. The customer now said, "We want products that will last longer. We'll have to pay more for them but will still want them and at the lowest price possible." Customers wanted better-quality products but still demanded competitive prices. The 1983 K Mart Corporation Annual Report stated that "Consumers today are well educated and informed. They want good value and they know it when they see it. Price remains a key consideration, but the consumer's new definition of value includes quality as well as price."

Corporate Strategies

In 1980, K Mart management introduced a program that it called "K Mart for the 80s." As part of an overall reexamination of corporate strategies, this program resulted in several new approaches to revitalizing the company. The area receiving initial attention was in improvement in apparel display. Name brands were added because management recognized that the customer transferred the product quality of branded goods to perceptions of private-label merchandise. In the eyes of K Mart management, "If you sell Wrangler, there is good quality. Then the private label must be good quality." A similar program was developed in hard goods.

Before 1980, the traditional K Mart layout was by product category. Often these locations were holdovers from the variety store past. Many departments would not give up prime locations. As part of the "K Mart for the 1980s" program, the "shoppe" concept was introduced. Management recognized that it had a sizable "do-it-yourself" store. As management in the Planning and Research group discussed the issue, it became evident that "nobody was aware of the opportunity. The hardware department was right smack in the center of the store because it was always there. The paint department was over here, and the electrical department was over there. All we had to do," management contended, "was put them all in one spot, and everyone could see that we had a very respectable 'do-it-yourself' department." The concept resulted in a variety of new departments such as "Soft Goods for the Home," "Kitchen Korners," and "Home Electronic Centers."

The program also involved using and revitalizing the existing stores by remodeling and updating them. Initial effort was concentrated in key major markets such as Indianapolis, Atlanta, Denver, Chicago, Detroit, and Buffalo. Stores also were identified in smaller markets that had rapid growth and significant new competition. A key to implementing this program was merchandising assortments that required changing the firm's preconceived notions about what the customer would or would not buy and under what conditions. The new look featured a broad "poppy red" and gold band around interior walls as a "horizon"; new racks—round, square, and honeycombed—that displayed the full garment; relocation of jewelry and women's apparel to areas closer to the entrance; and redesigned counters to make them look more upscale and hold more merchandise.

In the mid 1970s and into the 1980s, K Mart acquired and developed several smaller new operations. K Mart Insurance Services, Inc., acquired as Planned Marketing Associates in 1974, offered a full line of life, health, and accident insurance policies in insurance centers located in twenty-seven K Mart stores primarily in the South and Southwest. The acquisition of Furr's Cafeterias, Inc., in 1980 with 117 cafeterias in the Southwestern United States, was part of a new direction as K Mart sought business opportunities that could be evaluated in terms of the firm's historical expertise or common knowledge base. The cafeteria business fit in well because there were cafeterias within K Mart stores. In 1983, the company acquired Bishops Buffets, Inc., a chain of thirty cafeterias based in Cedar Rapids, Iowa. This company fit geographically and philosophically with the Furr's venture.

In 1982, K Mart initiated its own off-price specialty apparel concept called Designer Depot. A total of twenty-eight Designer Depot stores were opened in 1982, to appeal to customers who wanted quality, upscale clothing at a budget price. A variation of this concept, called Garment Rack, was opened as apparel that normally would not be sold in Designer Depot. A distribution center was added in 1983, to supplement both of the above ventures. K Mart attempted an unsuccessful joint venture with the Hechinger Company of Washington, D.C., a warehouse home center retailer. After much deliberation, however, K Mart chose instead to acquire Home Centers of America, based in San Antonio, Texas. The division would build 80,000-square-feet warehouse home centers named Builders Square. It would capitalize on K Mart's real estate, construction, and management expertise as well as Home Centers of America's merchandising expertise.

K Mart acquired Waldenbooks, a chain of 877 book stores, from Carter Hawley Hale, Inc., in 1984. The acquisition was part of a strategy to capture a greater market share with a product category that K Mart already retailed. K Mart had been interested in the book business for some time and took advantage of an opportunity in the marketplace to build on its common knowledge base.

The Planning Function

Corporate planning at K Mart was the result of executives, primarily the senior executive, recognizing change. The senior executive's role was to get others to recognize that nothing is good forever. "Good planning" was perceived as the result of those who recognized that at some point they would have to get involved. "Poor planning" was done by those who didn't recognize the need for it; when they did, it was too late to survive. Regularly conducted and timely good planning was assumed to improve performance. K Mart's Director of Planning and Research contended, "planning, as we like to stress, is making decisions now to improve performance tomorrow. Everyone looks at what may happen tomorrow, but the planners are the ones who make decisions today. That's where I think too many firms go wrong. They think they are planning because they are writing reports and are aware of changes. They don't say, 'because of this, we must decide today to spend this money to do this to accomplish this goal in the future.' "[4]

The Director of Planning and Research believed that K Mart had been very successful in the area of strategic planning. "When it became necessary to make significant changes in the way we were doing business," he suggested, "that was accomplished on a fairly timely basis." When the organization made the change in the 1960s, it recognized a very powerful investment opportunity and capitalized on it—far beyond what any other firm would have done. "We just opened stores," he

---

[4]Michael Wellman, interview with Director of Planning and Research, K Mart Corporation, 6 Aug. 1984.

continued, "at a great, great pace. Management, when confronted with a crisis, would state, 'It's the economy, or it's this, or that, but it's not the essential way we are doing business.' " He continued, "Suddenly management would recognize that the economy may stay like this forever. We need to improve the situation and then do it."[5] Strategic planning was thought to arise out of some difficult times for the organization.

K Mart had a reasonably formal planning organization that involved a constant evaluation of the marketplace, the competition, and available opportunities. Management felt a need to diversify because K Mart would not be a viable company unless it grew physically. Management felt that the firm could grow physically with the K Mart format forever. It needed physical growth and opportunity, particularly for a company that could regularly open 200 stores. The Director of Planning and Research felt that, "Given a 'corporate culture' that was accustomed to challenges, management would have to find ways to expend that energy. A corporation that is successful," he argued, "has to continue to be successful. It has to have a basic understanding of corporate needs and be augmented by a much more rigorous effort to be aware of what's going on in the external environment."

A planning group at K Mart reports directly to the Chairman of the Board through its Director of Planning and Research. The group represents a number of functional areas of the organization. Management describes it as an "in-house consulting group" with some independence. The planning group comprises (1) financial planning, (2) economic and consumer analysis, and (3) operations research. The chief executive officer is the primary planner.

The Challenge

On April 6, 1987, K Mart Corporation announced that it agreed to sell most of its fifty-five Kresge and Jupiter variety stores in the United States to McCroy Corporation, a unit of the closely held Rapid American Corporation of New York. The move left the firm with approximately 4,000 retail units including discount department stores, restaurants, home improvement centers, financial and real estate service centers, and specialty shops in the United States, Canada, Australia, China, and Puerto Rico.

In the light of a corporate climate of asset-disinvestment and asset redeployment, the firm was at the crossroads, in terms of corporate strategy. The question was, what to do now? (See Exhibits 30–1 to 30–4 on the following pages.)

---

[5]Michael Wellman, interview.

K Mart Corporation Financial Structure 1983 Annual Report

EXHIBIT 30–1A
Consolidated Statements of Income

($Millions)	Fiscal year ended		
	January 25, 1984	January 26, 1983	January 27, 1982
Sales	18,597.9	16,772.2	16,527.0
Licensee fees and rental income	191.3	169.5	151.6
Equity in income of affiliated retail companies	51.7	44.5	44.4
Interest income	38.0	54.6	45.7
Subtotal	18,878.9	17,040.8	16,768.7
Cost of merchandise sold (including buying and oc-cupancy costs)	13,447.4	12,298.6	12,360.4
Advertising	424.6	401.7	385.7
Selling, general and administrative expenses	3,880.1	3,602.9	3,424.0
Provision for store closings		44.5	
Interest expense			
Debt	84.1	97.7	114.9
Capital lease obligations	189.0	176.5	160.8
Subtotal	18,025.2	16,621.9	16,445.8
Income before estimated income taxes	853.7	418.9	322.9
Estimated income taxes			
U.S.	304.7	131.7	73.9
Foreign	4.8	3.1	4.4
State and local	35.5	19.6	17.1
Tax effects of timing differences	21.5	7.6	11.8
Subtotal	366.5	162.0	107.2
Income from retail operations	487.2	256.9	215.7
Equity in income of insurance operations	5.1	4.9	4.6
Net income for the year	492.3	261.8	220.3
Earnings per common and common equivalent share*	$3.80	$2.06	$1.75

*Dollar value given.

EXHIBIT 30–1B

Consolidated Statements of Income Retained for Use in the Business

($Millions)	Fiscal year ended		
	January 25, 1984	January 26, 1983	January 27, 1982
Income retained for use in the business at beginning of year	2,204.9	2,067.4	1,966.0
Net income for the year	492.3	261.8	220.3
Cash dividends declared—$1.08, $1.00, and $.96, respectively	(135.1)	(124.3)	(118.9)
Cumulative retained earnings of Bishop Buffets, Inc., at the date of acquisition	7.0		
Income retained for use in the business at end of year	$2,569.1	$2,204.9	$2,067.4

EXHIBIT 30–1C
Consolidated Balance Sheets

Assets ($Millions)	January 25, 1984	January 26, 1983
Current assets		
Cash (includes temporary investments of $762.9 and $449.4, respectively)	1,027.7	553.8
Accounts receivable	134.8	115.8
Merchandise inventories	3,581.6	3,294.9
Operating supplies and prepaid expenses	44.4	39.1
Total current assets	4,788.5	4,003.6
Investments in and advances to		
Affiliated retail companies	211.8	216.4
Insurance operations	128.6	114.3
Other assets and deferred charges	80.5	72.5
Property		
Land	57.6	56.6
Buildings	174.4	179.5
Leasehold improvements	303.9	276.4
Furniture and fixtures	1,738.0	1,589.1
Construction in progress	57.5	41.6
	2,331.4	2,143.2
Less depreciation and amortization	976.6	858.0
Total property owned	1,354.8	1,285.2
Leased property under capital leases, less accumulated amortization of $767.2 and $701.1, respectively	1,618.9	1,651.7
Total property	2,973.7	2,936.9
Total current assets and property	8,183.1	7,343.7

EXHIBIT 30–1C *(continued)*

Liabilities and shareholders' equity	January 25, 1984	January 26, 1983
Current liabilities		
Long-term debt due within 1 year	3.2	5.1
Obligations under capital leases due within 1 year	70.6	65.7
Accounts payable—trade	1,717.2	1,513.4
Accrued payrolls and other liabilities	294.0	263.0
Taxes other than income taxes	172.9	163.1
Dividends payable	34.0	31.1
Income taxes	228.9	135.0
Total current liabilities	2,520.8	2,176.4
Obligations under capital leases	1,822.3	1,824.4
Long-term debt	711.2	596.0
Other long-term liabilities	127.8	94.0
Deferred income taxes	60.9	51.6
Shareholders' equity		
Common stock	125.9	124.5
Capital in excess of par value	293.4	271.9
Income retained for use in the business	2,569.1	2,204.9
Cumulative foreign currency translation adjustment	(48.3)	
Total shareholders' equity	2,940.1	2,601.3
Total liabilities and shareholder's equity	8,183.1	7,343.7

EXHIBIT 30–1D
Consolidated Statements of Changes in Financial Position

($Millions)	Fiscal year ended		
	25 January 1984	26 January 1983	27 January 1982
Cash provided by (used for)			
Operations			
Net income for the year	492.3	261.8	220.3
Noncash charges (credits) to earnings—			
Depreciation and amortization			
Property owned	167.8	157.4	140.7
Leased property under capital leases	96.7	93.7	88.9
Provision for store closings		44.5	
Deferred income taxes	21.5	7.6	11.8
Equity in undistributed income of affiliated retail companies and insurance operations	(16.8)	(15.9)	(16.5)
Increase in other long-term liabilities	33.8	21.2	19.1
Other	.8	6.4	5.5
Total from net income	796.1	576.7	469.8
Cash provided by (used for) current assets and current liabilities—			
Increase in inventories	(286.7)	(159.8)	(289.2)
Increase in accounts payable	203.8	260.4	192.8
Net change in other current assets and other current liabilities	106.6	130.2	(95.3)
Net cash provided by operations	819.8	807.5	278.1
Financing			
Increase in long-term debt and notes payable	123.4	197.2	168.2
Reduction in long-term debt and notes payable	(10.4)	(181.4)	(4.0)
Obligations incurred under capital leases	78.9	141.8	197.9
Reduction in capital lease obligations	(75.5)	(63.0)	(59.1)
Sale of common stock under stock option, purchase and employees' savings plans and conversion of debentures (includes $5.4 for acquisition of Bishop Buffers, Inc., in 1983)	22.9	8.2	11.0
Net cash provided by financing	139.3	102.8	314.0

EXHIBIT 30–1D *(continued)*

	Fiscal year ended		
($Millions)	25 January 1984	26 January 1983	27 January 1982
Dividends paid	(132.2)	(123.0)	(117.5)
Investments			
Property additions—			
Property owned (includes $10.0 in 1983 relating to acquisition of Bishop Buffets, Inc.)	(377.9)	(306.4)	(361.4)
Leased property under capital leases	(37.8)	(85.0)	(178.2)
Proceeds from the sale of property	91.4	49.7	38.2
Increase in investments in and advances to affiliated retail companies and insurance operations	(24.5)	(3.8)	(68.2)
Other—net	(4.2)	(3.2)	(2.8)
Net cash used for investments	(353.0)	(348.7)	(572.4)
Net increase (decrease) in cash and temporary investments	$473.9	$438.6	$(97.8)

EXHIBIT 30–2
Financial Performance, K Mart and S. S. Kresge Company, 1960 to 1983

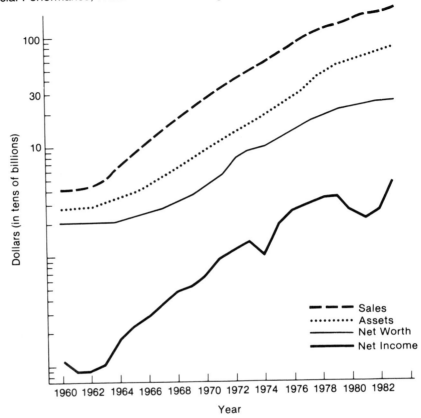

EXHIBIT 30–3

Financial Performance, K Mart and S. S. Kresge Company 1960 to 1983

Year	Sales ($000s)	Assets ($000s)	Net Income ($000s)	Net Worth ($000s)
1960	418,200	269,343	11,120	205,757
1961	432,838	274,293	8,863	205,791
1962	452,561	281,897	9,014	205,493
1963	510,531	315,265	10,278	209,109
1964	692,499	344,272	17,150	212,700
1965	862,441	394,015	23,470	229,597
1966	1,102,688	442,740	28,609	251,803
1967	1,401,168	525,536	34,915	275,632
1968	1,757,750	657,825	47,611	319,450
1969	2,185,298	797,526	54,089	367,519
1970	2,595,155	926,227	66,994	456,761
1971	3,139,653	1,095,948	96,116	548,469
1972	3,875,183	1,383,439	114,674	779,726
1973	4,702,504	1,652,773	138,251	924,512
1974	5,612,071	1,896,110	104,772	1,016,600
1975	6,883,613	2,377,541	200,832	1,197,825
1976	8,483,603	2,865,572	266,574	1,441,793
1977	10,064,457	3,428,110	302,919	1,687,817
1978	11,812,810	4,836,260	343,706	1,915,666
1979	12,858,585	5,642,439	357,999	2,185,192
1980	14,204,381	6,102,462	260,527	2,343,172
1981	16,527,012	6,673,004	220,251	2,455,594
1982	16,772,166	7,343,665	261,821	2,601,272
1983	18,597,900	8,183,100	492,300	2,940,100

Source: Fortune Financial Analysis.

Analytical Problem

Prepare a position paper, titled "K Mart Corporation: Corporate Strategy at the Crossroads," for general distribution to the business community. The paper should include an analytical consideration of the following issues:

1. Evaluate the strategies that K Mart has introduced as part of "K Mart for the 1980s." How much impact will these strategies have on the competitive environment as the firm seeks to maintain its position and to grow in the future?

2. How much importance is placed on the planning function at K Mart? What are some constraints that are likely to decrease the effect of planning on the organization's development?

3. Why do you think planning is important to an organization like K Mart?
4. How does planning fit into the management process at K Mart?
5. Discuss the importance of changes in the external environment. How much impact do they have on strategic plans in retail firms like K Mart?
6. What conclusions can you draw from a review of K Mart's financial performance from 1960 to 1984?
7. What new directions are needed to "position" K Mart to meet the challenges of the next 20 years?
8. Review alternative strategies that K Mart might implement as part of its "K Mart for the 1980s" program.

Bibliography

Bussey, John. "K Mart Is Set to Sell Many of Its Roots to Rapid-American Corp's McCory." *Wall Street Journal,* 6 April 1987.

Carruth, Elanore. "K Mart Has to Open Some New Doors on the Future." *Fortune,* July 1977, 143–150, 153–154.

Dewar, Robert E. "The Kresge Company and the Retail Revolution." *University of Michigan Business Review,* 2 July 1975, 2.

"It's Kresge . . . Again." *Chain Store Executive,* November 1975, 16.

Key, Janet. "K Mart Plan: Diversify, Conquer: Second Largest Retailer Out to Woo Big Spenders." *Chicago Tribune,* 11 Nov. 1984.

Main, Jerry. "K Mart's Plan to Be Born Again." *Fortune,* 21 Sept. 1981, 74–77, 84–85.

Wellman, Michael. Interview with Director of Planning and Research, K Mart Corporation, 6 Aug. 1984.

"Where K Mart Goes Next Now That It's No. 2." *Business Week,* 2 June 1980, 109–110, 114.

"Why Chains Enter New Areas." *Chain Store Executive,* December 1976, 22, 24.